THE
SPIRITUAL GOSPEL

THE
SPIRITUAL GOSPEL

THE INTERPRETATION OF THE
FOURTH GOSPEL IN THE
EARLY CHURCH

BY

MAURICE F. WILES

FELLOW OF CLARE COLLEGE AND LECTURER IN DIVINITY
IN THE UNIVERSITY OF CAMBRIDGE, FORMERLY
LECTURER IN NEW TESTAMENT STUDIES
UNIVERSITY COLLEGE, IBADAN

CAMBRIDGE
AT THE UNIVERSITY PRESS
1960

PUBLISHED BY

THE SYNDICS OF THE CAMBRIDGE UNIVERSITY PRESS

Bentley House, 200 Euston Road, London, N.W. 1
American Branch: 32 East 57th Street, New York 22, N.Y.

©

CAMBRIDGE UNIVERSITY PRESS

1960

Printed in Great Britain at the University Press, Cambridge
(Brooke Crutchley, University Printer)

CONTENTS

ACKNOWLEDGEMENTS

I wish to express my thanks to Professor Henry Chadwick for advice and encouragement and to the Rev. Barry Mackay for help with the proof-reading.

M. F. W.

UNIVERSITY COLLEGE
IBADAN
11 April 1959

ABBREVIATIONS

The following standard abbreviations have been used:

A.C.O.	*Acta Conciliorum Oecumenicorum*, ed. E. Schwartz
C.S.E.L.	*Corpus Scriptorum Ecclesiasticorum Latinorum*
D.C.B.	*Dictionary of Christian Biography*
E.T.	English Translation
Exp. T.	*Expository Times*
G.C.S.	*Die Griechischen Christlichen Schriftsteller der ersten drei Jahrhunderte*
J.T.S.	*Journal of Theological Studies*
P.G.	*Patrologia Graeca, Cursus Completus*, ed. J.-P. Migne
P.L.	*Patrologia Latina, Cursus Completus*, ed. J.-P. Migne
R.B.	*Revue Biblique*
Rev. Bén.	*Revue Bénédictine*
R.H.E.	*Revue d'Histoire Ecclésiastique*
R.S.R.	*Recherches de Science Religieuse*

The following additional abbreviations have been used in references to commentaries on the Gospel:

I. ANCIENT

O.	Origen, ed. A. E. Brooke (Cambridge, 1896)
Chr.	John Chrysostom, *P.G.* 59
T.	Theodore of Mopsuestia, *Corpus Scriptorum Christianorum Orientalium: Scriptores Syri*, Series 4, Tomus III, interpretatus est J. M. Vosté (Louvain, 1940)
T. Frag.	Greek fragments in R. Devreesse, *Essai sur Théodore de Mopsueste* (Vatican, 1948), pp. 305–419
Cyr.	Cyril of Alexandria, ed. P. E. Pusey (Oxford, 1872)
Tract. Joh.	Augustine, *Corpus Christianorum*, Series Latina 36 (Turnhout, 1954)
Corderius	Corderius, *Catena Patrum Graecorum in S. Johannem* (Antwerp, 1630)
Cramer	Cramer, *Catena in Evangelia SS. Lucae et Johannis*, Oxford, 1841

ABBREVIATIONS

2. MODERN

Barrett   C. K. Barrett, *Gospel according to St John* (London, 1955)

Bernard   J. H. Bernard, *I.C.C.* (2 vols., Edinburgh, 1928)

Dodd   C. H. Dodd, *Interpretation of the Fourth Gospel* (Cambridge, 1953)

Hoskyns   E. C. Hoskyns, *The Fourth Gospel* (2nd ed., London, 1947)

Lightfoot   R. H. Lightfoot, *St John's Gospel* (Oxford, 1956)

Macgregor   G. H. C. Macgregor, *The Gospel of John* (Moffatt Commentary) (London, 1928)

Temple   W. Temple, *Readings in St John's Gospel* (London, 1947)

Westcott   B. F. Westcott, *The Gospel according to St John* (2 vols., London, 1908)

See the Bibliography for fuller details of articles

INTRODUCTION

COMMENTARIES AND COMMENTATORS

Theological scholarship in recent years has shown an especial interest in the interpretation of the Fourth Gospel and in patristic exegesis of the Bible. Within the brief period between 1953 and 1956, three major works on the Fourth Gospel have been published in England.[1] On the continent the work of Père Daniélou and others has shown a revival of interest in early Christian exegesis. This study is devoted to the exegesis of the Fourth Gospel in the early Greek fathers in the hope that it will be of value in both fields of study.

The Fathers knew well the fascination of the Fourth Gospel. Origen describes the Gospels as the first-fruits of all Scripture, and the Gospel of St John as the first-fruits of all the Gospels,[2] and we have in fact more than one work of major importance in commentary upon it. There are some books of the Bible whose interpretation has been so completely revolutionised by modern critical methods that the exegesis of earlier centuries is unlikely to add much of value to our understanding of them. There is probably no book of which this is less true than the Fourth Gospel. It is of such a nature that it seems to reveal its secrets not so much to the skilful probings of the analyst as to a certain intuitive sympathy of understanding. We need not, therefore, despair of finding amongst such early interpreters significant examples of a true insight into the meaning of the Gospel.

It is also a particularly valuable field within which to study the pattern of early exegesis. One of the most interesting features of such a study is the contrast between the schools of Alexandria and of Antioch. From Alexandria, we have considerable portions of the commentary of Origen, the most renowned of her exegetes, and practically the whole of the commentary of Cyril, the most powerful of her leaders. From Antioch, we have (in translation) the com-

---

[1] C. H. Dodd, *The Interpretation of the Fourth Gospel* (1953); C. K. Barrett, *The Gospel According to St John* (1955); R. H. Lightfoot, *St John's Gospel* (1956).
[2] O. 1, 6.

mentary of Theodore of Mopsuestia, the most renowned of her exegetes, and the homilies of John Chrysostom, the greatest of her preachers. We have thus abundant material for a comparative study of the methods of the outstanding representatives of the leading exegetical schools of the period.

Primary attention in this study has been given to the three commentaries of Origen, Cyril and Theodore. Theodore's commentary has only come to light in comparatively recent times, and is therefore not so generally well known.[1] There is an obvious fascination in comparing the work of Theodore with that of Origen, the two most famous exegetes of Antioch and Alexandria, in commentary upon the same book of the Bible.[2] In many respects however, Cyril, though not so pure an example of Alexandrian scholarship, provides a better standard of comparison. In the first place his commentary has survived in a far more complete form than that of Origen. Secondly, Cyril and Theodore were contemporaries, whereas Origen's commentary is at a remove of almost two centuries from that of Theodore. Thirdly, Cyril is far less prone to personal eccentricities of exegesis, which often mar the work of Origen and which render it less readily usable for the purpose of comparative study.[3]

Our main concern, therefore, will lie with these three commentaries, with their method in the work of interpretation and with the meaning that they find in the text of the Fourth Gospel. But before embarking upon such an analysis of their thought, a brief survey must be given of our knowledge about the historical occasions of their composition. Moreover, although these three works

[1] It was discovered in 1868 and first published in Syriac by Chabot in 1897. It was not translated into Latin until 1940. See J. M. Vosté, 'Le Commentaire de Théodore de Mopsueste sur Saint Jean, d'après la Version Syriaque'. See also p. 5 n. 3 below.

[2] Cf. J. Guillet, 'Les Exégèses d'Alexandrie et d'Antioche : Conflit ou Malentendu?', p. 260. Guillet carries out an interesting comparison of Origen's and Theodore's interpretations of Psalm iii.

[3] The most important factor making for the more controlled nature of Cyril's exegesis is his recognition of the principle that not everything that is said in the Bible need necessarily have a spiritual sense. See A. Kerrigan, St Cyril of Alexandria: Interpreter of the Old Testament, p. 50 n. 2, who quotes a clear affirmation of Cyril to this effect from Glaph. in Gen. bk. IV (P.G. 69, 192 B). The Commentary on St John also contains a warning against forcing a spiritual meaning out of passages which ought to be treated historically (Cyr. in John ix. 4; II, 154, 7–12).

are the most important for our purpose, they were not isolated phenomena. They stand within a developing tradition of interpretation, within which other writings of importance have come down to us in complete or fragmentary form. These too must be included in our preliminary survey.

The earliest commentary on the Gospel known to us is that of Heracleon, a Valentinian Gnostic, who probably wrote about A.D. 170.[1] We cannot be certain that his work represents a full commentary on the Gospel, but it seems most probable that it does. It is clear from Origen's quotations that he dealt at least with continuous passages of the Gospel of some length. Origen's remark that Heracleon makes no comment on John iv. 32 suggests that this is exceptional and that his commentary is normally verse by verse.[2] It is true that there are long sections of Origen's commentary (including the whole of the last two surviving books) in which he makes no reference to Heracleon whatever. It is therefore possible that Heracleon's work was incomplete, but there are other more probable explanations. In view of the length of time and the varied and unsystematic nature of Origen's writing of his own commentaries, it seems more likely either that he grew tired of referring to Heracleon (his later books are certainly less expansive than his earlier ones) or that he did not always have his commentary readily available for reference.

Origen's commentary was begun at a comparatively early stage in his literary career before his departure from Alexandria. The most likely date is about A.D. 225. The first five books were composed there, but the work was interrupted by the upheaval surrounding his final removal from Alexandria.[3] The method of composition appears to have been by dictation to stenographers—a fact which helps to explain its prolixity and unsystematic character.[4] Only eight and a half books have survived; by the last of these (Book 32), Origen has reached Chapter xiii of the Gospel. If, therefore, he covered the whole of the Gospel, the completed work must have been of prodigious length. However, as Jerome speaks only of thirty-two books and there is an almost complete lack of surviving fragments

[1] Cf. G. Salmon in *D.C.B.* vol. II, p. 900; A. E. Brooke, 'The Extant Fragments of Heracleon', pp. 33–4.   [2] O. 13, 34.   [3] O. 6, 1–2.   [4] O. 6, 2.

of the later texts of the Gospel, it seems most likely that the work was never finished.[1]

We do not possess any other commentary from the third century, though the period was one of importance for the development of the interpretation of the Gospel.[2] The theology of Irenaeus, worked out in conscious opposition to Gnosticism, involved a serious grappling with the meaning of the Fourth Gospel. Not only Gnosticism, but modalist and monarchian heresies also were forcing the Church to pay ever-increasing attention to the problem of its correct interpretation. With the impact of Arianism this pressure was increased. It seems that a considerable number of commentaries were written in the course of the fourth and early fifth centuries, but in most cases only fragments of them have survived.

Probably the earliest of these was written by Asterius the Sophist in support of the Arian cause.[3] It is described by Theodore as a prolix work, which contrives to say nothing of any value for a true understanding of the Gospel, but achieves its great length by spending many words on matters that are entirely obvious.[4] Such judgments need always to be received with caution, and Theodore himself is certainly unusually brief by contemporary standards. It is perhaps more significant that Theodore still finds it necessary to refer to the work of Asterius more than half a century after its publication. Theodore of Heraclea, who receives high praise as an exegete from both Jerome and Theodoret, also appears to have written a commentary on the Gospel about the middle of the fourth century. But as he too was a supporter of the Arian cause, it is not surprising that only small fragments of his work remain.[5]

[1] Jerome, *Ep.* 33, 4.

[2] The catalogue of works recorded on the statue of Hippolytus shows him as having written a work on the Fourth Gospel, but it has not survived (cf. A. d'Alès, *Théologie de Saint Hippolyte*, Introduction, p. iv).

[3] The surviving fragments of the works of Asterius are to be found in G. Bardy, *Recherches sur Saint Lucien d'Antioche et son École*, pp. 341–54. Although they do not seem to include actual fragments of the commentary, they do include quotations which throw some light on his exegesis of the Gospel.   [4] T. 2, 4–11.

[5] Jerome, *De Vir. Ill.* 90; Theodoret, *H.E.* II, 3. (See C. H. Turner, 'Greek Patristic Commentaries on the Pauline Epistles', pp. 497–8 and 'The Early Greek Commentators on the Gospel according to St Matthew', p. 107, where he speaks of Theodore as 'one of the earliest and ablest exegetes of the Antiochene school'.)

But the majority of the commentaries stood in the tradition of Nicene orthodoxy and especially within the tradition of Alexandrian exegesis. Didymus the Blind, head of the catechetical school of Alexandria, Apollinarius of Laodicea, who was orthodox at least on the issue of Arianism, and Ammonius, one of the celebrated 'Tall Brothers', all appear to have written commentaries on the Gospel, and fragments of their work are to be found in the Catenae.[1]

In the last decade of the fourth century we have another exposition of the Gospel in the Antiochene tradition. The homilies of John Chrysostom on the Gospel were delivered in Antioch itself before his departure from the city in A.D. 398. Although delivered as sermons, they appear to have been preached to a well-instructed congregation and contain thorough and careful exposition fully worthy of comparison with more specific works of commentary.

The commentaries of Theodore and of Cyril, both of which are to be dated early in the fifth century, thus find their place within a succession of no mean magnitude. Theodore's commentary is to be placed in the later part of his life, probably in the first decade of the fifth century.[2] Of the original Greek text only fragments survive. Like others of his works, however, it was translated at an early date into Syriac. This version has now been rendered into Latin by Père Vosté and thus made more easily accessible.[3] In his introduction

---

[1] In the case of Didymus, we have the express statement of Jerome (*De Vir. Ill.* 109). In the other two cases our judgment is based solely on the extent of material attributed to them surviving in the Catenae. Apollinarius is not strictly an exegete within the Alexandrian tradition; C. H. Turner ('Greek Patristic Commentaries on the Pauline Epistles', p. 500) says of him that 'his exegetical position was therefore influenced more by his geographical connexion with the city of Antioch than by his opposition to the teaching of its school in the sphere of theology'. None the less the work of commentary on the Fourth Gospel is so essentially theological an exercise that it is not surprising that the Catena fragments should reveal a closer affinity to Cyril of Alexandria than to any other writer in this particular sphere.

[2] J. M. Vosté, 'Le Commentaire...', p. 541; 'La chronologie de l'activité littéraire de Théodore de Mopsueste', pp. 77–80.

[3] *Corpus Scriptorum Christianorum Orientalium: Scriptores Syri*, Series 4, Tomus 3 interpretatus est J. M. Vosté. The surviving Greek fragments have been collected by R. Devreesse and printed as an appendix to his *Essai sur Théodore de Mopsueste*. The reliability of the Syriac translation is generally agreed. Vosté ('Le Commentaire...', p. 534) speaks of its 'fidélité admirable'. F. A. Sullivan, who is in general inclined to be critical of the Syriac translations, believes it to be 'quite faithful to the Greek text', though he regards the translations of ch. i and the last section of the Gospel following

5

to the commentary, Theodore not only refers to the earlier work of Asterius, but also to his desire to write in defence of Basil against Eunomius; this shows that he too has the Arian controversy much in mind. He carefully distinguishes the work of the commentator from that of the preacher. The task of the commentator is to make clear the meaning of the text. If that meaning is obvious, it is not his job (as it is the preacher's) to elaborate upon it. On the other hand, he must be prepared to spend much time on the more difficult texts. In particular this means that he will have to dwell in detail on any texts which have been perverted in current heretical teaching.[1]

Cyril's commentary is one of his earlier works. There is difference of opinion about its exact date, but there seems to be general agreement that it is to be dated before the outbreak of the Nestorian controversy in A.D. 428.[2] The anti-Arian purpose, which is present in the work of Theodore, is still more explicit in the work of Cyril. His avowed purpose is a δογματικωτέρα ἐξήγησις, which will counter the false teaching of heresy at every point.[3] Like Theodore, therefore, he sees it as his especial duty to unmask the errors of heretical interpretation, and to that end he includes in the commentary a number of excursuses, which are often only very loosely attached to the actual text of the Gospel. But he goes further than Theodore in including in the commentator's task a full, positive exposition of the doctrinal implications of the Gospel.

xx. 23 as less precise than the main body of the work (*The Christology of Theodore of Mopsuestia*, p. 125). Many of the Greek fragments for the second half of the Gospel are in the form of an epitome rather than direct quotation and are clearly less reliable than the Syriac.

[1] T. 2, 12–27.
[2] For summaries of recent discussions of the date of the Commentary, see J. Liébaert, *La Doctrine Christologique de Saint Cyrille d'Alexandrie...*, pp. 191–6; H. Chadwick, 'Eucharist and Christology in the Nestorian Controversy', p. 151 n. 4.
[3] Cyr., Praefatio (1, 7, 13).

CHAPTER I

THE AUTHORSHIP AND PURPOSE
OF THE GOSPEL

Towards the close of the second century, there appears considerable and widespread testimony to the Johannine authorship of the Gospel. Theophilus of Antioch quotes the opening phrases of the prologue as the words of John, one of the inspired men.[1] He does not explicitly say that the John was the disciple of the Lord, though that may well have been his intention. Ptolemaeus, whose exposition of the prologue is quoted by Irenaeus, expressly attributes it to 'John, the disciple of the Lord'.[2] Heracleon also believed the Gospel on which he was commenting to be the work of a disciple.[3] In fact the considerable Gnostic interest in the Gospel was probably motivated at least in part by the desire to find in it apostolic authority for their teaching.[4]

In addition we have four fuller accounts of the writing of the Gospel. The anti-Marcionite prologue describes the Gospel as dictated by John to his disciple Papias 'while still in the body'. This presumably implies that it had something of the character of a last will and testament of the aged disciple.[5]

The Muratorian Canon ascribes the writing of the Gospel to the disciple John at the encouragement of his fellow-disciples and bishops. The Gospel is said to incorporate not only the recollections of John but of all the apostles. The writing down was the work of John and the Gospel was, therefore, published under his name.[6]

[1] Theophilus, *Ad Autolycum*, 2, 22.
[2] Irenaeus, *Adversus Haereses*, 1, 8, 5 (Harvey, vol. 1, p. 75).
[3] O. 6, 3. Origen is disputing Heracleon's assertion that John i. 18 is to be attributed 'not to the Baptist but to the disciple'.
[4] J. N. Sanders, *The Fourth Gospel in the Early Church*, p. 65.
[5] *Rev. Bén.* XL (1928), p. 198.
[6] H. Lietzmann, *Kleine Texte für theologische Vorlesungen*, No. 1, *Das Muratorische Fragment*, p. 5. None of these sources can be dated with precision, but they can all be placed with a considerable degree of confidence in the second half of the second century.

Clement of Alexandria gives a similar, less elaborate but more significant account. He writes: 'But, last of all, John perceiving that the external facts had been made plain in the Gospel, being urged by his friends and inspired by the Spirit, composed a spiritual Gospel.'[1]

Finally Irenaeus declares that the Gospel was written after the others, by John, the disciple of the Lord, who also leaned on Jesus' breast, while he lived at Ephesus.[2]

Over against this testimony, we hear of only one other suggested attribution of authorship. The heretical Alogoi, in their opposition to the Gospel, are said by Epiphanius to have ascribed it to Cerinthus.[3] It has been argued that the tentative use made of the Gospel by Justin 'makes it difficult to believe that he regarded the Fourth Gospel as Scripture or as the work of an apostle'.[4] However, even the fact of Justin's knowledge of the Gospel cannot be regarded as proved beyond doubt. If, indeed, the tradition was unknown earlier in the second century it had established itself securely by the end of the century, and from that time on was the universally accepted view in need neither of question nor of proof.

Irenaeus' description of Ephesus as its place of origin has further support of about the same date in statements of Polycrates[5] and of Clement.[6] Here again only one dissentient voice has survived in all the early literature. Ephrem Syrus records a tradition that John wrote the Gospel at Antioch, where he lived until the reign of Trajan.[7] But apart from this one isolated exception the connection of the Gospel with Ephesus appears regularly as a part of the unvarying tradition.

The other feature which is common to more than one of these early traditions is the allotment of some part in the origin of the Gospel to others in addition to the individual apostle himself. The different forms of this part of the tradition were inconsistent with one another, but that the Gospel was written in some sense at the prompting of others was also generally accepted.

---

[1] Eusebius, *H.E.* 6, 14, 7. [2] Irenaeus, *Adv. Haer.* 3, 1, 1 (vol. 2, p. 6).
[3] Epiphanius, *Pan. Haer.* 51, 2–3. [4] Sanders, *op. cit.* p. 31.
[5] Eusebius, *H.E.* 5, 24, 2–3. [6] *Ibid.* 3, 23, 6–19.
[7] Sanders, *op. cit.* p. 7; M. Goguel, *Introduction au Nouveau Testament*, vol. II, pp. 180–1.

For all the later commentators, therefore, it is an accepted fact that the author of the Gospel is none other than John, the son of Zebedee. To speak of finding confirmation of this fact from the internal evidence of the Gospel itself would be misleading. One cannot confirm that about which one is not in any doubt. Rather the commentator, knowing the secret of the authorship, is enabled to recognise the hidden evidences of his firsthand authority, which he has deliberately left within his record.

Irenaeus, as we have seen, identifies John with the beloved disciple and this identification is universally assumed. The 'other disciple' known to the high-priest of John xviii. 15 is also assumed to be John without the need for any discussion of the matter.[1] The indirect method of referring to himself is regarded as a suitable means of emphasising the unimpeachable nature of his authority without at the same time abandoning a proper humility.[2]

Similarly he has given evidence of the unquestionable nature of his testimony in John xix. 35. Different reasons are suggested as to why such emphasis should be laid on the witness to this particular occurrence. Theodore suggests that the issue of water and blood was not visible to all the bystanders, but was a personal revelation to himself alone.[3] Chrysostom declares that so degrading an occurrence in the life of Christ demanded by its very nature especially reliable testimony.[4]

John xxi. 24 is generally regarded as John's own seal of authority. His claim to be the one whom Jesus specially loved is a part of the guarantee of his utter reliability. Jesus, the Truth, would not so have loved one who would desert the truth. His humility is shown in the continued maintenance of his anonymity.[5]

The Muratorian Canon had pointed to the opening words of the first epistle of John as evidence for eyewitness authorship of the Gospel,[6] but the 'we beheld' of John i. 14 does not appear to be so

[1] T. 233, 23–6; Chr. 83, 2; Cyr. in John xviii. 15 (III, 29, 26–7). Cf. Westcott, vol. II, p. 273.
[2] Chr. 83, 2; Cyr. in John xviii. 15 (III, 29, 27–30, 24).
[3] T. 242, 27–34. [4] Chr. 85, 3.
[5] Cyr. in John xxi. 24 (III, 169–70). Cf. Irenaeus, Adv. Haer. 3, 5, 1 (vol. II, pp. 18–19).
[6] H. Lietzmann, op. cit. pp. 5–7.

used. The extreme doctrinal importance of the verse naturally monopolised the commentator's interest at that point.[1]

The author, therefore, was John, the Galilean fisherman and the beloved disciple. As a Galilean fisherman, he ought not to be expected to be a polished author. Origen is not afraid to assert of him that he does not express his point at one place with perfect clarity because he is no professional writer.[2] To Origen of course this is but one example of the general truth that there is nothing remarkable about the form or style of Scripture as a whole, but that God has entrusted his treasure to an earthen vessel so that its effectiveness might be recognised as due not to the wisdom of men, but to the power of God.[3] Chrysostom actually argues that John must have belonged to the poorest category of fisherman. No reason, he says, other than extreme poverty would have persuaded a father to allow his son to follow his footsteps in so mean a trade. Moreover, John fished not in the sea, but in a small lake; he had to mend his own nets and is described by St Luke in Acts iv. 13 as without learning.[4]

More significance, however, attaches to the fact of Christ's special love for John, which has earned him the title of Beloved Disciple. This has a greater importance as providing a clue towards the character and intention of his work. At its simplest level, Chrysostom declares that this love was the essential motive of his writing.[5] More important is the spiritual proximity to the mind of Jesus implicit in such a privileged position. Origen finds this most vividly portrayed in the picture of John reclining at supper on the bosom of Jesus. Just as it is the fact that the only-begotten Son is in 'the bosom of the Father' that constitutes him able to reveal God to men, so John's reclining upon the bosom of Jesus symbolises his ability to declare the deepest truths of the Gospel.[6] John's unique and exalted

---

[1] Cyr. *in* John xiii. 23 (II, 366, 30–367, 5) quotes the verse in the singular form ('I beheld. . .') applying it specifically to the evangelist, but he interprets it of his spiritual understanding rather than of his historical testimony.

[2] O. 13, 54.

[3] *De Principiis*, 4, 1, 7; extract in *Philocalia* from Book 4 of the *Commentary on St John* (Fragment no. 15 in Brooke's edition of the Commentary).

[4] Chr. 2, 1.   [5] Chr. 88, 2.

[6] O. 32, 20 (John xiii. 23). Cf. Origen, *In Can. Can.* bk. 1 (*P.G.* 13, 87B: *G.C.S.* ed. Baehrens, p. 93).

position is reflected in the unique and exalted character of his Gospel.

All our three principal commentators express the purpose of the Gospel not as something standing alone, but by comparison with the first three Gospels. It is striking to find that they make no use of John's own avowal of his purpose in John xx. 31.[1] All the expositions of the Gospel's purpose are in effect developments of the dictum of Clement, that it is intended to be a spiritual Gospel in supplementation of the earlier ones, whose concentration had been upon the bodily facts.

Origen develops this idea with characteristic verbal ingenuity. Matthew is a book of the 'genesis' of Jesus Christ; Mark is the beginning of the Gospel; and Luke is a record of all that Jesus began to do and to teach. All therefore leave the completion of the record to the one who had enjoyed the privileged position on the breast of Christ. And the essence of this completion of the Gospel records is to make unequivocally clear the divinity of Jesus. This is John's paramount purpose.[2]

Theodore states that the Christians of Asia recognised that the omission of certain miracles and certain elements of teaching might lead in future generations to men losing sight of Christ's divinity. It was to rule out the possibility of any such misapprehensions in the future that John undertook his task of writing.[3]

Cyril gives a very similar account of the Gospel's origin and purpose. The only difference is that the danger of false teaching is not future but already present. The eternal generation of the Son and the pre-existence of the Logos are already being attacked in John's own lifetime.[4] John's purpose is therefore a full and careful statement of Christ's divinity, in correction both of present and of future heresies.[5]

Thus there is complete agreement that the purpose of the Gospel is so to supplement the other Gospels as to place beyond all

[1] Irenaeus, *Adv. Haer.* 3, 16, 5 (vol. II, p. 86) does refer to this verse as an expression of John's purpose, but it is significant that it is only the Christological aspect of the verse as showing John's foresight of a particular form of Christological heresy that he is concerned with. The desire to impart faith and life is not developed.
[2] O. 1, 6.   [3] T. 3, 16–4, 8.   [4] Cyr. bk. 1 (Preface) (1, 14, 17–15, 10).
[5] Cyr. *in* John i. 1 (1, 31, 5–17).

reasonable doubt the doctrinal truth of Christ's divinity. Although the other commentators are evidently well aware of the fact, it is only Chrysostom who states explicitly that John also lays more stress than the other evangelists on the lowly aspects of Christ's humanity in the ordinary course of his ministry, as distinct from his passion, thus ensuring also a true belief in the incarnation.[1]

[1] Chr. 63, 2.

CHAPTER II

THE FOURTH GOSPEL AND THE
SYNOPTIC GOSPELS

The purpose of the Gospel was, as we have seen, conceived and expressed in terms of a comparison and contrast with the other three Gospels. So it is no surprise to find more detailed questions of the relationship of St John's account to that of the other three evangelists constantly recurring in treatments of the Fourth Gospel. Differences between St John's Gospel and the Synoptics seem to have been recognised as a possible stumbling-block to faith from the very beginning. The Muratorian Canon appears to wish to reassure the believer on this score.[1] Origen refers to some people, probably within the Church, who think that the discrepancies between the different Gospel records show that the evangelists are not absolutely reliable.[2] One of the reasons given by the Alogoi for their rejection of the Fourth Gospel was the impossibility of squaring its chronology with that of the Synoptics, in particular the impossibility of finding a place in the Johannine record for the forty days in the wilderness.[3]

The longer period of ministry required by the Johannine account was noticed by Irenaeus and put by him to positive use against the Valentinians. They had asserted a connection between the passion and the twelfth aeon, on the ground that Jesus suffered in the twelfth month after his baptism. Irenaeus objects by pointing out that, according to St John, Jesus visited Jerusalem for four distinct passovers, and that therefore the ministry must have extended over a much longer period than a single year.[4]

---

[1] See Barrett, pp. 96–7.
[2] O. 6, 34 (see A. Harnack, *Der Kirchengeschichtliche Ertrag* . . ., Pt. 2, p. 28).
[3] Epiphanius, *Pan. Haer.* 51, 4.
[4] Irenaeus, *Adv. Haer.* 2, 22, 3 (vol. 1, pp. 328–9). Irenaeus regards John v. 1 as referring to a passover as well as ii. 13, vi. 4 and xiii. 1. Irenaeus in fact believed in a very much longer ministry even than that required by the Johannine account. On the basis of John viii. 57, he believed that Jesus was about fifty years old at the time of his death (*Adv. Haer.* 2, 22, 6; vol. 1, p. 332).

Thus the Church was aware of the issue from the earliest period, but it is naturally in the later writers, when the Fourth Gospel was fully and unquestionably accepted, that we find a more careful and systematic attack upon the problem.

The general difference of character and of subject-matter presented no problem. This very fact had largely determined the accepted understanding of the purpose of the Gospel as a whole, and it was therefore itself easily and completely explicable in terms of that purpose. Where John includes incidents or teaching not recorded by the others, he is simply supplementing them, particularly in such a way as to enhance the divinity of Christ.[1] Where he omits incidents already recorded, the motive is obvious, especially in the case of such incidents as the temptation story or the agony in the garden, which emphasised the humanity of Christ.[2] Where he does repeat what has already been written, it is in order to develop new and important theological teaching on the basis of the old story, as with the feeding of the five thousand.[3] This was John's particular role in the dispensation of the Holy Spirit.[4] Here was no difficulty, but rather corroborative evidence of the overruling wisdom of the Spirit.

Difficulty, however, was most acutely felt when the work of comparison was carried down into matters of detail. Eusebius, Epiphanius, and Augustine set themselves specifically to the task of resolving all apparent points of conflict.[5] Nothing is to be gained by following out in full detail the tortuous ingenuity of their reasoning. It is, however, of interest to note that Eusebius is prepared to allow himself the possibility of a copyist's error as a principle to which appeal may be made in the resolution of these conflicts. Yet this is normally one of two or more possible methods of solution, and not the one to which his own personal preference is given.[6]

It is a sign of the historical realism, and of the fundamental honesty

---

[1] Cyr. bk. I (Preface) (I, 12); Chr. 4, I.

[2] Origen, *Matt. Comm. Ser.* 92; 126; *Luc. Hom.* 29.

[3] T. 4, 30–5, 13; 45, 10–15.

[4] Eusebius, *Supplementa Quaestionum ad Marinum*, 9 (*P.G.* 22, 1001 A).

[5] Eusebius, *Quaestiones Evangelicae* (*P.G.* 22, 877–1016); Epiphanius, *Pan. Haer.* 51, 5–31; Augustine, *De Consensu Evangelistarum.*

[6] Eusebius, *Quaestiones ad Marinum*, 2, 7 (*P.G.* 22, 948 B); *Supplementa Minora Quaestionum ad Marinum*, 4 (*P.G.* 22, 1009 AB).

of Origen and of Theodore as commentators, that they alone are prepared to admit quite frankly the impossibility of such methods leading to a complete and successful solution of every difficulty. In their fearless rejection of all facile solutions they are at one, but that is as far as the similarity between them extends.

Origen declares that the Johannine and synoptic chronologies cannot be harmonised. The Johannine account leaves no room for the temptation story;[1] the different datings of the cleansing of the Temple cannot be harmonised at a straightforward historical level.[2] In addition there are clear discrepancies in the differing accounts of the call and naming of Peter, and differing assertions on the subject of the overlapping of the ministry of Jesus with that of John.[3] The discrepancies in fact are of such magnitude that they might well undermine our whole faith in the trustworthiness of the Gospel records.[4] That they need not do so is due to one cardinal principle. The factual differences are designed to express different spiritual truths. Correct chronological sequence may be disregarded for better representation of spiritual meaning.[5] Spiritual truth can, in fact, be preserved in material falsehood.[6] In Scripture as a whole, but especially in St John's Gospel, there is an admixture of the un-historical with a view to spiritual teaching.[7] Origen, therefore, admits the presence of extensive disagreements only to deny that they represent any serious problem at all. In fact, the greater the variety of accounts, the greater the range of spiritual meaning.

This does not, of course, exclude the possibility of historical harmonisation as well. In answer to an objection of Celsus about the inconsistency in the Gospel records of the number of angels who appeared at the time of the resurrection, Origen declares that the Gospel statements can be justified both as historical events and as manifesting some allegorical meaning concerning the truths made clear to people who have been prepared to see the resurrection of the

---

[1] O. 10, 3.   [2] O. 10, 20–2.

[3] O. 10, 8. In O. Frag. 21 he does harmonise the initial calls of Peter, but does not there discuss the different occasions of the naming. Chrysostom claims that the Johannine account makes the synoptic record of the sudden call of Peter by the lakeside more easily credible (Chr. 18, 3).

[4] O. 10, 3.   [5] O. 32, 2.

[6] O. 10, 4–6.   [7] O. Frag. 74.

Logos. He does not, however, develop the argument in detail then and there, because he regards it as an activity more proper to commentaries on the Gospels than to a work of apologetics.[1] In similar vein within the commentary on St John itself he asserts that the comparison of similar texts in the different Gospels is essential for two reasons—first, to show the harmony of things that appear to be in conflict, and secondly, to make clear the precise individual meaning of each apparently similar text.[2] It is, therefore, no surprise to find that within his commentaries there are indeed examples of harmonisation which are characteristic both in their ingenuity and in their improbability. He argues that there must have been different occasions when the Baptist spoke of himself as being unworthy to bear his successor's shoes and as being unworthy to loose them.[3] Similarly he decides in favour of the view that there must have been three separate occasions of the anointing of Jesus by a woman at dinner.[4] But such argumentation is not required by his fundamental position, and is rather the natural overflow of a restless inquiring mind, always ready to notice the most subtle distinctions of detail, and always overready to build a whole edifice of interpretation upon them.

Theodore does not adopt any such position which would enable him to evade the historical problem. For him the discrepancies are not so extensive, but the problem that they raise is more real. The chronologies he does not believe to be incompatible at all. The fundamental principle to which he appeals is that the Synoptic Gospels have in fact no true chronology. It is only John who is really concerned with chronology, as the precision of his dates bears witness.[5] The exact dating of the first miracle at Cana of Galilee proves that the temptation cannot have followed immediately upon the baptism.[6] The emphatic statement in John iii. 24 that John the Baptist was not yet cast into prison shows that everything recounted in chapters ii and iii of St John's Gospel must have happened before

---

[1] *Contra Celsum*, 5, 56.   [2] O. 6, 24.
[3] O. 6, 34 (John i. 27).   [4] *Matt. Comm. Ser.* 77 (John xii. 1–8).
[5] T. 5, 14–35; 33, 22–33 (John i. 35). Cf. Temple, p. xi, 'We do not have to choose between two incompatible chronologies, for the Johannine chronology is the only one that we have'.
[6] T. 39, 1–13 (John ii. 1).

the start of the ministry described by the Synoptics.[1] In all probability the cleansing of the Temple was performed on two occasions; alternatively the explanation is to be found in the fact that Matthew and the others are simply not concerned about the question of date.[2]

Theodore does not, therefore, admit the existence of any conflict in chronology. But discrepancies in matters of fact he does not deny. He insists that they do not apply to essential issues, but occur only over matters of detail.[3] Such discrepancies ought not to be the occasion of surprise. There are clear reasons why they ought rather to be expected. In the first place Mark and Luke were not themselves disciples, and therefore their records have not got the full evidential value of the firsthand witness.[4] The same distinction of Matthew and John as the more important Gospels, in view of the position of their authors as actual eye-witnesses, had been made by Eusebius in his discussion of apparent conflicts within the Gospel records. But to Eusebius this only suggested that in the dispensation of the Holy Spirit they had been chosen to record the things of greater importance, while less important matters were left for the secondary evangelists.[5] Theodore, however, finds in the distinction ground for regarding Mark and Luke as less reliable witnesses in matters of factual detail. The only exception that he mentions is in the precise recording of the double cock crow associated with Peter's denial. Here Mark gives the fuller and more strictly accurate account, but

[1] T. 53, 11–23 (cf. also Eusebius, *H.E.* 3, 24, 7–13; Chr. 17, 1). On this point, however, Theodore is strangely inconsistent. He appears to have forgotten that he has earlier asserted that there is a gap between John ii. 11 and ii. 12 during which several things happened which John has omitted as already recorded by others (T. 42, 18–24). The main motive for this earlier assertion appears to be the feeling that the cleansing of the Temple requires some degree of notable public ministry before it (T. 43, 5–10).

[2] T. 53, 23–33. Chrysostom also believes that there were probably two separate occasions, and gives the additional reasoning that the wording of the Johannine rebuke ('a house of merchandise') is milder than the synoptic wording ('den of robbers') and is therefore more suited to an earlier occasion (Chr. 23, 2). More surprising is Chrysostom's assertion that the two accounts of Jesus' walking on the water in Matthew and in John refer to different occasions (Chr. 43, 1; John vi. 19–21).   [3] T. 244, 13–28.

[4] T. 238, 34–239, 7; 244, 34–245, 2.

[5] Eusebius, *Quaestiones ad Marinum*, 4, 1 (*P.G.* 22, 953 A).

this can easily be explained on the basis of Mark's close connection with Peter.[1]

Secondly, a considerable proportion of these points of conflict occur in the records of the passion. But at the time of the crucifixion all the disciples except John had forsaken Jesus and fled. He alone, therefore, was in a position to know the exact detail of those last hours.[2] In any event, the kind of points over which there are differences are just the kind of points over which men do habitually differ in the remembering of events. Differences in point of the precise time of an event, for example, are just the sort of thing that one should expect.[3] But Theodore goes beyond the attempt to show that these differences are not to be the occasion of surprise. He too, like Origen, desires to give them some positive value. They ought, he says, even to be welcomed, because they are clear evidence that there has been no deliberate collusion on the part of the evangelists.[4] The marginal element of discrepancy is in fact good evidence of the veracity of the evangelists and thus of the overall historical reliability of their accounts.

None the less Theodore is by no means averse to the activity of finding resolutions of apparent conflicts. If Matthew says that the woman with the alabaster cruse of ointment anointed Jesus' head, while John says she anointed his feet, then doubtless she must have done both. John, knowing that Matthew has already recorded the anointing of the head, deliberately gives only the additional information about his feet to provide a fuller account of the quality of her love.[5] When John says that Jesus carried his own cross, there is no conflict there either. Jesus started out carrying the cross, which was transferred to Simon of Cyrene *en route*, as the precise wording of Luke in fact implies.[6] Such comparatively reasonable instances of harmonisation he does offer, but, because he does not regard it as essential to find a complete solution to every conflict, he is free of the temptation to work out unduly complicated and far-fetched explanations of apparent differences. Mark's account of the exact time of the resurrection can in fact be squared perfectly with that

[1] T. 189, 10–13.
[2] T. 245, 2–3.
[3] T. 239, 7–9.
[4] T. 244, 23–34; 252, 15–32.
[5] T. 168, 7–28 (John xii. 1–8).
[6] T. 240, 7–27 (John xix. 17).

of the other evangelists, but it would not be a matter of any great moment if it could not.[1] The same is true of his record of the precise hour of the crucifixion.[2]

Cyril is comparatively unconcerned with the issue. John's purpose was to supplement the other Gospels by providing a deeper, more doctrinal, account. Therefore, when we find differing accounts of some incident, the important thing is to show how John has brought out the most vital significance of the happening.[3] His concentration is therefore directed towards the theological meaning of the Johannine record in itself. In this respect his approach to the Gospel is more adequate than that of any other of the early commentators. Comparisons of chronology he does not raise at all. He does very occasionally point to apparent conflicts in points of detail. Like Theodore, he insists that these apparent conflicts concern only unimportant matters of detail, and not essentials, but from that fact he draws a very different conclusion. To Theodore it suggested that the inconsistencies, being in matters of detail only, could be admitted without undue concern. Cyril, on the other hand, argues that it is impossible to believe that the evangelists, while agreeing so completely in all matters of importance, should then contradict one another in something so insignificant. He therefore finds it necessary to indulge in the somewhat improbable argument that there were many attendants present at the crucifixion, and while one lot gave Jesus a sponge of vinegar on a reed, others gave him the sponge on a piece of hyssop.[4] Cyril's strength as a commentator lies, therefore, not so much in the way in which he meets the detailed problem of the relation between John and the Synoptics, but rather in his comparative readiness to ignore it.

While he does thus virtually ignore the more obvious points of conflict in the varying accounts of the same incident, he does occasionally raise less obvious points, which require treatment of a rather different kind. John declares that when the word became flesh, he was 'full of grace and truth'; yet Luke ii. 52 speaks of Jesus advancing in wisdom and grace. The problem is met by

[1] T. 246, 16–36; 251, 21–252, 7.   [2] T. 239, 9–17 (John xix. 14).
[3] Cyr. *in* John xii. 14–15 (II, 306, 7–9).
[4] Cyr. *in* John xix. 29 (III, 94, 6–29).

drawing a distinction between what is said of Jesus as Logos and what is said of men's growing estimation of him—a distinction of which he makes use in other places in interpreting the Christology of the Fourth Gospel as a whole.[1] Again, he contrasts Jesus' action in visiting Samaria with his own limitation of his mission to the lost sheep of the house of Israel according to Matt. xv. 24. Here he points to John's phrase 'He *must needs* pass through Samaria'. This is an indication of a deeper purpose behind the action of Jesus. He goes not simply to preach to the Samaritans, but to enact the transference of the blessing of God away from Israel. This too is part of a consistent interpretation of the symbolism of the Fourth Gospel, of which Cyril makes widespread use in other contexts.[2] In these cases, therefore, Cyril is free from any criticism of special pleading, because his solutions are entirely in line with his overall theological interpretation of the Gospel.

Finally we find in all the commentators an occasional appeal to the Synoptic Gospels in order to provide the explanation or interpretation of some happening or saying in the Fourth Gospel. Thus Theodore, Chrysostom, and Cyril all ascribe the hesitation of Philip, in responding to the request of the Greeks to see Jesus, to his memory of Jesus' words in Matt. x. 5, forbidding the disciples to 'go into any way of the Gentiles'.[3] Heracleon had an allegorical interpretation of Jesus' going down to Capernaum in John ii. 12, which was based on the fact that Jesus was not recorded to have done anything there. Origen objects to the interpretation on the

---

[1] Cyr. *in* John i. 14 (I, 143, 28–144, 9). Cf. p. 132 n. 4 below.

[2] Cyr. *in* John iv. 4 (I, 263, 1–25). Origen tackles the same basic difficulty in O. 13, 52, though the Matthaean text with which he contrasts the action of Jesus is Matt. x. 5 and not xv. 24. The difference of method in meeting the problem is interestingly representative of the difference between them as commentators. Origen offers two lines of solution. (1) Matt. x. 5 can be given a purely allegorical intepretation. (2) If we observe the wording of the two accounts carefully, we will notice that the injunction is against entering 'any city of the Samaritans'. John never asserts that Jesus did enter the city, only that he abode with them for two days, that is, with those who had come out of the city to him at the well. Origen here shows great ingenuity and acute observations of detail, but lacks the theological depth of Cyril. Chrysostom asserts that the Evangelist has made special mention of the woman's coming out of the city, expressly to meet any Jewish cavil that he was disobeying his own injunction given in Matt. x. 5 (Chr. 31, 4).

[3] T. 170, 34–171, 6; Chr. 66, 2; Cyr. *in* John xii. 21–2 (II, 310, 12–21).

ground that in the Synoptic Gospels Capernaum is the scene of very much activity on the part of Jesus.[1] Such comparisons do not always further the cause of the best exegesis. In his consideration of Jesus' saying 'A prophet is not without honour save in his own country', Cyril makes no explicit reference to the Synoptic version of the saying, but it is presumably due to his memory of its setting there that he completely misinterprets the passage in John as a reference to Nazareth.[2]

[1] O. 10, 11.
[2] Cyr. *in* John iv. 44 (1, 300, 6–12). Chrysostom refers it to Capernaum on the strength of Luke x. 15 (Chr. 35, 1, 2).

CHAPTER III

HISTORICITY AND SYMBOLISM

I. THE PROBLEM OF HISTORICITY

One of the bewildering features of modern Johannine studies is the radically divergent answers that are given to the question of the historical character of the book. While one interpreter may regard it as the romantic creation of the mystical imagination, another believes it to be absolutely rooted and grounded in history. The cleavage of opinion does not find such violent expression in the early centuries, but nevertheless it is already present. The only early writers who accept at all the possibility of there being differing degrees of historicity attaching to different parts of the scriptural record are, as we have seen, Origen and Theodore. The two stand in opposing camps in their assessment of the Gospel's historicity. For Origen the Gospel has a special admixture of the unhistorical.[1] For Theodore it has the greatest historical reliability as a firsthand account.[2]

Origen was always on the alert to find a deeper meaning in the words of Scripture. When Heracleon gives simply the natural straightforward meaning of a text, Origen's repeated criticism is that this is πολὺ ἁπλούστερον, that it does not go nearly deep enough.[3] Many incidents are recorded for doctrinal purpose, and not as a strict historical account.[4] He himself, therefore, is always ready to move on to symbolic or allegorical meanings, to the complete exclusion of the historical sense if necessary. No doubt he regarded the bulk of the record as historical and even insists upon its historicity on occasions, but the claim of Père de Lubac that he never denies the literal historical meaning does not seem to stand up to the evidence.[5] De Lubac also asserts that on occasions Origen actually attacks the process of getting rid of the literal meaning of the Gospel by

---

[1] O. Frag. 74.
[2] T. 244, 34–245, 7.
[3] O. 6, 39; 19, 19.
[4] O. Frag. 20.
[5] H. de Lubac, Introduction to *Origène: Homélies sur la Genèse*, pp. 5–6.

allegorising.[1] But again the evidence does not confirm his assertion. The passages concerned do criticise a false allegorising, but the ground of criticism is not that they are getting rid of the literal sense. He is not attacking allegorism itself in defence of history, but a too facile allegorism which does not see through to the full and true spiritual meaning.

Origen sometimes points out that the evangelist has given clear indications that a passage requires allegorical interpretations, but in practice he does not appear to need any special pointers before going behind and beyond the literal meaning.[2] The kind of deeper meaning that he finds varies from the most arbitrary allegorising to a profound understanding of the symbolism of the Gospel. Examples of the former are particularly to be found in his treatment of numbers and of place-names, though they are not restricted to such cases.[3] For instance, the deeper meaning of the saying about the latchet of Christ's shoe, which Origen prefers to Heracleon's own simple interpretation, is an allusion to the incarnation and to the descent into Hades.[4] Over against this must be set such penetrating comments as his interpretation of the words in John xiii. 30, 'He...went out straightway, and it was night'. Judas went out not simply from the house in which the supper was being held, but altogether from Jesus himself, like those of whom it is said in the epistle that 'they went out from among us'. The night into which he went was symbolic of the darkness in his own soul, or the darkness which pursued but could not overtake the true light.[5] In each case a deeper meaning is

[1] H. de Lubac, 'Typologie et Allégorisme', p. 214; *Histoire et Esprit*, pp. 124 and 202. The texts to which he appeals are O. 13, 9 and O. 20, 20.

[2] O. 13, 30; 32, 4. H. N. Bate ('Some Technical Terms of Greek Exegesis', p. 60) suggesst that herein lies the real difference between the allegorising of Alexandria and of Antioch, namely that the Antiochenes really do accept the principle that the context must give special evidence to justify an allegorical interpretation before allegorising is to be allowed. J. Guillet in his comparative study of the exegetical methods of Origen and Theodore finds them at one in their use of obscurities or apparent inconsequentialities in the literal sense as evidence of a hidden sense (p. 264). An example from Theodore's commentary is his comment on John xv. 15: 'Evidenter et hoc, sicut alia multa, figurate est dictum. Nam si attente verbum istud consideremus, ne verum quidem apparet' (T. 203, 4–6).

[3] O. 2, 33 contains a specific assertion of the profit to be gained from the interpretation of names.   [4] O. 6, 35 (John i. 27).

[5] O. 32, 24.

found in the detail of the narrative, but they are deeper meanings of profoundly different character.

Such recognition of a deeper meaning is not, of course, exclusive of a simpler historical meaning. Sometimes Origen's comment draws specific attention to meanings of both kinds. The night by which Nicodemus came to Jesus was both the historical means of avoiding the observation of other Pharisees and a symbol of the night of his own ignorance.[1] The same phrase has both literal and symbolic significance. On another occasion he suggests that it is a regular scriptural usage for the same word appearing twice within a single context to alternate between a literal and spiritual meaning. While he describes this as a general practice of Scripture, he presumably found it particularly evident in the Fourth Gospel, as all his illustrations are drawn from it. He cites the references to harvest in iv. 35, to the drinking of water in iv. 7 and 10, and to seeing and not seeing in ix. 39.[2]

Origen, in fact, does not regard the Fourth Gospel as requiring a spiritual manner of interpretation radically different from that applicable to Scripture as a whole. He is as free with his allegorical interpretations when dealing with the first three Gospels as when dealing with the fourth.[3] The only difference is that he seems to find the Fourth Gospel lending itself more readily to his general manner of interpretation; it is there particularly that he finds pointers towards and clear illustrations of his method. The method itself is of universal application, but it is in the firstfruits of all Scripture that its appropriateness is most patently evident.

[1] O. Frag. 34 (John iii. 1).

[2] *Comm. Rom.* 3, 7. Origen, however, is not consistent in his treatment of John iv. 35. In his commentary he agrees that the first half of the text sounds like a simple historical statement, but goes on to argue that as such it simply cannot be fitted into the gospel chronology. John iv. 35, he argues, cannot be as much as eight months after the events of chapter ii, which a literal interpretation of the text would require. This, he suggests, ought to convince people that 'many of the things spoken by the Saviour may be of purely intellectual purport and void of literal or bodily meaning' (O. 13, 39). For this argument to be valid, Origen has to forget his other principle that it may be the chronological sequence that is not historical. Cf. p. 15 above.

[3] H. Smith, *Ante-Nicene Exegesis of the Gospels*, pp. 34–6. In so far as Origen's Commentary on St Matthew is less allegorical than that on St John, the reason seems more likely to be the later date of the former work than any supposed difference in the character of the two gospels. Cf. R. Hanson, *Origen's Doctrine of Tradition*, p. 29.

Theodore, on the other hand, has, as we have seen, an especial respect for the historical accuracy of the Gospel. This applies particularly to the question of chronology. The only exception to strict chronological order in the Gospel is the words of Jesus at the close of chapter xii. These, he says, must actually have been spoken before the withdrawal of Jesus recorded in xii. 36, but have been placed after it at the very end of the whole section so as to provide a final emphatic indictment of the Jews' failure to believe.[1]

When curious historical details enter into the narrative, Theodore is keen to give a historical explanation of them. Thus Christ's seamless robe woven from the top, which suggested to Origen the wholeness of Christ's teaching, to Cyprian the unity of the church, and to Cyril the virgin birth of Christ, receives from Theodore no other comment than that such methods of weaving were common in the time of Christ, although in his day they had died out except for soldiers' uniforms.[2]

More important is the appeal to incidental points of detail as corroborative evidence of the historical accuracy of the Gospel. Theodore finds this particularly illustrated by the range of vivid detail in the whole story of the raising of Lazarus.[3] In this Cyril is completely at one with him.[4] It is, in fact, Cyril who makes the most frequent use of this particular argument. He employs it especially in connection with the many place-names and precise time references to be found in the Gospel. John's memory of the occasion of the teaching in chapter vi as having been given in the synagogue at Capernaum is evidence that he is not likely to be at fault about the content of the teaching.[5] His description of the time of Jesus' arrival at the well of Sychar as 'about the sixth hour' is

---

[1] T. 180, 8–23.

[2] Origen, *Matt. Comm. Ser.* 128; Cyprian, *De Unitate Ecclesiae*, 7; Cyr. *in* John xix. 23 (III, 89, 11–22); T. 241, 6–16. Even Chrysostom, while emphasising mainly the precision with which the prophecy is fulfilled and the characteristic cheapness and simplicity of such a robe, does mention that some people see in it an allegorical allusion to the divinity from above possessed by the crucified (Chr. 85, 1–2).

[3] T. 156, 2–10.

[4] Cyr. *in* John xi. 31 (II, 278, 10–13).

[5] Cyr. *in* John vi. 59 (I, 547, 14–18). Cf. also his comment on Bethabara in John i. 28 (I, 165, 6–10).

a clear sign of his passionate concern for absolute accuracy, even in the most insignificant matters.[1]

Again, the incidental historical detail may be regarded as a guarantee not so much of the accuracy of the Evangelist as of the truly divine character of the events that he records. This argument is employed alike by Theodore, Cyril and Chrysostom. John the Baptist's sojourn in the desert was to ensure that his witness to Jesus could not be regarded as having the bias of personal friendship or acquaintance.[2] The water-pots used at Cana of Galilee were ones after the Jews' manner of purifying to ensure that they had never held wine and could have had no lees lurking at the bottom, and they were filled to the brim to ensure that no wine could have been added afterwards.[3] Lazarus was allowed to remain dead four days, so that no one could claim that he had never really died.[4] Jesus was laid in a new tomb, so that there could be no question about the identity of the one who was risen.[5] On other occasions the value of the recorded detail is found in the way that it reveals more fully the reasonableness and the intrinsic probability of the narrative. The season of Nisan is a time when there would be much grass on which the people could sit.[6] Winter is a season when men would be likely to congregate at Solomon's porch.[7] The sixth hour is the hottest hour of the day, a time when it would be natural to sit down and rest by a well.[8]

But for anyone who takes seriously the historical character of the Gospel, the demonstration of its historical reasonableness and intrinsic probability is clearly too big a problem to be settled by the appeal to a few such incidental details. It is essential to show the discourses and activity of Jesus not merely as having a coherent theological interpretation but also as being credible occurrences in

[1] Cyr. *in* John iv. 6 (I, 266, 27–267, 3). Cf. also his comment on the eight days in John xx. 26 (III, 144, 5–9).
[2] T. 31, 8–21 (John i. 31).
[3] Chr. 22, 1–2; T. 40, 21–3 (John ii. 6–7). O. Frag. 29 adds that this is also why Jesus ordered the servants and not the disciples to do the filling.
[4] Cyr. *in* John xi. 17 (II, 271, 19–22).
[5] T. 243, 8–14; Cyr. *in* John xix. 41 (III, 106, 26–30); Chr. 85, 4.
[6] T. 94, 9–14 (John vi. 10).
[7] Cyr. *in* John x. 23 (II, 249, 12–14).
[8] Cyr. *in* John iv. 6 (I, 266, 21–7).

their original historical setting. This is a problem of which all the commentators, and Theodore in particular, are acutely aware. The first important principle of which they make use is the ability of Jesus to read the thoughts and hearts of men. With the help of this principle, it is always possible to strengthen the coherence of the discourses. Any apparent jump in thought, which might at first sight be supposed to have been baffling to an original audience, can always be explained as the answer of Jesus not to the spoken words of his interlocutors but to their unspoken thoughts.[1]

The second principle is one of even more far-reaching significance and capable of a very wide range of application. This is the very reasonable assumption that the aim of Jesus in his actions and his discourses was the practical aim of converting his hearers to the truth. If Jesus acts openly by sending the blind man all the way to Siloam instead of healing him on the spot or by ordering the paralytic to violate the law by carrying his bed on the sabbath, it is all with this purpose in view, that the attention of the largest possible number of people may be drawn to the greatness of the miracle.[2] If, on another occasion, he rejects the suggestion of his brothers to show himself openly and delays his own attendance at the feast, his overall intention is still the same. He wishes to give an opportunity for the fury of his opponents to subside and for the interest of his friends to grow, so that all may be better prepared to respond to his teaching.[3] The precise form taken by his dialogues with the Jews can be better understood when we recognise that his aim is to woo them gradually from their natural psilanthropism to a full acknowledgement of his divinity. This principle, as we shall have occasion to see later, was of particular importance, not merely in demonstrating the historicity of the dialogues but also in making possible a uniform Christological exegesis.[4]

[1] Chr. 40, 1; Cyr. *in* John v. 37–8 (I, 375); *in* John vi. 43 (I, 505, 20–506, 10); *in* John viii. 43 (II, 88, 25–89, 8).

[2] T. 134, 5–23 (John ix. 7; v. 8).

[3] T. 111, 4–18 (John vii. 8–10). Cf. a Catena fragment of Theodore of Heraclea who describes the withdrawal of Jesus at the end of his public ministry in John xii. 36 as an act of φιλανθρωπία designed to give his enemies a chance to reflect (Cramer, p. 332).

[4] Cyr. *in* John xii. 49–50 (II, 339, 32–340, 14). For the Christological application of this principle, see pp. 139–40 below.

Even when all these principles are pressed into full service, there are still considerable elements within the discourses which must have been largely unintelligible to their hearers, if we regard them as strict history. It is further evidence of Theodore's honesty and of his historical sense that he alone appears to recognise that a real problem still remains. It is a problem with which he is prepared to grapple, but which he is clearly uncertain just how to handle.

Figurative language, it is true, was not something foreign and unfamiliar to the Jews,[1] yet Jesus' use of it is on occasions designed to conceal a truth for which his hearer or hearers are not ready.[2] There is nothing therefore surprising in the failure of the Jews to understand him at such points. Even the disciples frequently failed to understand him until his words received confirmation in later events.[3] This is a principle which John himself has made explicit in his reference to Jesus' saying about the destruction of the temple of his body and its raising again in three days. It is a principle capable of wide application. Much of Jesus' teaching only became intelligible after his resurrection and ascension, and in such cases the purpose of Jesus' words was not the benefit of his immediate hearers, but the profit of future generations for whom they were later to be recorded in writing.[4] This is the primary means which Theodore employs to overcome the difficulty, and he can justifiably claim the precedent of the Evangelist's own example. On the one occasion when he does not use this line of argument, the alternative adopted is very much less satisfactory. The allegory of the good shepherd at the beginning of chapter x was not understood by the Jews, because in it the claim of Jesus to a superiority over all the other messengers of God was wrapped up in parabolic form. Jesus' use of an obscure and indirect method of teaching in this instance was deliberately adopted to avoid the appearance of pride involved in the open assertion of such a claim.[5] Such a combination of arguments seems to render the delivery of the allegory at all entirely pointless.

For Theodore, therefore, much of the failure of the Jews to understand and respond to the message of Jesus was easily accounted for

[1] T. 106, 8–10.
[2] T. 49, 27–30 (John iii. 11).
[3] T. 114, 37–115, 2.
[4] T. 81, 4–12; T. 106, 9–10; T. 146, 24–35.
[5] T. 141, 28–36 (John x. 1–6).

and not such as ought to be a matter of surprise. Not so with Cyril. For him the failure of the Jews to understand is always culpable. When the Evangelist declares of the allegory of the good shepherd 'This parable spake He unto them, but they understood not what things they were which He spake unto them', he means the 'This' to be emphatic. The parable was one of incomparable clarity and free from every kind of difficulty, and yet they failed to comprehend.[1]

There emerges therefore at this point a cleavage between the exegesis of Theodore and of Cyril. This cleavage becomes clearest in their differing treatment of the issue of the faith of the disciples in Jesus' own lifetime. Here there is a complete conflict of interpretation. At the very outset of the ministry John the Baptist acclaims Jesus as the Son of God, because he has seen the Spirit descending and remaining on him at his baptism. Cyril declares that the title Son of God signifies perfect Godhead and identity of substance with the Father. This, it is implied, is the intention both of the Evangelist and the Baptist.[2] Theodore says that the words apply not to Christ's divine nature, but to his human nature which receives the honour of the title Son of God by virtue of its union with the only-begotten in the Spirit, just as we too are made sons of God by the regenerating power of the Spirit at our baptism.[3] There is an underlying difference of Christological belief here, with which we shall be concerned later. But there is also a hestitation on Theodore's part about attributing to the Baptist a full recognition of the eternal relationship of Father and Son, which Cyril does not share.

This becomes far clearer in the case of the disciples and the friends of Jesus themselves. For Cyril, the acclamations of Nathanael, of Martha, and of Thomas are full affirmations of faith in the

---

[1] Cyr. *in* John x. 6 (II, 211, 5–17). Cf. also Cyr. *in* John vi. 60–2 (I, 547–50). The only instance in Pusey's edition of Cyril's commentary in which Cyril admits that Jesus allows himself to run the risk of being unintelligible or misunderstood by his hearers for the sake of giving beneficial instruction to later generations is an occasion in conversation not with his opponents but with his disciples; they misunderstood his reference to the death of Lazarus as a sleep, which must have had the ulterior motive of giving us an example of the avoidance of boasting (Cyr. *in* John xi. 11; II, 269, 8–14). The passage, however, belongs to the part of the commentary surviving only in fragmentary form, and its authenticity is clearly open to question.

[2] Cyr. *in* John i. 34 (I, 191, 15–20).

[3] T. 33, 5–21 (John i. 34).

uniqueness and divinity of Christ. He finds support for this view in the detailed form of each passage. Nathanael's faith is an appropriate response to the omniscience displayed by Christ, because it is the property of God alone to search out the hearts of men.[1] In the cases of Martha and Thomas, the presence of the definite article is evidence of the completeness of the faith affirmed.[2] There is one passage in the Gospel that appears at first sight to militate against this interpretation. In John xiv. 7 Jesus says to the disciples 'If ye had known me, ye would have known my father also. From henceforth ye know Him and have seen Him.' Cyril argues that the main burden of the saying is of general application rather than applicable to the disciples only. The only ignorance being ascribed to the disciples is a failure to recognise the deeper metaphorical meaning of the saying that Christ is the way. 'Henceforth' does not mean 'from this particular moment', but 'from the time of my coming to reveal God', 'from the time of the incarnation as a whole'. The saying is therefore not inconsistent with the Johannine and Matthaean traditions that the disciples recognised Jesus during the time of his ministry as the Christ, the Son of the living God.[3]

For Theodore, this kind of interpretation is ruled out as a historical absurdity. The disciples did not reach so complete a faith so soon.[4] Words which might appear to suggest that they did must be capable of a less exalted interpretation. Nathanael's response cannot represent a full assertion of Christ's inherent deity, for he had displayed no greater power of knowledge than we can find recorded of the prophets, as in the story of Elisha's rebuke of Gehazi.[5] Martha is a Jew accepting Jesus as the awaited Messiah, and the Jewish expectation was of a human rather than of a divine figure.[6] Even the

[1] Cyr. in John i. 49 (I, 199).

[2] Cyr. in John xi. 27 (II, 275, 8–16); Cyr. in John xx. 28 (III, 151, 20–152, 12).

[3] Cyr. in John xiv. 7 (II, 414–17).

[4] T. 159, 33–6; T. 169, 35–170, 2 (John xii. 16); T. 192, 29–193, 4 (John xiv. 10). Cf. Theodore, Cat. Hom. 8, 3, which cites in evidence John viii. 19, xiv. 9, xvi. 25, xvi. 24 and xvi. 12–13.

[5] T. 37 (John i. 49). In this instance Chrysostom is in full agreement with him. His main reason is that the other interpretation would destroy the significance of Peter's confession at Caesarea Philippi. He does not, therefore, need to minimise the confessions of Martha and of Thomas in the same way (Chr. 21, 1).

[6] T. 161, 1–12 (John xi. 27).

exclamation of Thomas is an exclamation of gratitude to God for the wonder of the miracle of the resurrection, rather than an affirmation of faith in the divinity of Jesus. The sudden reversal of belief, which would be involved if the latter meaning were the true one, makes such an interpretation hardly plausible.[1] For Theodore also it becomes impossible to accept the ἀπάρτι of John xiv. 7 as referring to that precise moment. But his need, in contrast to that of Cyril, is to transfer the reference to a later rather than to an earlier moment. He declares that Christ's reference is to the time of the coming of the Spirit, and that was the moment from which the disciples' true faith began.[2] He has a clear conception of the gradual development of the disciples' faith, which was not complete or firmly established until Pentecost. Any statements in the Gospel that appear to conflict with this historical scheme must be interpreted into conformity with it. Thus, while Cyril has no difficulty in accepting the insufflation of John xx. 22 as a real ἀπαρχή of the Spirit, Theodore interprets it simply as a promise of the future gift. The word 'Receive' here means 'You will receive'.[3]

Cyril and Theodore, therefore, are at one in their unqualified acceptance of the full historicity of the Gospel. In this respect there

---

[1] T. 256, 29–35 (John xx. 28). This particular feature of Theodore's exegesis was one that caused especial offence, and was used against him to secure his condemnation at the fifth general council in A.D. 553. (Cf. R. Devreesse, *Essai sur Théodore de Mopsueste*, p. 221 n. 4 and pp. 247–51.)

[2] T. 191, 16–19.

[3] Cyr. *in* John xx. 22–3 (III, 133–8); T. 254, 29–255, 4. Cyril here follows the tradition of Origen who regards the two occasions as representing gifts of the Spirit differing in quantity; he finds this implied by the difference between the words 'Receive' and 'Be baptised' (*Con. Cel.* 7, 51). Eusebius states that the first gift was the gift of authority to forgive sins only, while at Pentecost other gifts of the Spirit, such as the power to work miracles, were given. He finds evidence of the partial nature of the first gift in the absence of the article in John xx. 22 (*Supplementa Minora Quaestionum ad Marinum* 9 and 10; *P.G.* 22, 1013 B–1016 B). Chrysostom seems prepared to accept either Theodore's or Eusebius' line of interpretation (Chr. 86, 3). Cyril uses this incident to account for Thomas being allowed to touch the risen Christ, whereas Mary was forbidden. Mary was forbidden because she had not yet received the Holy Spirit; Thomas was allowed because he had, even in his absence, received the Spirit as given to the twelve (Cyr. *in* John xx. 17; III, 119, 6–30; *in* John xx. 27; III, 145, 21–146, 6). This at least seems preferable to Origen's curious suggestions that it was due to Mary's being a woman, or to Christ's needing the cleansing of the Father after the passion (O. 13, 30; O. 6, 55).

is no difference between them. The difference derives from Theodore's greater historical realism. He is conscious, as Cyril is never conscious, of the difficulties involved in the maintenance of this axiomatic faith in the historicity of the Gospel. He also takes the problem far more into account in the actual course of exegesis, with results that on occasion distract from the fullest appreciation of the Gospel's real content.

2. THE PRESENCE OF SYMBOLISM

God does nothing in vain, and therefore every detail of Scripture, however small and insignificant, is intentional and capable of bringing benefit to the careful reader.[1] No early exegete would have had any doubt about this principle. We have already seen how the presence of such details in the Fourth Gospel was used in confirmation of the accurate knowledge of the writer and of the intrinsic probability of the events described. But this does not exhaust the use made of them. It is the Alexandrines who give most frequent and most explicit expression to this principle of the importance of detail, and for them its significance was to be found primarily (though, as we have seen, not exclusively) in its symbolic or allegorical potentialities. The very same kind of detail that we have seen used in the cause of historicity is employed by Cyril in the presentation of a deeper spiritual exegesis. The record of Jesus and his disciples baptising in close proximity to where John the Baptist was doing the same was intended to teach the similarity without identity of John's baptism and Christian baptism.[2] The 'much grass' of John vi. 10 is a picture of spiritual refreshment, as the 'green pasture' of Psalm xxiii. 2 suggests.[3] The night through which the disciples fished to no purpose is the darkness of the dispensation before Christ.[4] The night into which Judas departed was a cloak for his unholy thoughts and a picture of the hell to which he was going.[5]

[1] O. 20, 36; Cyr. *in* John iv. 31 (I, 291, 12–15); Chr. 36, 1.

[2] Cyr. *in* John iii. 23 (I, 232–3).

[3] Cyr. *in* John vi. 10 (I, 415, 14–21). For Theodore's very different kind of comment, see p. 26 above.

[4] Cyr. *in* John xxi. 1–6 (III, 157, 23–158, 17).

[5] Cyr. *in* John xiii. 30 (II, 375, 11–13).

The loss of Malchus' right ear was a symbol of the Jews' loss of right hearing in refusing to accept the teaching of Christ.[1] In both these last two cases, which are the only ones in which the equivalent comment of Origen survives, we find that the earlier Alexandrian commentator had already given the same interpretation.[2] The language is not particularly close, and it would therefore suggest not necessarily that Cyril is in direct dependence here on the writings of Origen, but rather that in this kind of comment he was continuing a general Alexandrian tradition of exegesis, of which Origen was the chief exponent. He follows the same tradition in his continuation of the practice of an allegorical interpretation of the numbers in the Gospel record. Here also there was clear precedent in the writings of Origen, but in this case there is an even less close correspondence in the detail of their exegesis. Cyril's interpretations of numbers are no less arbitrary than those of Origen, but they have normally a more specifically Christian content. The tenth hour at which the two disciples followed Jesus is not just a holy number, as with Origen, but a symbol of the lateness of Christ's coming.[3] The five fishes, which for Origen are associated with the meanings of scripture on the basis of the traditional five senses, are for Cyril a symbol of the law expressed in the fivefold book of Moses.[4] Cyril further differs from Origen in not employing this kind of interpretation at all in the case of place-names.[5]

It need hardly be added that such symbolic interpretations of detail did not exclude the historical meaning, or the possibility of that particular detail having some especial significance in its literal, historical sense also. Sometimes the two different kinds of interpretation simply stand side by side as separate comments. Thus for Cyril the newness of the tomb in which Christ was laid is primarily a symbol of the newness of the conquest of death that he was

[1] Cyr. *in* John xviii. 10 (III, 25, 11–18). Cf. Apollinarius *in* John xviii. 10 (Cramer, p. 378).

[2] O. 32, 24; *Matt. Comm. Ser.* 101.

[3] O. 2, 36; Cyr. *in* John i. 39 (I, 194, 17–26).

[4] Origen, *Comm. Matt.* 11, 2; Cyr. *in* John vi. 9 (I, 417, 10–418, 1).

[5] This is the more surprising in that he does make considerable use of the etymologies of names in his exegesis of the Old Testament and also in his commentaries on St Matthew and St Luke (see A. Kerrigan, pp. 376–83; H. Wutz, *Onomastica Sacra*, vol. II, pp. 1058–61).

accomplishing, yet he also adds as a subsidiary comment that which for Theodore and Chrysostom was the central thing, namely that it ensured that it was Christ and none other who came out from the tomb.[1] The eighth day of Christ's second appearance to the disciples after the resurrection is both evidence of the accuracy and precision of the Evangelist, and a picture of the weekly appearance of Christ in the body among his disciples at every Christian Eucharist.[2] At other times there is a more organic link between the points emphasised in the two different kinds of comment. The clearest examples of such an organic relation between the historical and the deeper meaning are the occasions on which Jesus is said to withdraw himself from the Jews because of their opposition and unbelief. This was an intelligible and proper historical action. It was also a picture of the withdrawal of God's favour from the Jews and its transference to the Gentile world. The literal and the deeper meanings have a clear and definite relation to one another.[3]

This last example introduces us to a new and more important feature in Cyril's spiritual interpretation of the Gospel. It is more than just a symbolic or allegorical interpretation of an isolated detail within the Gospel record; it represents the recognition of a symbolism within the Gospel of a much broader and more comprehensive kind. There are two great themes of God's dealings with men, which Cyril believes to underlie many of the stories and much of the activity of the Gospel.

The first theme is the inadequacy of the law, which is only a type finding its fulfilment in Christ. The deeper meaning of the miracle of the water into wine is the superiority of the Gospel over the letter of the Mosaic law, which is inadequate to meet the requirements of men. There is certainly much to be said for this interpretation. Cyril, however, is inclined to press the detail of the story in an arbitrary allegorical manner. The third day is the fulness of time, and the ruler of the feast is the Christian priest, who is first partaker of the fruits.[4] Also he finds the same fundamental meaning in other

---

[1] Cyr. *in* John xix. 41 (III, 105–6). Cf. p. 26 above.

[2] Cyr. *in* John xx. 26 (III, 144, 5–145, 20).

[3] Cyr. *in* John vi. 1 (I, 398–403); *in* John vii. 1 (I, 579–82); *in* John x. 40 (II, 262–3).

[4] Cyr. *in* John ii. 11 (I, 203–5).

places, where it is far less likely to be the correct interpretation. Thus the fruitless night fishing of the seven disciples in John xxi is a picture of the same ineffectiveness of the Mosaic law to complete the work of capturing men wholly for the service of God. The superiority of the command of Christ is symbolised by the right-hand side of the boat, where the catch is finally made.[1] However much the theme of the law's inadequacy may be present in the real thought of the Gospel, it seems hardly likely that it is the true meaning of this particular story.

But the Gospel is not the conclusion of God's economy, of God's dealings with men. The stories of the Gospel are therefore not only the antitype completing the foreshadowing of the Old Testament law. They can themselves also be types, with a forward-looking reference. Thus, the second great theme that Cyril develops is the way in which the activity of Jesus foreshadows the Gentile mission. Here, as we have seen, the deeper meaning is normally related to the closely allied historical fact of actual withdrawals from Jewish opposition.[2] This idea is not original to Cyril, but had already been suggested by Origen with reference to the same historical context.[3] Cyril, however, develops the idea very considerably. As with the concept of the inadequacy of the law, this development takes the twofold form of the elaboration of historical detail within the setting of this wider symbolism and the discovery of the same symbolism in other less plausible contexts. The first form of elaboration is well illustrated by Cyril's whole treatment of the narrative of chapter vi. The opening verse, as we have seen, symbolised for him the inauguration of the Gentile mission. He attempts therefore to interpret the succeeding narrative consistently within the same historical perspective. Christ's withdrawal alone to the mountain is therefore interpreted of the ascension; his coming to the disciples on the lake pictures his second coming at night, when he will have the world, pictured by the sea, beneath his feet and will bring the boat of the Church speedily and safely to heaven; and those who came to him the next day with fine words but inadequate faith are a type of those who in the day of judgment will say to him, 'Lord, Lord', but who

[1] Cyr. *in* John xxi. 1–6 (III, 156–60).
[2] Cf. p. 34 above.
[3] *Comm. Matt.* 10, 23 (John vi. 15).

will be rejected.[1] There is a real attempt here to provide a unified, spiritual exegesis, but the greater the elaboration of the pattern the less likely appears the interpretation. The second form of the development is the discovery of the symbolism in a wide range of contexts. It is present, for example, even in the interpretation of the first miracle at Cana, which is primarily interpreted in terms of the inadequacy of the law. The setting of the marriage feast to which Jesus was invited in Galilee of the Gentiles is a picture of the Gentile Church to be, replacing the Jewish synagogue, which rejected the heavenly bridegroom.[2] More striking still is the interpretation of the healing of the man born blind as a picture of Christ's mission to the Gentiles, a people who unlike Israel have never enjoyed the gift of light.[3] This interpretation is no chance allegorisation of one detail in the opening verse of the story. Whether valid or not, it is for Cyril an important element in the total meaning of the sign, to which he constantly returns in the course of his exposition.[4]

Thus the two outstanding features of Cyril's spiritual exegesis are the broad comprehensiveness of its conception and the specifically Christian character of the content of meaning disclosed by this method.[5]

It is in this sphere of spiritual exegesis that we most naturally expect to find a striking difference between the exegesis of Cyril and of Theodore. Such a difference is indeed present, but it does not mean that Theodore is bound solely and completely to a purely literal manner of interpretation. This can be most simply illustrated from his interpretation of the words, 'Arise, let us go hence', in

[1] Cyr. *in* John vi. 15 (1, 425, 9–27); *in* John vi. 18–21 (1, 430, 8–432, 13); *in* John vi. 26 (1, 436, 16–438, 5).

[2] Cyr. *in* John ii. 11 (1, 204, 15–22).

[3] Cyr. *in* John ix. 1 (11, 134–5). This had also been suggested earlier by Origen (*Is. Hom.* 6, 3).

[4] Cyr. *in* John ix. 6–7 (11, 156, 10–16); *in* John ix. 28 (11, 185); *in* John ix. 38 (11, 202, 3–203, 13).

[5] The one example to be found in Pusey's edition of Cyril's commentary of a piece of exegesis in the truly Philonic, psychological tradition is an interpretation of Lazarus, Martha and Mary in terms of νοῦς, σάρξ and ψυχή (Cyr. *in* John xi. 44; 11, 292, 15–23). But the passage is a fragment of very doubtful authenticity and ought almost certainly to be rejected. Origen's interpretation is in terms of the lapsed Christian, the practical life and the contemplative life respectively. (O. Frag. 80.)

John xiv. 31. In view of the fact that the discourse continues in the next two chapters, he cannot accept the words in their most literal sense of ordinary physical departure from the upper room. To that extent he is less literal at this point in his exegesis than many other commentators both ancient and modern.[1] On the other hand he does not go to the length of a fully fledged spiritual interpretation of the kind which is suggested by Cyril, who finds in the words reference to a spiritual transition from the love of the world to choosing the will of God, from slavery to sonship, from the earth to the heavenly city, from sin to righteousness, from uncleanness to sanctification.[2] Theodore's interpretation is not purely literal, but it remains within the historical sphere. The meaning which he finds in the words is an expression of a readiness to go and meet his murderers without regret or fear of death. It is thus a fitting climax to the disclosure of God's purpose for the future given in the preceding verses.[3]

Theodore is perfectly capable of recognising deeper meanings and symbolic allusions in the Gospel. He sees that the reference to the resurrection in John ii. 19 shows that the cleansing of the Temple really depicts the abolition of the whole sacrificial system.[4] He recognises and develops a theological allusion to the creation story in the insufflation after the resurrection.[5] No doubt these are commonplaces of interpretation, but they show that Theodore was alive to symbolic and theological meanings in the Gospel.

He does not normally indulge, as Cyril does, in spiritual interpretations of the factual details of the historical narrative.[6] He does, however, frequently take individual words or concepts which are of a deliberately metaphorical character and draw out detailed symbolic significance from them. In some cases, he is simply developing more fully the intention of the metaphorical usage. In

---

[1] E.g. Chr. 76, 1; Westcott, vol. II, p. 187; Temple, p. 249.
[2] Cyr. *in* John xiv. 31 (II, 531–3). A similar spiritual interpretation in terms of transition from worldly to heavenly thoughts is attributed to Gregory Nazianzen (Cramer, p. 353).   [3] T. 200, 21–7.
[4] T. 43, 27–9.   [5] T. 253, 36–254, 9 (John xx. 22).
[6] The only exception is the interpretation of the clay used in healing the man born blind as a symbol of the creator. This is a very early exegesis which appears in Irenaeus, *Adv. Haer.* 5, 15, 2 (vol. II, p. 365) (John ix. 6). Cf. p. 55 below.

others, his interpretation seems quite extraneous to the real meaning of the phrase and of the passage. Just as it was a lifeless serpent that saved the Israelites from death, so it is through his apparent mortality and his death that Christ brings life.[1] When John the Baptist speaks of himself as the friend of the bridegroom and Jesus as the one who has the bride this is because Jesus is the bridegroom who takes the Church as his bride.[2] When in turn Jesus describes John the Baptist as a λύχνος, the word is well chosen because a lamp is no longer needed once the sun is risen.[3] The description of Jesus himself as φῶς has an especial appropriateness, because like Jesus the sun dies and rises again through the power of its own inherent nature.[4] The image of the pangs of travail to describe the temporary sorrow of the disciples at the time of the crucifixion was well chosen because through the resurrection there came to birth a new man, a new humanity born for immortality.[5] Once again, it is true that many of these interpretations can be found paralleled in earlier writers.[6] None the less, when taken together they reveal clearly the kind of symbolism that is most characteristic of Theodore's exegesis of the Gospel.

Theodore therefore does not eschew symbolic interpretations altogether, but the practical and literal bent of his exegesis does detract at times from the value of his comments. The particular nature of his approach to Scripture is less suited to the interpretation of this Gospel than of almost any other book of the Bible. This weakness shows itself primarily in his failure to grasp and give full expression to the realised eschatology of the Gospel, the sense of present spiritual achievement in the person of Jesus. In John i. 51 Jesus promises to Nathanael the vision of the angels of God ascending and descending on the Son of Man. Theodore interprets this as the literal angelic visitations at the temptation, in Gethsemane, at the

[1] T. 51, 13–18 (John iii. 14–15).
[2] T. 55–8 (John iii. 29).   [3] T. 88, 1–10 (John v. 35).
[4] T. 175, 26–36 (John xii. 35–6).   [5] T. 215, 13–21 (John xvi. 21).
[6] For the serpent, cf. Epistle of Barnabas xii. 7. This is not strictly a comment on the Gospel, but the point emphasised is the same as that emphasised by Theodore— αὐτὸς ὢν νεκρὸς δύναται ζωοποιῆσαι. Chrysostom also develops the imagery of the serpent, but in a different way—the venomless nature of the brazen serpent suggests the sinlessness of Christ (Chr. 27, 1). That there is a reference to the church as the

time of the resurrection and of the ascension.[1] Cyril has a reference to the ministry of the angels at the time of the temptation, but his primary interpretation is in wider terms of the angelic ministry as a whole carried out at Christ's command for the salvation of men.[2] In John v. 25 Jesus declares that 'the hour...now is when the dead shall hear the voice of the Son of God; and they that hear shall live'. Theodore refers simply to the widow of Nain's son, to Jairus' daughter and to Lazarus.[3] Again Cyril does refer to the case of Lazarus, but his main interpretation is of the change from spiritual death to spiritual life already at work in those who have faith in Christ.[4] Both exegetes recognise that the saying of Jesus in John xiii. 31, 'Now is the Son of Man glorified', refers to the passion. But for Theodore the glory is to be seen in the portents which accompanied the crucifixion, whereas for Cyril the cross itself is the glory.[5] When in John xiv. 18 and xiv. 28 Jesus promises to his disciples that he will come to them, Theodore finds its fulfilment in the historical happenings of the post-resurrection appearances.[6] For Cyril the reference is to his coming in the person of the Holy Spirit.[7]

These examples are of a fairly diverse character, and yet they have something significant in common. In every case Theodore's horizon of thought seems to be limited to the field of individual historical occurrences. Cyril seems to rise closer to the theological meaning of the Gospel. On occasions Theodore's characteristic approach enables him to make some minor point of possible value, which Cyril overlooks. Thus while Cyril gives only a spiritual interpretation of the command to 'Lift up your eyes and look on the fields

---

bride of Christ in John iii. 29 is generally assumed (cf. O. Frag. 45; Chr. 29, 3). For the development of the distinction between λύχνος and φῶς, cf. Chr. 40, 2 where Chrysostom makes a similar but slightly different point. The light of the sun is intrinsic; that of a λύχνος is not. For the association of the man born after travail with the new man brought into being at the resurrection, cf. Chrysostom (Chr. 79, 1) and a Catena fragment attributed to Apollinarius and Theodore of Heraclea (Cramer, p. 366).

[1] T. 38, 17–25. Cf. Chr. 21, 1.   [2] Cyr. *in* John i. 51 (1, 200).
[3] T. 84, 20–3.
[4] Cyr. *in* John v. 25 (1, 344–6).
[5] T. 186, 31–187, 3; Cyr. *in* John xiii. 31 (II, 377, 5–378, 9) (cf. pp. 83–4 below).
[6] T. 196, 3–9; 199, 1–5.
[7] Cyr. *in* John xiv. 18 (II, 470–3); *in* John xiv. 28 (II, 511–12).

that they are white already to harvest', Theodore suggests a more historical reference to the approaching Samaritans, ready for the harvesting of conversion.[1] Theodore's comment here may well be a true one, though the matter is clearly open to doubt.[2] What is not in doubt is that Theodore's natural tendency to favour this kind of more literal interpretation is a serious handicap to his discovering the deeper meaning of the gospel as a whole. Sometimes it even betrays him into comments which show a complete misunderstanding of the text. Thus he cannot accept any reference to the wind in John iii. 8, because we do know where the wind comes from and goes to and moreover the wind has no will to blow where it lists.[3] This is an extreme instance of a pedantic literalism. It is not typical in itself, but it is a striking example of what is his besetting weakness.

[1] Cyr. *in* John iv. 35 (1, 295–6); T. 66, 37–8. Chrysostom makes the same point as Theodore (Chr. 34, 2). Origen pours scorn on a literal interpretation of this passage by Heracleon. He does not quote it in full, but it appears to have been similar in purport to that of Theodore (O. 13, 41).

[2] Amongst modern commentators it has the support of Westcott (vol. 1, p. 166), Bernard (vol. 1, p. 157), Macgregor (p. 111) and Hoskyns (p. 247).

[3] T. 48, 35–49, 6.

CHAPTER IV

THE SIGNS

The first half of the Gospel is built up almost entirely of a series of signs and interpretative discourses. Theodore recognises the existence of this structure, but fails to do justice to its organic and theological character. He declares simply that it was Jesus' custom to follow his miracles with doctrinal instruction, because the greatness of his actions would serve as confirmation of his words.[1] He shows no special understanding of or interest in the actual concept of the sign. This finds most adequate treatment in Origen's commentary. The word 'sign' is used of things which are indicative of something beyond the mere fact of their occurrence. Therefore a sign need not be miraculous, as Biblical usage bears out. In fact every Biblical miracle is also a sign, but this is an empirical and not a logical fact. The phrase 'signs and wonders' is not a mere tautology, because one can distinguish in thought between the symbolic and the marvellous aspect of any miracle. It is the fact that the miracles of the Fourth Gospel are so carefully and explicitly referred to as signs that shows unquestionably that they require a deeper, spiritual interpretation.[2]

Two other passages from outside the commentary include relevant comments on the nature of a sign. In one passage Origen explains the words of Christ in John ii. 4 that his hour had not yet come to mean that the appropriate hour for his signs had not yet arrived. This, says Origen, is because signs are for unbelief, and unbelief can only be said to be present where there has already been preaching—a ministry on which Christ had not yet started at that time. This shows a recognition of a connection between the miracles and teaching of Jesus, but at no deeper theological level than that described

[1] T. 138, 30–2. Theodore's comment on the future witnessing of the Spirit and of the disciples promised in John xv. 26–7 provides an interesting parallel. The Spirit will provide the miracles in confirmation of the words spoken by the disciples (T. 206, 17–25).
[2] O. 13, 64.

by Theodore.[1] In another passage, Origen asserts that every sign in the Old Testament looks forward to something in the New, whereas the signs of the New Testament refer either to something in the age to come or to some historical occurrence subsequent to the time of the sign itself.[2] This is not a very satisfactory description of Origen's own method of interpreting the signs. The reference to later historical occurrences does occur in his work and is of importance in view of the use made of it by later exegesis and particularly by Cyril,[3] but the eschatological reference is certainly more characteristic of him. The ultimate significance for Origen is always to be found beyond history.[4]

In this chapter we shall take each of the main signs in the Gospel in turn and inquire how the earliest commentators understood their symbolic meaning.

1. JOHN ii. 1–11. THE TURNING OF THE WATER INTO WINE

The story is naturally referred to in teaching about marriage, but it is never suggested that this is the essential meaning of the sign.[5] Three main types of interpretation are to be found.

(a) Christ shows himself to be one with the Creator. This interpretation is found in Irenaeus, in whose writings this theme receives repeated emphasis.[6] It appears also in Origen,[7] Athanasius[8] and Chrysostom.[9]

(b) The marriage feast is a symbol of joy. This is the main interpretation given to the sign in Origen's commentary. Christ

---

[1] In Ps. cxliv (cxlv). 15 (J. B. Pitra, Analecta Sacra, vol. III, p. 356).

[2] Comm. Matt. 12, 3.　　　　　　　　[3] Cf. p. 35 above.

[4] O. 10, 18 οὐ γὰρ νομιστέον τὰ ἱστορικὰ ἱστορικῶν εἶναι τύπους, καὶ τὰ σωματικὰ σωματικῶν, ἀλλὰ τὰ σωματικὰ πνευματικῶν καὶ τὰ ἱστορικὰ νοητῶν.

[5] Tertullian (De Monogamia, 8, 7) even argues that the singleness of the occasion was deliberately intended to teach against second marriage. Cyril develops the significance of the reference to marriage in two ways. Christ is undoing the curse on childbirth of Gen. iii. 16 and he is declaring the blessing that he brings to be also for the generations yet unborn. But both these remain subsidiary to his main interpretation of the sign (Cyr. in John ii. 1–4; I, 201, 3–24).

[6] Irenaeus, Adv. Haer. 3, 11, 5 (vol. II, pp. 43–4).

[7] O. Frag. 30 (O. Frag. 28 links the idea of creatorhood with the presence at a marriage, instead of with the creation of the wine).

[8] Athanasius, De Incarnatione, 18.　　　　[9] Chr. 22, 1–2.

is the bringer of joy to his companions.[1] This is in line with a common idea in Origen that while bread is the basic source of strength, wine is essentially the source of joy.[2] In the early Gnostic writers it is particularly the picture of the ultimate heavenly joy.[3] A similar idea reappears in Cyril, when he sees the sign as depicting future participation in the heavenly banquet.[4] In his case, however, it is not the main emphasis which he gives in interpreting the story.

(c) Christ transforms the water of Judaism into the new wine of Christianity.

This is especially an Alexandrian tradition of interpretation, though there is considerable variety in the detail of its understanding. It occurs first in a difficult passage of Clement, where the watery element of the law receives the addition of Christ's blood, the two together constituting a ποτὸν ἀληθείας.[5] In Origen, the law is not the water but the old wine that has failed and which is replaced by the good wine of the Gospel. The location of the sign in Cana of Galilee shows that the effective realisation of the sign is to be found in the calling of the Gentiles.[6] It is in a very similar form, as we have seen, that the interpretation reappears in Cyril.[7] Cyprian's interpretation is on the same lines, though it is expressed in terms of the failure of the Jews rather than of the law, and it adds the further idea that the calling of the Gentiles is to the marriage of Christ and his Church.[8] Chrysostom gives a spiritual interpretation which is allied to these, but which is far more general in its reference and lacks the historical perspective. There are those who are as weak as water, but if they are brought to the Lord, he can transform their wills into the stronger consistency of wine.[9]

[1] O. 10, 12; 13, 57; 13, 62.   [2] E.g. O. 1, 30.
[3] Clement, *Excerpta ex Theodoto*, 65 (cf. W. von Loewenich, *Das Johannes–Verständnis im zweiten Jahrhundert*, p. 99). Heracleon also asserts that the eating of the Passover referred to in John ii. 13 signifies ἡ ἀνάπαυσις ἡ ἐν γάμῳ. We have not got his interpretation of John ii. 1–11, but it must almost certainly have been along these same lines.   [4] Cyr. *in* John ii. 14 (1, 207, 19–208, 6).
[5] Clement, *Paidagogos*, 2, 2, 29.
[6] O. Frag. 74. But contrast O. 13, 62, where within a general interpretation in terms of joy Origen says 'Before Jesus the Scripture was indeed water, but after Jesus it has become wine for us'.
[7] Cyr. *in* John ii. 11 (1, 203–5). Cf. pp. 34–6 above.
[8] Cyprian, *Ep.* 63, 12.   [9] Chr. 22, 3.

In more than one of the passages discussed, the idea of the Eucharistic sacrament is clearly present in the context. It is not, however, suggested that the sign itself has a direct sacramental significance, except in one passage of Irenaeus, where the anxiety of Mary to induce Jesus to perform the miracle is ascribed to a desire to taste the Eucharistic cup before the time.[1] Theodore discusses the details of the miracle at some length, but makes no attempt to give any spiritual interpretation of the sign as a whole.[2]

2. JOHN ii. 13–22. THE CLEANSING OF THE TEMPLE

The earliest interpretation of this passage is that of Heracleon. His interpretation of the particular incident is set within an allegorical understanding of the movements of Jesus in the chapter as a whole. Capernaum, where Jesus is not recorded to have acted at all, is the abode of the ὑλικοί, Jerusalem of the ψυχικοί, and the Temple itself, which he identifies with the holy of holies, of the πνευματικοί. In the forecourt of the Temple are to be found those ψυχικοί who are outside the Pleroma but not altogether outside salvation. Jesus' purging of the Temple with a scourge of cords is an image of the purifying power of the Holy Spirit. This understanding of the passage is elaborated with appropriate allegorical interpretations of the third day and the forty-six years.[3]

Origen, who devotes almost the whole of his tenth book to this story, offers a variety of interpretations of it. He sees in it a picture of the ever necessary work of Christ in purging his Church.[4] Alternatively he suggests that it may represent the entry of Jesus in triumph into the Jerusalem that is above and his freeing it of the presence of the so-called 'spiritual hosts of wickedness in the heavenly places' which had residence there before his ascent.[5] Primarily, however, he interprets it in terms of the coming of the word of God to the individual human soul.[6] It is in terms of this interpretation that he is thinking when he suggests that the different details of the records of the four Evangelists may be designed to

---

[1] Irenaeus, *Adv. Haer.* 3, 16, 7 (vol. II, p. 88).　　[2] T. 39–42.
[3] O. 10, 11; 33; 37–8.　　[4] O. 10, 23.
[5] O. 10, 29.　　[6] O. 10, 28.

correspond to the varied conditions of different human souls and the consequent variety of the action of the word of God upon them.[1]

But in addition to these fully spiritualised lines of interpretation, he insists that as a sign it symbolises the end of the Jewish sacrificial system. It is more than a prophetic protest against abuses; it marks the abolition of the whole system of literal observance of the law.[2] This interpretation finds further confirmation in his recognition that the promised sign of the raising of the temple of Christs' body refers not only to the resurrection but also to the founding of the Church.[3]

This symbolic sense is that given by most later commentators. We find it in Isidore, who says that the command to take hence the sacrificial animals is on the ground that they are no longer needed, because the law of the letter is giving place to the law of the spirit.[4] Cyril, rather surprisingly, does not develop the idea in terms of his favourite theme of the abolition of the law, but in the wider terms of a judgment upon unfaithful Israel, set in deliberate proximity to the call of a Gentile church typified by the immediately preceding miracle at Cana of Galilee.[5] As we have already seen, even Theodore gives expression to the basic understanding of the sign as signifying the abolition of the sacrificial system.[6]

3. JOHN iv. 1–42. THE WOMAN AT THE WELL OF SAMARIA

The gift of water, which is the heart of this sign, is interpreted in two main ways—either as teaching or as the Holy Spirit. Cyprian interprets the sign of the unrepeatability of baptism, but as he expressly states that baptism is intended by every mention of water in the Scriptures, no great importance can be attached to his interpretation here.[7]

[1] O. 10, 31.
[2] O. 10, 24.
[3] O. 10, 35.
[4] Corderius, p. 78.
[5] Cyr. *in* John ii. 14 (1, 208, 7–23).
[6] T. 43, 22–29 (cf. p. 37 above).
[7] Cyprian, *Ep.* 63, 8. In practice Tertullian does not lag far behind in the acceptance of such a principle. It enables him to find baptismal allusion even in such an unlikely passage as John ii. 1–11 (*De Baptismo*, 9, 4). (See also Gaudentius of Brescia, Tract. 8 and 9; *C.S.E.L.* 68, pp. 73 and 89.)

(a) The Interpretation as Teaching

This general heading covers a fairly wide range of interpretations with considerable variation in the detail of their exegesis. It occurs in its simplest form in Eusebius.[1] It also represents the main line of Origen's understanding of the story, though his interpretation of the passage is not uniform. He does interpret it, as we would expect, in a straightforward way of the contrast of the law and the Gospel, of a literal and spiritual understanding of Scripture.[2] This, however, is not the interpretation given in his commentary. Heracleon had interpreted the passage in this way, and had deduced from it the conception of the absolute supersession of the old by the new. Origen criticises him for failing to recognise the positive typological value of the old.[3] It is probably in order to bring out unmistakably the difference between his own understanding of the passage and that of Heracleon that he avoids the simple contrast of old and new, which he employs elsewhere. Instead he draws a contrast between the teaching of Scripture (whether understood spiritually as when drunk by Jacob and his sons, or at a lower level as when drunk by his cattle, or even misunderstood altogether as when drunk by the Samaritan woman before her conversion) on the one hand and the interior teaching of Christ, which goes beyond what either is or can be recorded in writing, on the other.[4]

Heracleon's interpretation is not just an isolated piece of allegorising. Although we have only fragments of his interpretation handed on by Origen, we can see that he was attempting to interpret the sign as a whole. The woman's previous husbands (six in number according to Heracleon) are all forms of false entanglement with matter, while the husband she is to bring is her Pleroma in conjunction with which, through the agency of the Saviour, her goal will

---

[1] Eusebius, *Dem. Ev.* 6, 18, 48–9. It also appears in O. Frag. 54, but R. Devreesse ('Notes sur les Chaînes Grecques de Saint Jean', p. 208) has shown that this should be attributed to Photius and not to Origen.

[2] *Gen. Hom.* 7, 5; O. Frag. 56.   [3] O. 13, 10.

[4] O. 13, 5–6. This clearly has a certain affinity with the second type of interpretation in terms of the Holy Spirit. In elaboration of the meaning of this interior well Origen cites 1 Cor. ii. 16 ('We have the mind of Christ'), but he does not identify it with the Holy Spirit.

be achieved.[1] The promise of the new worship in spirit and in truth is clear evidence of the falsity of the old, whether it be heathen worship of the devil as symbolised by the worship on Mt Gerizim or the Jewish worship of the creator God as symbolised by the worship at Jerusalem.[2] The whole passage is understood to be a picture of God's dealing with those of a πνευματικός nature,[3] and, in the conclusion of the story, Christ reaches out through the woman representing the πνευματικός Church to achieve the salvation of the people of the city, who are ψυχικοί living more deeply embedded in the ordinary life of the world.[4]

Origen's interpretation of the husbands is not radically different. He interprets them of the five senses which rule the soul before its coming to faith in Christ.[5] Elsewhere, presumably in conjunction with a more simple contrast of law and Gospel, they are interpreted of the five books of the law, which alone the Samaritans accepted.[6] In the interpretation of the worship in spirit and in truth, he is once more in direct conflict with Heracleon. The relevant opposite to truth for Origen here is not falsehood but type. The new worship is spiritual reality as contrasted with bodily type.[7] The worship of Mt Gerizim is the misguided worship of heretics and the worship of Jerusalem is the pedestrian worship of the ordinary Church member.[8] Those who ultimately leave the city and come to Christ are those won from heterodoxy to an acceptance of the true teaching.[9]

(b) The Interpretation as the Holy Spirit

Little requires to be said of this interpretation. It is adopted by Irenaeus, Chrysostom, Theodore and Cyril.[10] In no case is the interpretation elaborated. The contrast is understood simply to be between the physical water of Jacob's well literally understood, and the gift of the Spirit.[11]

[1] O. 13, 11.　　[2] O. 13, 16; 19.　　[3] O. 13, 10; 16.
[4] O. 13, 51.　　[5] O. 13, 9.　　[6] O. Frag. 57.
[7] O. 13, 13; 18.　　[8] O. 13, 16.　　[9] O. 13, 51.
[10] Irenaeus, *Adv. Haer.* 3, 17, 2 (vol. II, p. 93); Chr. 32, 1; T. 63, 18–23; Cyr. *in* John iv. 14 (I, 271, 26–272, 6).
[11] Augustine, who follows this same line of interpretation, does go in for considerable elaboration. For example, the first water is interpreted as the water of pleasure drawn up in the vessel of lust (*Tract. Joh.* 15, 16).

There is thus a clear tendency for later exegesis to move towards a more standardised and a more specifically theological interpretation of the passage.

The interpretation of the promise of living water in vii. 37–9 goes hand in hand with the interpretation of this passage. Cyprian and writers associated with him interpret it of baptism;[1] Origen and Eusebius of divine knowledge.[2] In view of *v*. 39, these interpretations are linked with the idea of the Spirit. Baptism of course is the means by which the Holy Spirit is received.[3] Origen, after setting out the Holy Spirit and instruction as two possible alternative interpretations, goes on to draw the two together on the strength of the fundamental association of each with the practice of baptism.[4] Here also later exegesis shows a shift of emphasis. The imagery is conceived of as bearing a more direct reference to the Holy Spirit. Theodore still insists that the reference is to the grace and operation of the Spirit rather than the actual person and nature of the Spirit himself.[5] But this is for purely theological rather than exegetical reasons. The water now symbolises the Spirit rather than baptism or teaching, though the old associations are not completely forgotten. Cyril, who interprets the passage of the Spirit's gifts, sees in it an especial reference to the gift of teaching.[6] Elsewhere Cyril goes further and asserts that water is frequently used in Scripture to signify sanctification through the Spirit or even the Holy Spirit himself.[7] He also recognises that the practice of the feast provides an acted background to the saying, though he regards it as an Old

---

[1] Cyprian, *Ep.* 63, 8; 73, 11; ps-Cyprian, *De Rebaptismate*, 14; *De Montibus Sinai et Sion*, 9.

[2] Origen, Sel. *in* Ps. cxxxv (cxxxvi). 6 (*P.G.* 12, 1656CD); Eusebius, *Dem. Ev.* 6, 18, 49; *in* Ps. xcii (xciii). 2–3 (*P.G.* 23, 1189A).

[3] Cyprian. *Ep.* 63, 8; ps-Cyprian, *De Rebaptismate*, 14.

[4] O. Frag. 36.

[5] T. 115, 30–2. Cf. Theodore, *Cat. Hom.* 10, 9; Chr. 32, 1.

[6] Cyr. *in* John vii. 38 (1, 688–9).

[7] Cyr. *in* John iv. 10 (1, 269, 20–3); *in* John vi. 35 (1, 475, 20–3). Here, as so often, what is primarily a later emphasis is already present in one strand of the teaching of Origen. In giving his interpretation of 'being born of water and the Spirit' in John iii. 5, he goes so far as to suggest that water ἐπινοίᾳ μόνῃ, ἀλλ᾽ οὐχ ὑποστάσεως διαφορὰν ἔχει πρὸς τὸ πνεῦμα, and cites this passage in evidence (O. Frag. 36).

Testament type rather than as having a function equivalent to the miracles of Jesus in the other discourses.[1]

4. JOHN iv. 46–54. THE HEALING OF THE NOBLEMAN'S SON

This story seems to have had a particular importance for the early Gnostics. The same general line of interpretation is attributed by Irenaeus to the Valentinians and by Origen to Heracleon. The nobleman is the demiurge, who, with his servants the angels, welcomes the coming of Christ to heal the creation of its sin. In the case of the Valentinians, this is in fact given by Irenaeus as their interpretation of the healing of the centurion's servant in Matthew and Luke.[2] However, elsewhere Irenaeus speaks of the healing of the centurion's son as occurring in St John's Gospel. This may be a mistake rather than a conscious identification of the two stories, but it shows at least that the two stories were not clearly distinct in his mind.[3] Heracleon's interpretation is woven into his total pattern of interpreting the Gospel. The detailed record of the location of the nobleman's son at Capernaum shows him to be in an intermediate position near the sea, that is, bordering on matter, and the geographical movements of Jesus are also given a spiritual interpretation which links them with the activity and movements of Jesus already interpreted in chapter ii.[4] The reference to signs and wonders as necessary to promote belief is appropriate to those of ψυχικός nature. This gives the miracle a certain topical connection with the preceding sign, in which a woman of πνευματικός nature has been shown as responsive to the word alone without the additional evidence of miracle.[5]

The starting-point of Origen's interpretation is the recognition of the fact that the story is meant to be understood as a pair with the first miracle at Cana. The first miracle had been interpreted by him in terms of Christ's gift of joy to his companions at the feast. The

---

[1] Cyr. *in* John vii. 37 (I, 685–8). For the variant punctuations and consequent differences of detailed exegesis of this text, see C. H. Turner, 'The Punctuation of John vii. 37–8', and Hoskyns, pp. 320–3.

[2] Irenaeus, *Adv. Haer.* 1, 7, 4 (vol. 1, p. 64).

[3] *Ibid.* 2, 22, 3 (vol. 1, p. 328). Origen explicitly distinguishes the two incidents in O. 13, 62.

[4] O. 13, 60.   [5] O. 13, 61.

49

second miracle is clearly one of healing. This is hardly the natural sequence, but Origen accepts it and gives his interpretation in two forms, one historical of God's dealings with the world and one psychological of God's dealings with the individual soul. The healing of the nobleman's son is therefore a picture either of the Saviour's second coming to the world for the final redemption of Israel after the fulness of the Gentiles has come in, or else it is the Logos' second visitation of the soul to purge it of the residuum of sin.[1] He does not find it easy to interpret the detail of the story in conformity with his general outline. He has to admit that it is by no means certain that the nobleman was a Jew, and yet he symbolises Abraham seeking the Saviour's help for his sinful child, the Jewish people.[2]

He does also suggest another quite different interpretation which has close affinities with that of the Gnostics. The nobleman is one of the angelic powers referred to as 'the rulers of this world', and his son that section of the world's population that comes under his authority. Some of these powers were converted by the coming of Christ, and their conversion is reflected in the conversion of whole cities or nations.[3]

Cyril also attempts to interpret the link between this story and the earlier miracle at Cana, but he does so at a purely historical level. The people at Cana have been prepared by the former miracle and are therefore of a disposition which can be helped by Christ.[4] In effect, both he and Theodore interpret the sign as a simple story of the birth of faith. In Cyril's words, it is the story of a double healing —the nobleman as well as the child.[5] Theodore emphasises particularly that the belief of $v.$ 50 is merely the acceptance of Christ's word; complete belief is reached only in the climax of $v.$ 53.[6]

---

[1] O. 13, 57.　　　　　　　　　　[2] O. 13, 58.
[3] O. 13, 59.
[4] Cyr. *in* John iv. 46 (1, 301, 7–13).
[5] Cyr. *in* John iv. 50–1 (1, 303, 6–16).
[6] T. 68–9 (cf. p. 90 below). Cf. also Chr. 35, 2.

5. JOHN V. 1–16. THE HEALING OF THE MAN AT THE POOL OF BETHESDA

There is no clear or uniform tradition of the interpretation of this miracle. That which recurs most frequently is an understanding of it in terms of baptism. This occurs first, as is to be expected, in Tertullian and Cyprian. Tertullian is concerned primarily with the typological significance of the angel at the pool as a feature of the pre-Christian dispensation, and does not refer directly to Christ's act of healing.[1] Cyprian's interest is in the injunction of *v.* 14 'Sin no more, lest a worse thing befall thee', which he applies to the need of perseverance after baptism as an essential for salvation.[2] But these clearly presume an understanding of the healing itself as a symbol of baptism. The same basic idea is present in Chrysostom, who points out that paralysis is especially common as a picture of sin.[3]

Cyril works the miracle into his scheme of interpretation based on the movements of Jesus. After the passover of chapter ii, which figured the death of Christ, Jesus exercised his ministry among the Samaritans and in Galilee of the Gentiles. His return to Jerusalem therefore depicts a second visitation of Christ for the salvation of Israel after the fulness of the Gentiles has been gathered in. This is almost at the end of time, after a long period of weakness, symbolised by the thirty-eight years of paralysis—thirty-eight being just short of forty, the number symbolic of completeness.[4] This has some striking similarities with Origen's interpretation of the healing of the nobleman's son. Unfortunately we have not got Origen's interpretation of this passage. It may be that Cyril is drawing upon him, but if so he has certainly succeeded in giving a more satisfactory schematic interpretation of the sequence of miracles as a whole.

Other commentators more naturally see in it the healing offered to Christ's people at his first coming. For Apollinarius the significance of the number thirty-eight is that it falls just short of forty, the

---

[1] *De Baptismo*, 5; *Adversus Judaeos*, 13, 26.

[2] *Testimonia*, 3, 27; *Ep.* 13, 2.

[3] Chr. 38, 1–2. Chrysostom does not develop the baptismal significance of the healing at all fully in his homilies on the Gospel. He treats the whole incident much more fully in his twelfth homily against the Anomaeans (see especially *P.G.* 48, 804).

[4] Cyr. *in* John v. 1–9 (1, 304–9).

4-2

number indicative of punishment (for example, forty years in the wilderness, forty days of flood, forty stripes). So the miracle pictures Christ's coming when the world's time is nearly complete and by his work of grace cutting short the punishment of the law.[1] Augustine sees in it the offer of healing to a people living under the five arches of the Pentateuch suffering from its imperfections as again represented by the thirty-eight years of the paralysis.[2]

Theodore does not attempt to give the miracle any symbolic interpretation.[3] For him it is a miracle deliberately demonstrative of Christ's divine authority. Only one man is healed, because that is sufficient for the act of revelation; more would have appeared like deliberate self-glorification.[4] The healing of the man is far from spiritually perfect, because his informing the Jews about Jesus was an act of treachery. Theodore pours scorn upon any interpretation which attributes the man's action to good motives.[5]

6. JOHN vi. THE FEEDING OF THE FIVE THOUSAND AND THE WALKING ON THE WATER

The Eucharistic interpretation of this passage is so familiar to us that it comes as something of a surprise to find that it takes a comparatively subordinate place in the earliest exegesis, especially from Alexandria. Clement on one occasion speaks at length of the eating of Christ's flesh and the drinking of his blood commanded in this chapter as the assimilation by faith of Christ the Word.[6] Elsewhere in a difficult

---

[1] Cramer, p. 229. [2] *Tract. Joh.* 17, 2–7.

[3] In this he has the support of Hoskyns among modern commentators—one who is not usually slow to find symbolic significances. 'The story is an episode; and the Evangelist turns it neither into an allegory, nor into a symbol, nor into a myth' (Hoskyns, p. 253). With this, however, contrast the judgment of J. Daniélou, *Bible et Liturgie*, pp. 282–3: 'La tradition chrétienne est simplement l'expression du Nouveau Testament lui-même. Dans l'Évangile de saint Jean, en effet, l'épisode a un sens baptismal.'

[4] T. 69, 32–4. Augustine by contrast interprets the selection of one man only to be healed as symbolic of the unity of Christ's healing work (*Tract. Joh.* 17, 1).

[5] T. 72, 15–73, 9. This condemnation includes Cyril (*in* John v. 15; 1, 311, 25–312, 4) and Chrysostom (Chr. 38, 2), who both point out that the man told the Jews who it was who had healed him and not who it was who had commanded him to break the Sabbath.

[6] Clement, *Paidagogos*, 1, 6, 38–47.

section of the *Excerpta ex Theodoto* he suggests that the passage contains an allusion to the Eucharist or (and he seems to regard this as the more valuable line of interpretation) to Christ's body, the Church.[1] Similarly Origen comments on *vv.* 53 and 55 as follows: 'We are said to drink Christ's blood, not only in the sacramental rite but also when we receive his words, in which life consists, as he himself says "The words which I speak unto you they are spirit and they are life".'[2] In a more general discussion of the passage as a whole, Origen points out that Christ speaks of bread both as something other than himself and as something referring directly to himself. For him the latter is the more fundamental idea. The central theme of the passage is the soul's reception of Christ the Word.[3] This could be effected through the Eucharist or through the acceptance of Christ's words or teaching as the quotation from the *Homily on Numbers* clearly shows. There seems little room for doubt, however, that it is the latter sense which is emphasised in Origen's interpretation of the symbolism of the chapter and to which he attaches the greater value.[4] Some of the fourth-century Catena fragments continue to show the same broad line of interpretation. Didymus interprets the eating of the life of practical goodness, and the drinking of contemplation.[5] Theodore of Heraclea finds the deeper meaning of *v.* 54 in the λογικῶς feeding upon the flesh and blood of Christ, which comes through accepting and feeding upon the dogma of the incarnation.[6]

---

[1] Clement, *Excerpta ex Theodoto*, 13.

[2] *Num. Hom.* 16, 9.

[3] *De Oratione*, 27, 2–4.

[4] Cf. O. 32, 24; *Matt. Comm. Ser.* 85; *Lev. Hom.* 7, 5; *Comm. Matt.* 11, 14. On the whole question of Origen's evaluation of the Sacrament, see J. Daniélou, *Origène*, pp. 74–9 (E.T. pp. 61–8) and H. de Lubac, *Histoire et Esprit*, pp. 355–73. The strength of Daniélou's account is his clear recognition that bread is basically for Origen 'a figure not of the Eucharist but of the Logos himself' (E.T. p. 65). De Lubac is inclined to overstate Origen's interest in the physical sacrament, just as he does Origen's acceptance of the literal meaning of Scripture.

[5] Cramer, pp. 255–6. This interpretation of the imagery derives from Origen (cf. O. 1, 30).

[6] Corderius, p. 193. On this whole early tradition of exegesis, cf. Hoskyns, p. 306: 'The Patristic exegesis of the sixth chapter or references to its teaching... do not refer it *either* to teaching *or* to sacrament. They choose to emphasise now one aspect of the symbolism, now another, as it is convenient to them at the moment.'

In this early period the western Cyprian is the most explicitly Eucharistic in his interpretation of the passage.[1] The fifth century shows a general development towards this more specifically Eucharistic interpretation. Cyril gives a fuller and more developed Eucharistic interpretation than his Alexandrian predecessors.[2] The main burden of Theodore's and of Augustine's exegesis is similarly Eucharistic in character, though with Theodore the emphasis is much less marked.[3] There is thus a close parallel in the general development of the understanding of this passage and that of the water imagery in Chapters iv and vii.[4]

Two other points are worthy of note in the development of the symbolism of the whole passage. The multiplication of the loaves is, like the turning of the water into wine, understood as a sign of Christ's oneness with the Creator.[5] He did not need any initial loaves or fishes to make his miraculous provision possible. This is clearly evident from his post-resurrection provision of a meal by the lakeside without any fish at all to start with. His purpose, therefore, must have been to disprove any heretical disparagement of matter.[6]

Secondly, the Moses typology, which is clearly present in the later comparison with the manna, is also found in earlier details of the story. At the outset of the whole occurrence, Jesus crosses the Sea of Tiberias to get away from his persecutors as Moses crossed the Red Sea in escaping from the pursuing Egyptians.[7] When Jesus feeds the multitudes there is not just sufficient as with Moses or Elijah, but enough and to spare.[8] The same superiority is shown by the walking on the water. Moses prayed and the sea was driven back. Christ acted in his own power and the sea carried its master on its back.[9]

---

[1] Cyprian, *De Dominica Oratione*, 18.
[2] Cyr. *in* John vi. 53 (I, 529–32).
[3] T. 97–9; 105–6; Augustine, *Tract. Joh.* 26.
[4] Cf. p. 48 above.
[5] Irenaeus, *Adv. Haer.* 3, 11, 5 (vol. II, p. 44); Chr. 42, 2.
[6] Chr. 42, 3; 87, 2.
[7] Cyr. *in* John vi. 1 (I, 402, 19–403, 24).
[8] T. 94, 32–96, 3.
[9] Didymus *in* John vi. 25 (*P.G.* 39, 1648 AB).

7. JOHN ix. 1–41. THE HEALING OF THE MAN BORN BLIND

As with the miracles of the turning of the water into wine and of the feeding of the five thousand, Irenaeus emphasises the way in which the miracle displays the oneness of Jesus with the Creator. He links this particularly with the use of the clay, which recalls the manner of man's creation in Genesis ii. 7.[1] This allusion, and the significance attached to it, was universally adopted, and, as we have seen, reappears regularly even in the most unlikely authors.[2]

The pattern of the exegesis of the sign as a whole is best seen by the comparison of three contrasting interpretations.

(a) Theodore's interpretation is at a simple historical level. The Jews were blinded by their own lack of faith, and evil will.[3] This is revealed not only by the conclusion of the teaching of ix, but also by their failure to take Jesus at the end of viii, which is to be explained as due to some form of divine blinding.[4] The miracle has thus a most appropriate historical setting, in which the gift of sight is contrasted with the blindness of the Pharisees. No further symbolism (apart from the significance of the clay) is developed. Siloam means 'Sent', but it signifies no more than the literal sending of the man to the pool with the practical purpose of ensuring that a large crowd would be able to witness the greatness of the miracle.[5]

(b) Cyril sees in the miracle a picture of Christ's mission to the Gentiles.[6] This is the work he must work, while it is day, that is to say during the time of his incarnation.[7] It is also on the Sabbath, because the incarnation came at the end of the age, as the Sabbath is at the end of the week.[8] Healing is to be found in the water of baptism, but the interpretation of Siloam as 'Sent' shows that its

---

[1] Irenaeus, *Adv. Haer.* 5, 15, 2 (vol. II, p. 365).

[2] Cyr. *in* John ix. 6 (II, 157, 5–8); T. 133, 31–134, 5; Chr. 56, 2. Athanasius (*De Incarnatione*, 18) also uses this miracle as evidence of Christ's creatorship, but does not link the idea specifically with the use of the clay.

[3] T. 139, 9–13.   [4] T. 129, 1–12.

[5] T. 134, 5–23. Cf. Chr. 57, 1.

[6] Cf. p. 36 above.

[7] Cyr. *in* John ix. 4 (II, 153, 23–4). This is the natural understanding of the text and is given also by Theodore (T. 132, 33–133, 10).

[8] Cyr. *in* John ix. 6 (II, 156, 16–22).

healing power derives from the incarnation, from the fact of the sending of the only-begotten Son into the world.[1]

(c) Augustine's interpretation is more elaborate in the detail of its exegesis and still wider in its scope. The man born blind is not merely the Gentile world, but humanity itself blinded by original sin.[2] The day of Christ's working is not simply the period of the incarnation, but the whole period before the final judgment.[3] Two stages of the healing can be distinguished. First the catechumen is anointed with the teaching of the incarnation, depicted by the spittle. Then he must go on to the second stage of baptism into Christ, the one signified by the explanatory title 'Sent'.[4]

8. JOHN xi. 1–44. THE RAISING OF LAZARUS

This miracle receives so full a treatment and interpretation within the Gospel itself that little room is left for doubt about its fundamental meaning. It is recognised all along that it is concerned not merely with the problem of physical death, but with the closely allied problem of sin. This understanding is found as early as Irenaeus, who, like others after him, sees a picture of the bands of sin in the bandages with which Lazarus is still bound as he comes out from the tomb.[5] The other gospels contain two records of raisings from the dead, and often the three stories are mentioned together as of similar import. Yet the raising of Lazarus has clearly

[1] Cyr. *in* John ix. 7 (II, 157, 11–158, 4). The understanding of the washing in terms of baptism appears in Irenaeus (*Adv. Haer.* 5, 15, 3) (vol. II, p. 366) and in Tertullian (*De Baptismo*, 1), but surprisingly not in Cyprian. It receives more widespread acceptance than the baptismal interpretations of the references to water in iv and vii, and even that in v. The interpretation of 'Sent' as referring to the sending of Christ as the Son of God is found in Origen (O. Frag. 63) and Eusebius (*Dem. Ev.* 7, 1, 115). Origen also interprets it in terms of the apostles (*Is. Hom.* 6, 3), but in the light of John xx. 21 this may be regarded as a complementary rather than a contradictory interpretation.

[2] *Tract. Joh.* 44, 1. This interpretation is already present in Irenaeus, *Adv. Haer.* 5, 15, 3 (vol. II, p. 366).

[3] *Tract. Joh.* 44, 5. This interpretation is to be found in Origen, *Jer. Hom.* 12, 10; Ps. xxxvi (xxxvii) *Hom.* 3, 10 (*P.G.* 12, 1346 AB).

[4] *Tract. Joh.* 44, 2. This interpretation of the spittle is to be found in O. Frag. 63.

[5] Irenaeus, *Ad. Haer.* 5, 13, 1 (vol. II, p. 355). Cf. O. 28, 7; Cyr. *in* John xi. 44 (II, 292, 3–6).

much the greatest emphasis laid upon it. Origen sees in the resurrection of the one whom Jesus loved the restoration of one who has enjoyed the friendship (φιλία) of Jesus and then fallen into sin, of one who has received knowledge of the truth, been enlightened, tasted of the heavenly gift, been made partaker of the Holy Ghost, tasted the good word of God and the powers of the age to come, and then apostatised and gone back to his old way of life.[1] Augustine explicitly differentiates it from the Synoptic raisings by suggesting that Lazarus, who was four days dead, depicts the person who is rooted and settled in sin.[2]

Considerable emphasis is placed on the relationship of Christ to the Father in the performance of the miracle, but this is in a form which bears more directly on questions of Christology than of the understanding of the sign itself. Origen, with his usual love of subtle distinctions, suggests that the work of resurrection was strictly the work of the Father, while that of Christ was literally to awaken with his loud cry the reunited body and soul. But he admits that those who ignore the distinction and think more simply of the work of resurrection as the common work of Father and Son can claim that the miracle is thereby integrated into the thought of the Gospel as a whole.[3] As with so many other of the miracles, the action of Christ is seen to show a unity of action with the work of creation.[4] Another writer specifically links the loud cry with which Lazarus is called out from the tomb with the voice of command at the creation.[5] Cyril gives it a forward-looking reference as a prefigurement of the loud shout of the trumpet at the final resurrection.[6] He

[1] O. 28, 6–7. It is no doubt this same description of Lazarus as the one whom Jesus loved which prompts the comment of Apollinarius that only the friends (φίλοι) of God will enjoy resurrection. The comment is actually associated with v. 43 and the calling of Lazarus by name (Corderius, p. 295).

[2] *Tract. Joh.* 49, 3.

[3] O. 28, 9 (Origen refers to John xi. 25 and v. 21).

[4] Origen, *Comm. Matt.* 12, 2.

[5] Ps-Hippolytus, *On the Raising of Lazarus*, p. 226, 32–6. This comes from the part of the work surviving in Greek and could possibly be a genuine work of Hippolytus himself, but the attribution is very doubtful (C. Martin, 'Note sur l'homélie εἰς τὸν τετραήμερον Λάζαρον attribuée à saint Hyppolyte de Rome').

[6] Cyr. *in* John xi. 43 (II, 290, 6–24). Cyril uses the argument that the loud cry must have some deeper meaning because it contradicts the normal principle that

further brings out the general meaning of the sign by suggesting that the tears of Jesus are not so much for Lazarus as for the general fact of human sin and mortality typified by him.[1]

9. JOHN xiii. 1–17. THE WASHING OF THE DISCIPLES' FEET

Three main lines of interpretation of this sign are employed, which are in no way exclusive of one another.

(a) The sign is explicitly stated in the Gospel to be a deliberate illustration of humility. No interpreter of the Gospel would wish to question the validity of this interpretation. A few writers, particularly in the Antiochene tradition, appear to suggest that it is the complete meaning of Christ's action. This is true both of Chrysostom and of Theodore.[2] Theodore in fact asserts that Peter misunderstood the saying of Jesus in *v.* 8 as a reference to baptism, and had to have this misunderstanding removed by the further saying of Jesus in *v.* 10.[3] The mysterious saying in *v.* 7 that they will understand the meaning of his action later is simply a reference to the immediately ensuing explanation in *vv.* 12–15 that it is intended as an example of humility.[4] It is far more surprising to find that Cyril of Alexandria falls also within this category. His treatment of the sign is more satisfactory than that of Theodore. Where Theodore emphasises that the feet-washing is the action of *Domini nostri homo* (albeit, as *v.* 2 suggests, conscious of the destiny in store for him), Cyril shows that the essence of the humility lies in its being the action of one who is fully and consciously Lord of all. He even interprets the coming forth from God of which Jesus was conscious in the undertaking of the action not of his incarnation but of his eternal generation.[5] Cyril does admit a reference to

---

'he shall not strive nor cry aloud'. Theodore, who does little to develop the deeper meaning of the sign, has an interpretation of the cry similar to that of Origen (T. 163, 22–5).

[1] Cyr. in John xi. 36 (II, 282, 13–18). Cf. Cyril's comment that, in meeting the sorrows of Mary, the risen Christ is meeting the sorrows of womankind as a whole (Cyr. *in* John xx. 15; III, 115, 4–23; *in* John xx. 17; III, 120, 12–15).

[2] Chr. 70, 2; T. 181–4.   [3] T. 183, 17–20.

[4] T. 184, 1–10. This understanding of *v.* 7 does not necessarily go along with a restriction of the sign to the role of a lesson in humility (cf. *Tract. Joh.* 58, 2).

[5] T. 182, 16–24; Cyr. *in* John xiii. 2–5 (II, 345, 29–346, 9).

baptism in *v*. 8. But this is not the meaning of the sign being enacted. It is merely that Jesus, while engaged in this sign whose intention and meaning is the lesson of humility, has characteristically seized the opportunity to enlarge the range of his teaching for the general benefit so as to include also at this point the theme of baptism.[1]

(*b*) The Gospel gives no other explicit interpretation of the sign, but the water symbolism, and especially the being clean in *v*. 10, seems to suggest that the lesson in humility does not exhaust its meaning. Our earliest reference to the story in Irenaeus sees in it a picture of the cleansing brought by the New Man to undo the bondage of death inherited from the first Adam.[2] It is not explicitly identified with baptism, though this would be a natural implication of his words. Tertullian uses the story in the *De Baptismo*, but in such a way as to rule out a baptismal interpretation of it. The words of Jesus in *v*. 10 are an assertion of the unrepeatability of baptism. As the disciples have received John's baptism, the action of Jesus is not baptismal.[3] He does not go on to give any positive interpretation of the meaning of the sign. His reasoning against a baptismal interpretation was very influential. Cyprian, for all his claim that water is everywhere a symbol of baptism, in practice only uses the story as an illustration of humility.[4] Both Origen and Augustine, who see in the story a symbol of cleansing, regard it as referring not to baptism itself but to subsequent post-baptismal cleansing.[5]

Origen argues that the action of Jesus must have some deeper meaning of this kind; otherwise Peter's refusal in *v*. 8 would have been right and reverent.[6] In his commentary he gives two interpretations. The primary understanding of the passage is that the Christian, after his initial cleansing, needs the regular cleansing of those elements within him which have closest contact with the defiling world. Thus the feet are the appropriate part for cleansing.[7] Even with the disciples this cleansing was not completed at the supper. Peter's later denial is clear evidence that he needed yet

[1] Cyr. *in* John xiii. 8 (II, 347, 24–348, 8).
[2] Irenaeus, *Adv. Haer.* 4, 22, 1 (vol. II, p. 228).
[3] Tertullian, *De Baptismo*, 12.
[4] Cyprian, *Testimonia*, 3, 29; *Ep.* 14, 2.
[5] O. 32, 2; *Tract. Joh.* 56, 4.   [6] O. 32, 8.
[7] O. 32, 2. Cf. also Augustine, *Tract. Joh.* 56, 4.

further cleansing. This is implicit in the Evangelist's careful statement that Jesus *began* to wash the disciples' feet.[1] The second interpretation depends upon the shorter text of *v.* 10 which omits εἰ μὴ τοὺς πόδας. In this interpretation, Origen suggests that the disciples really were clean, and for that very reason, on the principle that 'to every one that hath shall be given and he shall have abundance', they are given the further cleansing of Jesus. Without this further cleansing, even the most perfect of men cannot be reckoned as clean in the fullest sense of the word.[2] Elsewhere Origen interprets the cleansing water as the dew of the grace of the Holy Spirit and as the word of teaching.[3] This interpretation is suggested in the first place by John xv. 3 where the cleansing of the disciples is attributed to the word of Jesus. It is in line with his interpretations of the water symbolism in iv and vii. 37–9.[4] Finally it provides the most satisfactory meaning to the command to the disciples to imitate the action of their Master within the life of the Church.

(*c*) The third line of interpretation is also found in Origen and is characteristic of Alexandria. In this interpretation the cleansing of the disciples' feet is their preparation for the work of the spread of the gospel. It is the fulfilment of the prophecy 'How beautiful are the feet of them that bring glad tidings of good things!'. This could be regarded as a special case of the second interpretation, but the emphasis now lies not on the cleansing as forgiveness but as preparation for the work of evangelism. It occurs in Clement,[5] in Origen[6] and in a Catena fragment ascribed to Theodore of Heraclea and Apollinarius.[7]

10. JOHN xix. 17–42. THE CROSS

The cross is more than a sign; it is also the thing signified. Nevertheless it retains many of the characteristics of the sign. Early writers were not slow to interpret the details of the story as having not only historical significance, but also symbolic meaning.[8] Such symbolic

---

[1] O. 32, 4.
[2] O. 32, 7.
[3] *Jud. Hom.* 8, 5.
[4] Cf. p. 48 above.
[5] Clement, *Paidagogos*, 2, 8, 63.
[6] O. 32, 7–8.
[7] Cramer, p. 339.
[8] See especially Origen, *Con. Cel.* 2, 69.

interpretations not infrequently lapse into the more arbitrary form of allegory, but many of them are closely related to the total meaning of the cross. In this section the attempt is made to present a brief summary of such symbolic interpretations of the detail of the story as appear to bear some real association with the understanding of the cross as a whole.

(*a*) xix. 17. Christ's carrying of his own cross is frequently understood as a fulfilment of the type of Isaac.[1] More unusually it is understood as a fulfilment of the prophecy of Isa. ix. 6—Christ carries his ἀρχή upon his shoulder.[2] This interpretation is presumably associated with the notion of Christ's reigning from the tree. It is therefore closely similar to the interpretation of Chrysostom in terms of Christ bearing the symbol of his own victory, as conquerors bear their own trophies.[3]

(*b*) xix. 18. Cyril interprets the two thieves as Jew and Greek. The element of arbitrariness in many of these interpretations is, however, well illustrated by the fact that he is uncertain whether they represent the nations as unrepentant and therefore receiving just condemnation, or as redeemed through being 'crucified with Christ'.[4]

(*c*) xix. 20. Cyril's second interpretation of the two thieves is in line with his understanding of the threefold language of the title as proclaiming the future universal rule of Christ.[5] This line of thought appears also in a slightly different form in Isidore who sees in it a picture of the foretold function of the cross in drawing all men to Christ.[6] Cyril also makes a somewhat unsatisfactory attempt to identify the title with the handwriting against us which was nailed to the cross according to Colossians ii. 14.[7] Augustine interprets the words of the title as referring to his Kingship of the true Israel of God, the circumcised in heart.[8]

---

[1] Melito, Frag. in Routh, *Reliquiae Sacrae*, vol. I, p. 122; Chr. 85, 1.
[2] Apollinarius in Corderius, p. 437.   [3] Chr. 85, 1.
[4] Cyr. *in* John xix. 18 (III, 82, 28–83, 27).
[5] Cyr. *in* John xix. 20 (III, 85–6).
[6] Isidore in Corderius, p. 439.
[7] Cyr. *in* John xix. 19 (III, 83–5). For a similar modern interpretation, cf. E. Stauffer, *New Testament Theology* (E.T.), p. 144.
[8] *Tract. Joh.* 117, 5.

(d) xix. 23–4. Mention has already been made of the varied interpretations of Christ's seamless robe.[1] None of these interpretations, however, appears to be very closely related to the meaning of the cross, and therefore they do not require to be developed here.[2]

(e) xix. 30. The phrase 'gave up His spirit' is almost universally interpreted of the essentially voluntary nature of his death—an idea clearly expressed earlier in the Gospel in x. 18.[3] Origen sees a similar meaning in the bowing of his head, 'as if making it rest on the bosom of his Father'.[4]

(f) xix. 34. This verse is the one which most clearly demands some kind of symbolic interpretation, as was universally recognised.[5] There are two main interpretations of the water and the blood. One sees in them the two baptisms of water and of martyrdom,[6] the other the two sacraments of baptism and of eucharist.[7] The importance of their coming out from the side of the dead Christ is that the life-giving sacraments receive their efficacy from Christ and particularly from his death.[8] A further symbolism is found in a parallel with the coming of Eve from the side of Adam. As the source of sin and death came from the side of the sleeping Adam, so the source of

[1] Cf. p. 25 above.

[2] But with this judgment contrast the judgment of Hoskyns (p. 529). In view of the close association of the robe with the Body of Christ, he claims that 'the ancient and modern interpretation of the robe as the Church may...rightly penetrate the author's meaning'.

[3] O. 19, 16; Tertullian, *Apologeticus*, 21, 19; T. 241, 35–242, 1.

[4] *Matt. Comm. Ser.* 138. For further comment on this verse, see p. 67 below.

[5] The patristic interpretation of this verse has received special attention. For full accounts see Westcott, 'Additional note on chapter 19' (vol. II, pp. 328–33); Hoskyns, pp. 534–5.

[6] Tertullian, *De Pudicitia*, 22, 10; *De Baptismo*, 16; Cyril of Jerusalem, *Catecheses*, 3, 10; Jerome, *Ep.* 69, 6; Rufinus, *Comm. in Symb.* 23 (Rufinus gives an alternative interpretation in which the blood is to condemn the faithless, who had said 'His blood be upon us and on our children').

[7] T. 242, 21–3 (this is the only point in which Theodore gives any symbolic meaning to the facts of the passion; even here he merely identifies the symbols without any development of the idea); Chr. 85, 3; Cyr. *in* John xix. 34 (III, 103, 14–20); Augustine, *Tract. Joh.* 120, 2.

[8] See the references in the previous note to Chrysostom, Cyril and Augustine. This point is made also by Origen (*Ex. Hom.* 11, 2), though in accordance with his general pattern of exegesis it is for him not specifically the sacraments which flow from the side of Christ, but more generally the thirst-quenching waters of the word of God.

healing came from the side of Christ in the sleep of death.[1] The parallelism is sometimes extended to include the conception that just as it was Adam's bride, Eve, who came out from his side, so it was Christ's bride the Church, constituted by the sacraments, which came from the side of Christ.[2]

(g) xix. 41. Origen links the newness of Christ's tomb with the ability of his corpse to give out streams of water and blood like a living body. He is a new kind of dead man and so ought to have a new tomb. In the light of his purity, it is appropriate to his death as the virgin's womb was to his birth.[3] Elsewhere he associates it rather with the newness of life to which the Christian who is buried with Christ is initiated.[4] This line of thought is developed by Cyril who sees in the fact of the new tomb set in a garden the renewing work of a second Adam.[5]

These interpretations are so varied that it has been more convenient to set them out in chronological sequence through the Gospel, rather than under subject headings. Nevertheless three main thoughts about the meaning of the cross seem to be represented.

(1) The cross is seen as a work of recapitulation, a work of the second Adam. Surprisingly there is no evidence of Irenaeus using the Johannine passion story in this way.

(2) The cross is the source of newness of life, to be found preeminently in the sacramental life of the Church. These two lines of thought are combined with particular aptness by Augustine.

(3) The cross is that which universalises the saving work of Christ.

[1] Cyril of Jerusalem, *Catecheses*, 13, 21; ps-Athanasius, *De Passione et Cruce Domini*, 25; Apollinarius in Corderius, p. 444 (Apollinarius also accounts for the fact that Jesus' first appearance was to a woman, i.e. Mary Magdalene, on the ground that he was undoing the work of a woman's evil counsel: *ibid.* p. 447; cf. also Cyr. *in* John xx. 15; III, 115); Antiochus of Ptolemais in Cramer, p. 395 (Antiochus adds a rather more forced parallelism between the soldier's spear and the sword at the door of paradise).
[2] Tertullian, *De Anima*, 43, 10. Cf. Augustine, *Tract. Joh.* 120, 2; *De Civ. Dei*, 22, 17.
[3] Origen, *Con. Cel.* 2, 69.   [4] Origen, *Comm. Rom.* 5, 8.
[5] Cyr. *in* John xix. 41 (III, 105, 27–106, 25).

11. JOHN xxi. 1–14. THE MIRACULOUS DRAUGHT OF FISHES

This sign from the epilogue to the Gospel receives less notice than the pre-resurrection signs. It is generally understood as signifying the work of being fishers of men to which the disciples had been called at the first.[1] Cyril, as we have seen, develops this idea in terms of the contrasted efficacy of Law and Gospel in bringing men to the service of God.[2] Augustine contrasts it with the similar miracle of Luke v. That, he says, symbolises the present work of the Church, whereas this, with its reference to the dragging of the net to the shore reminiscent of the Matthaean parable of the drag-net, symbolises the final harvest of souls.[3] Their suggested interpretations of the number of the fish are in harmony with their understanding of the incident as a whole. For Cyril, the hundred represents the fulness of the Gentiles, the fifty the remnant of Israel and the three the Holy Trinity, to whose glory the whole work is done.[4] Augustine gives two interpretations. According to the first 153 is shown to be the sum of all the numbers up to seventeen. This signifies the total number of believers saved by the divine grace working through the medium of law (ten) and Spirit (seven). His second interpretation in terms of the Trinity bears a rather less direct relation to his general interpretation.[5]

[1] Theodore of Heraclea in Corderius, p. 467.
[2] Cyr. *in* John xxi. 1–6 (III, 156–60). Cf. p. 35 above.
[3] *Tract. Joh.* 122, 6–7.
[4] Cyr. *in* John xxi. 11 (III, 162, 2–9).
[5] *Tract. Joh.* 122, 8. According to Isho'dad an interpretation in terms of the Trinity goes back to Origen (*The Commentaries of Isho'dad of Merv*, ed. M. D. Gibson, vol. I, p. 287).

CHAPTER V

LEADING IDEAS OF THE GOSPEL

Professor Dodd devotes the whole of the second part of his *Interpretation of the Fourth Gospel* to a study of the leading religious concepts in the Gospel, in the attempt to define as closely as possible the dominant ideas with which the Evangelist operates.[1] No such systematic treatment of these leading ideas is to be found in the general run of patristic commentaries. As with many modern commentaries, it is normally the introductory concept of the Logos which captures the attention and alone receives any thorough discussion or treatment. The one notable exception is the commentary of Origen. Origen objects that too many would-be exponents of the Christian faith concentrate their whole attention upon the idea of Christ as the Logos to the virtual exclusion of the many other titles ascribed to him. Yet these other titles are essential to a proper understanding of the significance of the title Logos.[2] He also insists that the title Logos must always be considered, not as an isolated phrase, but in the light of the specific assertions of the immediate Johannine context.[3] As a corrective therefore to this common but misleading approach, Origen deals in his very first book with many of the most important Christological titles used in the Gospel. He discusses the ideas of Christ as light,[4] as resurrection, as the way, the truth, and the life,[5] as Christ and king,[6] as teacher and Lord, as Son,[7] and as true vine and living bread.[8] The titles of door and good shepherd are also mentioned but not interpreted.[9] Origen, therefore, does give us in the form of this Christological inquiry a considered treatment of many of the leading notions of the Gospel at the start

[1] See especially the Preface and p. 133.
[2] O. 1, 21.
[3] O. 1, 36.
[4] O. 1, 25, 26.
[5] O. 1, 27.
[6] O. 1, 28.
[7] O. 1, 29.
[8] O. 1, 30.
[9] O. 1, 21. Origen in fact extends his discussion (O. 1, 31–6) to take in a considerable number of other Christological titles outside the scope of the Fourth Gospel itself.

of his commentary. Nor is this the sum of his contribution in this field. He is far more inclined than other commentators to indulge, at the appropriate point in the course of the commentary itself, in a full consideration of the significance of some particular word or idea of especial importance. In this chapter we shall attempt to see how some of these leading ideas of the Gospel were understood by the early commentators. In almost every case Origen will provide our starting-point, and it is in his writing alone that any thorough treatment will be found.

I. SPIRIT

The great majority of the occurrences of the word πνεῦμα are regarded without question as being references to the Holy Spirit, the third person of the Trinity. Thus both Theodore and Cyril have no doubt that when Nicodemus is taught the necessity of a birth of water and the Spirit, it is of the work of the Holy Spirit in baptism that Jesus is speaking.[1] Theodore, as we have seen, even disallows the basic meaning of wind in John iii. 8 altogether, and Cyril finds evidence in the passage of the eternal relation of the Holy Spirit to the Father.[2]

John xi. 33 and xiii. 21 speak of Jesus groaning and being troubled in spirit. We have not got Origen's comments on xi. 33, but he interprets spirit in xiii. 21 of the human spirit which Jesus assumed in taking on himself the fulness of human nature. Origen points out that in scriptural usage the soul is morally neutral, capable of good or bad, but the human spirit is always (with the one exception of Deut. ii. 20) used in a good sense.[3] Both Theodore and Cyril, however, interpret both these passages as referring not to Christ's human spirit, but to the Holy Spirit. Thus Jesus is troubled by the Spirit in xiii. 21, according to Theodore because it is the Spirit in him who gives him knowledge of Judas' future betrayal, or,

---

[1] T. 46–9; Cyr. *in* John iii. 3–5 (1, 217–19).

[2] T. 48, 35–49, 6 (cf. p. 40 above); Cyr. *in* John iii. 3 (1, 217) (cf. p. 79 below). We have not got Origen's commentary at this point. O. Frag. 37 deduces from the text that the Spirit is no mere ἐνέργεια of God but a distinct οὐσία with his own ἰδιότης ὑπάρξεως, but the relevant section of the fragment is of doubtful attribution and the language strongly suggests a later hand.

[3] O. 32, 18.

according to Cyril, because troubled is the least inadequate human term to express the Spirit's hatred of evil.[1] In view of these interpretations, it is surprising to find that πνεῦμα is never interpreted of the Holy Spirit in John xix. 30.[2]

Two important occurrences of the word remain in which an interpretation in terms of the Holy Spirit was hardly possible. The first is vi. 63. 'It is the spirit that quickeneth; the flesh profiteth nothing: the words that I have spoken unto you, they are spirit, and they are life.' Again we have not got Origen's comment, but there appears to be a generally accepted understanding of the passage in which πνεῦμα is identified with Christ's divine nature.[3] Cyril, in fact, is concerned to insist that the statement that 'the flesh profiteth nothing' is not literally true of Christ. His flesh, though not life-giving in its own right, becomes life-giving by virtue of its association with the life-giving Word.

Finally, and most distinctively, we have in iv. 24 the words 'God is Spirit, and they that worship Him must worship in spirit and in truth'. Origen fully recognises the importance of this text. It has, he says, every appearance of being a definition of the οὐσία of God. But if we were to take it as such we would be committing ourselves to the view that God is σῶμα. In its literal sense πνεῦμα is as physical a word as fire or light. Its use is therefore just as metaphorical in this case as in the others. The significance of the metaphor is this. Just as the literal πνεῦμα around us provides the essential breath of physical life, so God is called πνεῦμα because it is he who leads men to real (ἀληθινός) life.[4] So for Origen the assertion that God is πνεῦμα is not a straightforward assertion of the incorporeal nature of God. Rather God is incorporeal, in spite of the fact that he is called πνεῦμα.[5] In the second half of the text he does allow that the appropriate contrast with worship in the spirit is bodily or

---

[1] T. 185, 17–26: Cyr. *in* John xiii. 21 (II, 363, 17–20). Cf. also Cyr. *in* John xi. 33 (II, 279, 19–20).

[2] Cf. p. 62 above. This interpretation is mentioned and regarded as at least an attractive possibility by many modern commentators, e.g. Hoskyns (p. 532), Dodd (p. 428), Barrett (p. 460) and Lightfoot (p. 319).

[3] Tertullian, *De Resurrectione Mortuorum*, 37; T. 108–9; Cyr. *in* John vi. 63 (I, 551–2).

[4] O. 13, 21–3.　　　　　　　　　　　[5] Origen, *Con. Cel.* 6, 70.

67　　　　　　　　　　　　　　　　　　　　5-2

fleshly worship, but this is based more on the total context and on the conjunction with worship in the truth than on the inherent meaning of the word πνεῦμα itself.[1]

Tertullian agrees with Origen in asserting a physical element in the literal meaning of πνεῦμα. He writes 'Who will deny that God is a body, although "God is a Spirit"? For Spirit is body of its own kind, in its own form.'[2] The conclusion is the exact opposite of that of Origen, but the premises are identical. The later writers, however, all regard the assertion that 'God is Spirit' as intended to convey simply and directly the incorporeal nature of his being.[3]

2. TRUTH

The most frequent understanding of the term ἀλήθεια in Origen's interpretation of St John is in the sense of spiritual reality as contrasted with the type or shadow of the Old Testament Law. This is naturally his interpretation of John i. 17, where the explicit contrast in the Gospel is with the Law.[4] It is also his standard interpretation of the worship in spirit and in truth of John iv. 24.[5] In one passage he interprets in the same way the reference to 'all the truth' in John xvi. 13, to which the disciples are to be led by the Spirit of truth.[6] But elsewhere he interprets it of the doctrine of the Trinity as the crown of Christian truth.[7]

The title is ascribed directly to Jesus in John xiv. 6, and Origen therefore includes it among the Christological titles which he discusses in his first book. Here his interpretation is not in accordance with his most usual sense of spiritual reality but along more ordinary, intellectualist lines as suggested by the alternative exegesis of John xvi. 13. The description of Jesus as the truth asserts his complete omniscience, which he shares with his Father.[8]

[1] Origen, *De Principiis*, 1, 1, 4; *Con. Cel.* 6, 70.
[2] Tertullian, *Adv. Prax.* 7, 8.
[3] T. 64–5; Chr. 33, 2; Cyr. *in* John iv. 24 (1, 284, 25–6); *Responsiones ad Tiberium*, 2 (Pusey, III, 577); *ibid.* 10 (Pusey, III, 593); *Ep. ad Calosyrium* (Pusey, III, 604).
[4] O. 6, 3.   [5] O. 1, 6; 13, 13.
[6] *Con. Cel.* 2, 2.
[7] *De Principiis*, 2, 7, 3; *Jes. Nav. Hom.* 3, 2.
[8] O. 1, 27.

A corresponding fluctuation of meaning is to be found in the understanding of the adjectival form ἀληθινός. Christ is called the ἀληθινός light in contradistinction not to any false light but to the sensible (αἰσθητός) light of the sun.[1] The interpretation of the ἀληθινός vine, which follows only a few chapters later in the same book, is, however, conceived rather differently. The vine is called ἀληθινός because its stem contains the truth, and its branches, the disciples, in imitation of the stem bear the truth as their fruit. Here the reference seems to be to Christ as the truth in the more intellectualist sense.[2] Even where, as in the case of the ἀληθινός light, he does interpret the word of spiritual reality, he is hesitant to allow it the full sense of ultimate reality. In one passage, where he admits that the ἀληθινός light has appeared on the earth in the person of Jesus, he adds that God the Father is greater than truth and superior to the ἀληθινός light.[3] He cannot, therefore, be giving to the terms ἀλήθεια and ἀληθινός the full sense of ultimate reality. He makes the same point (although with a diametrically opposite exegesis of the term ἀληθινός) by insisting elsewhere in his commentary that the opposite of ἀληθινός is shadow, type or image, and that as when the word became flesh it involved itself in these things the fully ἀληθινός λόγος can exist only in heaven, and not in incarnate form. Here his Greek background appears to have got the better of his Christian exegesis, but it is interesting to note that, although this passage occurs in the commentary on the Gospel, the immediate passage under discussion is one from the Apocalypse and not the Gospel.[4]

The variety of interpretation which is characteristic of Origen's understanding of ἀλήθεια continues in the later exegetes with a growing emphasis on the intellectualist side, which is inclined to identify ἀλήθεια with orthodoxy. This is most marked in Theodore. The contrast with type or figure remains only in the prologue, where the Gospel contrast with law in i. 17 almost necessitated such an interpretation.[5] Christ is called the truth because his teaching is the source of true knowledge and the truth into which the disciples

[1] O. 1, 26 (John i. 9). Yet in O. 20, 28 when discussing John viii. 44 he develops the Gospel contrast between ἀλήθεια and ψεῦδος and relates it to the definition of Christ as ἀλήθεια in John xiv. 6.
[2] O. 1, 30 (John xv. 1).   [3] O. 2, 23.   [4] O. 2, 6.
[5] T. 26, 35–6 (John i. 17); T. 24, 14–25 (John i. 14).

will later be led by the Spirit of truth is the whole range of Trinitarian and Christological doctrine.[1] He gives no treatment of the corresponding form ἀληθινός apart from the somewhat inadequate definition of the ἀληθινός light as implying its continuance to the end of the world.[2]

Cyril provides something of a synthesis. The age in which he lived tends to suggest to him an interpretation in terms of orthodox Christian truth, but his Alexandrian background makes him less likely to overlook the meaning of spiritual reality in contrast to type or shadow. Sometimes one idea is dominant, sometimes the other, but there are signs of a fusion of the two. In commenting on John i. 17 the contrast with type is naturally the sense given, but this interpretation occurs also in less obvious contexts, as in the explanation of the words 'Ye shall know the truth, and the truth shall make you free'.[3] On the other hand the opposite sense is dominant when Christ's identification as the truth is interpreted in terms of his being the measure of a correct understanding of the nature of God.[4] Yet the two can come together. The true worshipper of John iv. 24 is one who has moved over from type to reality and whose worship is offered in strict accord with the divine teaching.[5] ἀλήθεια is the reality which replaced the preparatory shadows of the Old Testament Law and which finds expression in the truths of Christian orthodoxy.

In his treatment of the term ἀληθινός, we find the usual Alexandrian contrasts. The ἀληθινός vine is contrasted with the sensible (αἰσθητός).[6] The ἀληθινός bread is contrasted with the type of the manna.[7] The ἀληθινός light receives a fuller and more positive definition. It is that which is intrinsic light, which contains within its own nature

---

[1] T. 190, 36–191, 1 (John xiv. 6); T. 210–11 (John xvi. 13).

[2] T. 21, 36–8 (John i. 9).

[3] Cyr. *in* John i. 17 (I, 152); *in* John viii. 32 (II, 60, 12–17).

[4] Cyr. *in* John xiv. 6 (II, 409, 19–27).

[5] Cyr. *in* John iv. 24 (I, 284–5). Cf. also Cyr. *in* John xvi. 13 (II, 626–8). Chrysostom similarly uses both senses in his interpretation of 'sanctification in the truth'. It is a 'real' sanctification by sacrifice in contrast to the Old Testament sanctification by sacrifice, which was only a type. But it is also said to be effected by the gift of the Holy Spirit and by right dogmas (Chr. 82, 1: John xvii. 17 and 19).

[6] Cyr. *in* John xv. 1 (II, 544, 15–21).

[7] Cyr. *in* John vi. 32 (I, 458, 6–9; 467, 15–18).

the power to be and to give light. It must therefore be uncreated and clearly distinct from the realm of creation.[1] The long discussion of the term, which Cyril goes on to give, is concerned rather with the theological implications of this definition than with the narrower field of precise exegesis.

Thus the main lines of the interpretation of ἀλήθεια are in terms either of ultimate reality or of true knowledge or of a synthesis of the two. One interesting exception is worthy of mention. In a Catena fragment on John xiv. 6, Apollinarius gives a moral emphasis to the term. Jesus, he says, calls himself the truth because he is the perfection of ἀρετή.[2]

3. LIFE

The life, which Christ came to impart to men, was something more than mere physical existence. Origen expresses the distinction in a number of ways. There is an ἀδιάφορος ζωή, which is enjoyed even by the impious and by irrational animals, but there is a διάφορος ζωή which is enjoyed through identification with the risen Christ.[3] Elsewhere he speaks with similar intent of ἡ κυρίως καλουμένη ζωή or of τὸ ἀληθινὸν ζῆν.[4]

The distinction is essentially a qualitative or even a moral one. The διάφορος ζωή is necessarily good in contrast to the ἀδιάφορος ζωή which is amoral in character.[5] A life of sin can only be described paradoxically as a living death.[6] Only the good life is really life at all, and therefore the Gospel deliberately speaks of the commandment of God and of the knowledge of God not as conveying life, but as actually being αἰώνιος ζωή.[7] In the same way, Christ is spoken of directly as being the life.[8] Thus Origen is quite clear that ζωή, whether qualified as αἰώνιος or not, is intended to be a present qualitative experience of the Christian, conveyed to him by Christ.

Yet here again, as we have already seen in our study of the term ἀληθινός, his subordinationist tendencies give him pause. If Christ is αἰώνιος ζωή, does this mean that he is qualitatively identifiable

---

[1] Cyr. *in* John i. 9 (1, 96–7).
[2] Corderius, p. 356.
[3] O. 20, 39.
[4] O. 1, 27.
[5] O. 20, 39.
[6] O. 2, 16 (John i. 4).
[7] O. Frag. 95 (John xii. 50).
[8] O. 13, 3.

with the Father? Cyril draws the conclusion with alacrity and with emphasis. For him the Gospel shows clearly that Christ is ζωή ἐκ ζωῆς.[1] But Origen insists on the superiority of the Father. This he does in two ways. The first is really inconsistent with his main exegesis of the Gospel, when in one passage he suggests that only to God can τὸ κυρίως ζῆν be attributed, and that in their fullest sense the words cannot be used of Christ, who tasted death for every man.[2] His second way maintains the formal consistency of his exegesis, but involves the introduction of a difficult new idea. Christ is ζωή, but the Father is greater than ζωή; Christ is αἰώνιος ζωή, but the Father is something above and beyond (ὑπέρ) αἰώνιος ζωή.[3]

The source of life is linked with the two ideas of πνεῦμα and of λόγος. As we have already seen, πνεῦμα in its literal sense was for Origen the source of ordinary life; the description of God as πνεῦμα metaphorically understood is therefore intended to present him as the source of ἀληθινὴ ζωή.[4] Alternatively, ἀδιάφορος ζωή is that which is shared even by the ἄλογοι, and therefore διάφορος ζωή is logically linked to the λόγος as its source, whether that be understood of the pre-existent λόγος or of its embodiment in the words of the incarnate Christ.[5]

Neither Theodore nor Cyril approaches the same level of understanding of the Johannine conception of ζωή or of ζωὴ αἰώνιος which is apparent in Origen. Theodore's treatment of the idea is both scanty and unsatisfactory. The statement of John i. 4 that 'In Him was life' is not a statement about the nature of the λόγος, but simply of his function as the giver of life to all creation.[6] The αἰώνιος ζωή of which the Gospel speaks is always conceived simply as a future gift. His comment on the closing words of John x. 10 ('that they may have it abundantly') will serve as an example. 'These words', he writes, 'are intended as an allusion to the resurrection which He will give to men.'[7]

Cyril differs from Theodore in insisting that John i. 4 is an assertion about the nature of the λόγος, and this insistence is of

[1] Cyr. *in* John vi. 57 (I, 544). Cf. also Cyr. *in* John i. 4 (I, 74–9).
[2] O. 2, 17.   [3] O. 13, 3.   [4] O. 13, 23 (John iv. 24).
[5] O. 20, 39 (John viii. 51).   [6] T. 19, 15–25.
[7] T. 143, 32–4. Cf. also his comments on John iii. 36, iv. 14 and viii. 51 in T. 59, 63 and 127.

importance for his exegesis of the theme of ζωή throughout the Gospel.[1] Like Theodore, he normally assumes that the reference of αἰώνιος ζωή is to a future life.[2] But in two respects his comments go deeper than those of Theodore. Having insisted that the λόγος is in the fullest possible sense ζωή by nature, he recognises that the gift of life comes through Christ's giving of Himself. As a result, he does acknowledge the present possession of the gift of life, but the idea comes in rather as a corollary than as the fundamental exegesis.[3] Secondly he does recognise that there is a frequent use of the term ζωή in the Gospel, which is qualitative in character, and which is to be distinguished from another and simpler usage of the word. But the distinction has reference to the future and not to the present experience of life. All men, good and bad alike, will be restored to life, but for some that restoration will mean only the beginning of eternal punishment, which is more properly called death than life. The gospel promise of life is, therefore, the promise not merely of the fact of resurrection, but of real life which is a future unending experience of bliss.[4]

4. LIGHT

Origen has two substantial discussions of the concept of light, both at a comparatively early stage in his commentary. In each case he begins with a classification of the most important uses of the term; in the first instance he lists 'light of the world', 'the light of men', 'the true light' and 'light of the Gentiles',[5] and in the second 'light of men', 'light' without further qualification and 'true light'.[6] These terms he says are clearly parallel and some would go so far as to regard them as identical, but it is a matter that requires careful investigation.[7]

---

[1] Cyr. *in* John i. 4 (I, 74, 1–7).
[2] E.g. Cyr. *in* John v. 24 (I, 344, 17–18). John v. 24 reads ὁ πιστεύων... ἔχει ζωὴν αἰώνιον. Cyril writes τοὺς δέ γε πιστεύοντας, οὐ μετόχους ἔσεσθαι μόνον τῆς αἰωνίου ζωῆς, ἀλλὰ καὶ τὸν ἐκ τῆς κρίσεως διαφεύξεσθαι κίνδυνον....
[3] Cyr. *in* John iii. 36 (I, 259, 7–11); *in* John vi. 47 (I, 513, 4–6).
[4] Cyr. *in* John viii. 51 (II, 115, 14–29); *in* John x. 10 (II, 220); *in* John xi. 25–6 (II, 274–5). Cf. p. 156 below.
[5] O. 1, 25. The last term in this list is of course drawn from outside the Johannine record.
[6] O. 2, 23 (John i. 4; i. 5; viii. 12).
[7] O. 1, 25.

The first point that needs to be made in such an investigation is that all these instances have to do with light not in its most literal sense, but in a metaphorical or spiritual one.[1] The sun is the light of the αἰσθητὸς κόσμος, Christ is the light of the νοητὸς κόσμος.[2] This is the significance of the title 'true light', ἀληθινός being here intended as the opposite of αἰσθητός.[3] True light has not, therefore, a sense which is distinct from the other usages with which it is listed, but merely makes explicit what is implicit in them all.

Having made this point clear, Origen does proceed to draw a distinction between 'light of the world' and 'light of men'. In both cases the reference must be to the intellectual enlightenment of reason and of will, but as Origen did not believe that men were the only rational beings in the universe, the term 'light of the world' is for him necessarily a wider and more inclusive term. He does, however, recognise that this distinction is based on a belief of a somewhat tentative character, and he is therefore not prepared to quarrel with the alternative exegesis which would equate the two terms completely.[4] In fact, in his second discussion of the terms he comes near to accepting this equation himself.

In this second discussion, he brings in the term 'light' without further qualification, which had not entered into his previous treatment. This suggests a different problem to his mind. God the Father is also spoken of as 'light', and this might lead the unwary to believe that there is no differentiation in οὐσία between Father and Son.[5] This Origen avoids by insisting that a light in which there is no darkness at all is different from a light which shines in the darkness and is pursued though not overcome by it. When, therefore, he goes on to equate 'the true light', 'the light of men' and 'the light

[1] O. 13, 23.
[2] O. 1, 25.
[3] O. 1, 26 (cf. p. 69 above).
[4] O. 1, 26. Cf. also Con. Cel. 5, 10.
[5] As in the case of ζωή, Cyril very readily draws such conclusions. The Gospel use of φῶς shows clearly that Christ is φῶς . . . ἐκ φωτός (Cyr. in John i. 9: 1, 96–7; in John viii. 12: 1, 711, 23–6), or that Father and Son have a common φύσις (Cyr. in John xii. 36; II, 326, 10–12). Basilides had drawn exactly the opposite conclusion; the Prologue has clear affinities with the opening chapter of Genesis, and the 'light which lighteth every man coming into the world' ought therefore to be identified with the light which came into being by the command of God according to Gen. i. 3 (Hippolytus, Elenchos, 7, 22, 4).

of the world', he presumably intends to imply not that they are all identical in connotation, but simply that they are identical in denotation as all referring to the Son rather than to the Father.

Finally in the same passage he discusses the relation between the terms 'life' and 'the light of men'. Here again his tentative conclusion is that there is identity of denotation, but a difference of connotation. The two always go together, but there is a logical priority in the idea of 'life' which provides a kind of substratum, upon which the enlightening process can operate.[1]

Theodore and Cyril do not indulge in such full treatments of the concept, but in this case they do recognise as fully as Origen its metaphorical and spiritual character. Theodore is more conscious of the sense of φῶς as the sun, which underlies the metaphor, but this does not detract from his handling of the term as a properly metaphorical concept.[2] Both he and Cyril show their fundamental understanding by the way in which they distinguish it from the concept of 'life' with which it is so closely associated in the prologue. Cyril punctuates the passage 'What was made, in it was life' and interprets 'life' in this context as the power of the creation to come into being and to continue in existence.[3] Theodore pours scorn on this interpretation; to him it seems absurd to speak of the existence of the inanimate creation as 'life'.[4] He, therefore, prefers to take the phrase 'which was made' with the preceding clause, and to interpret the words 'in Him was life' of the physical life of the animate creation.[5] So far their interpretations are in direct conflict. But both are in agreement that the reference to 'light' represents a narrowing of the field to the especially important gift of the light of reason to the rational creation.[6]

Both therefore give to 'the light of men' a wide and general interpretation. Origen had regarded 'the light of the world' as a term requiring in all probability an even wider interpretation. But here both Theodore and Cyril dissent. For them the term is one of historical rather than cosmological significance, and refers to the

[1] O. 2, 23.
[2] T. 133 (John ix. 5); T. 175 (John xii. 35–6). Cf. p. 38 above.
[3] Cyr. *in* John i. 4 (1, 75).   [4] T. 17, 28–38.
[5] T. 19, 15–25 (John i. 4).
[6] T. 19, 26–20, 2; Cyr. *in* John i. 5 (1, 81, 2–6).

range of Christ's mission being to the Gentiles and not only to the Jews.[1] Cyril does acknowledge the fact that Christ's power as φῶς νοητόν extends beyond the range of this world, but such power would have to be described as ὑπερκόσμιος and is not the intended meaning of the words spoken in the Gospel.[2] The difference here, therefore, is neither one of dogmatic belief nor one of the interpretation of the term φῶς, but arises from a conflicting understanding of the term κόσμος. To the interpretation of that term and of its correlatives we must now turn.

5. WORLD

Origen, as we have just seen, interprets the world of which Christ is the light as the νοητὸς κόσμος, the unseen world accessible only to the enlightened mind of man. This, however, appears to be the only occasion on which he gives this interpretation to the word κόσμος in the Gospel. He certainly believes the idea to be an important one in the thought of the Gospel, but reference to it is given obliquely by the implied contrast to this world. Origen's main discussion of the word and the ideas associated with it is by way of comment on John viii. 23. This verse includes two contrasted pairs of ideas— 'from below' and 'from above', and 'of this world' and 'not of this world'. To these he adds also 'of the earth' and 'from heaven' from John iii. 31. These phrases, he suggests, have differing connotations although they are identical in denotation. 'Below' and 'above' are used metaphorically of the nature of a man's beliefs; the contrast in terms of κόσμος is between the visible and invisible worlds. He finds additional corroboration of the fact that this world is coterminous with the realm of the below in the use of the word καταβολή of the creation in John xvii. 24. He differentiates his position sharply from that of the Gnostics by his insistence that men can be changed from below to above, from being of this world to being no longer of this world. This in fact was the very purpose of Christ's coming. The nature of the νοητὸς κόσμος itself is not made explicit, because the Gospel reference to it is indirect and negative. Origen, however, makes certain bold suggestions. The goal of man is the vision of

[1] T. 117, 18–30; Cyr. *in* John viii. 12 (I, 711, 27–712, 27).
[2] Cyr. *in* John ix. 5 (II, 155, 14–20).

this invisible world; but this hope may also be expressed in terms of the vision of God. He does not explicitly identify the two, but he is very near to it. He does suggest that in one sense at least the νοητὸς κόσμος may be identified with the Son. This world is a κόσμος by virtue of the λόγος and the wisdom by which its basic material is ordered. The νοητὸς κόσμος is the identical concept apart from matter. Yet Christ, the first-born of all creation, is the λόγος and the wisdom by which all things were made. In this sense, therefore, he may be identified with the νοητὸς κόσμος.[1] In commenting on the same text in the De Principiis, he is careful to distinguish between the νοητὸς κόσμος of Christian belief and that of the Platonic scheme. The latter, he declares, is an imaginary world and lacks the essential quality of reality. The world, which is Christ's true home, cannot be a purely phenomenological one, dependent for its existence on human thought. But beyond that it is neither possible nor desirable to speak with any definiteness. Origen's own conjecture on this occasion is that while of infinitely superior quality it should be conceived as contained within the limits of this world. His difficulty appears to be that despite his insistence on the non-physical nature of this other world, he still wishes to give it some spatial reference so as to make clear that it is not purely of an imaginary character.[2]

Important though this contrast is, it is not the one which is uppermost in the mind of Origen as he approaches the great majority of the gospel references to κόσμος. There is a second contrast between the meaning of the word as the whole frame of heaven and earth on the one hand and the inhabited earth on the other. This second sense, he declares, is especially characteristic of Johannine usage.[3] Elsewhere, in listing examples of this second use, he draws almost all his considerable series of examples from St John's Gospel and particularly from the seventeenth chapter. Some of these references are interpreted of the physical world itself and others of the men, or even of the sinful men, who live in it; in one case, he even suggests that 'the powers' specially linked with the inhabited world ought possibly to be included in the meaning of the phrase. These, however,

---

[1] O. 19, 20–2.   [2] De Principiis, 2, 3, 6.

[3] Con. Cel. 6, 59. Cf. the definition of κόσμος in O. 2, 29 as ὁ περίγειος τόπος ἔνθα εἰσὶν οἱ ἄνθρωποι.

are not regarded as different usages, but as all being illustrations of the one meaning—the inhabited world as distinct from the whole frame of heaven and earth.[1]

Theodore's commentary contains no particular discussion of the term. In commenting on John iii. 31 he asserts that the words 'from above' and 'from heaven' are not to be taken as literal statements about places but as descriptions of the eminence of Christ's nature.[2] In general he interprets the distinction between being of the world and not of the world in straightforward Christian terms of that spiritual rebirth, whereby men are translated from being members of Adam into members of Christ.[3]

Cyril has one important discussion of the issue in his commentary on John viii. 23, the same verse which had attracted the main surviving discussion in Origen's commentary. His conclusion is radically different from that of his Alexandrian predecessor. The phrases 'below' and 'of this world' are identical in meaning, as are also the contrasted pair—'above' and 'not of this world'. The contrast is not one of place, but expresses the complete contrast between the divine nature and derivative being (τὰ γενητά). But Cyril has then to meet an objection. The phrase 'I am not of this world' is likely to suggest to 'the enemy of the truth' (as indeed it had to Origen) that there is another world, to wit the κόσμος νοητός, from which Christ can be said to be. But this Cyril is not prepared to allow at any price. To say that Christ is from any sort of κόσμος, however exalted, is to place him on the wrong side of the great divide between the divine and the created world, and thus undermines the heart of Christian faith. The word 'this' does not necessarily imply a contrast with some 'other'. The contrast here is not between two different κόσμοι, but is a metaphorical description of the difference between created and divine nature. 'The word κόσμος in this context signifies the nature of created things as a whole.'[4]

---

[1] Comm. Matt. 13, 20. Cf. also Sel. in Ps. cxviii (cxix). 161 (P.G. 12, 1624B).

[2] T. 58, 29–30.

[3] E.g. T. 204 (John xv. 19); T. 227 (John xvii. 16).

[4] Cyr. in John viii. 23 (II, 12–18, especially 18, 4–5). Cf. also Cyr. in John iii. 31 (I, 240–6); in John xiv. 11 (II, 435, 24–436, 2). The reason for the anxiety of Cyril on this score may be well illustrated by the use made of the notion of Christ as light

The difference in exegesis arises from a difference of belief about the nature of the κόσμος νοητός. For Cyril the only possible contrast with the created world is the divine οὐσία itself. Thus for him the terms 'from above' and 'not of this world' always carry with them this full theological meaning. One example of the influence of this upon his exegesis will suffice. When Jesus speaks to Nicodemus of being born ἄνωθεν, this is a reference to the fact that rebirth is effected by the Holy Spirit and 'shows clearly that the Spirit is of the οὐσία of God and the Father'.[1] This is Cyril's primary understanding of the word, but he recognises that, in view of the involvement of created nature as a whole in the way of sin, κόσμος is also used in a pejorative sense to mean the opponents of the gospel of God.[2]

6. JUDGMENT

The portions of the Gospel on which Origen's commentary has come down to us do not include any of the principal passages which deal with the theme of judgment. We have, therefore, no full treatment of the idea in his commentary, and must rely largely upon the fragments for our knowledge of his understanding of the term.

He recognises that judgment in the obvious sense of the word was not the primary purpose of Christ's coming. His primary purpose was the salvation of the world. The work of judgment can be explained in two ways. It may be understood as a self-imposed judgment, which follows automatically upon failure to believe, and which is in that sense a result of Christ's coming. But Origen gives

of the world by Asterius, who had written 'The Son is the first of derivative beings (τῶν γενητῶν), and is one of the intellectual natures (τῶν νοητῶν φύσεων); and as the sun is one of the objects of vision, but also gives light to all the world by the decree of its maker, so the Son is one of the νοητοὶ φύσεις, but also Himself gives light to all those in the νοητὸς κόσμος' (Athanasius, *De Synodis*, 19: printed as Fragment 3 of Asterius in G. Bardy, *Recherches sur St Lucien d'Antioche et son École*, p. 343).

[1] Cyr. *in* John iii. 3 (I, 217). Origen points out the two different possible meanings of the word. He himself appears to prefer the sense 'from above' in that this meaning is clearly the right one elsewhere in the Gospel (O. Frag. 35; O. 19, 21). Chrysostom states that opinion was divided on the issue in his day (Chr. 24, 2). Cf. Westcott, Additional Note on John iii. 3 (vol. I, p. 136).

[2] Cyr. *in* John xvii. 25 (III, 11, 1–2).

an alternative explanation, which derives more from his own peculiar views on the nature of God's punitive activity than from the evidence of the Gospel itself. He suggests that the work of judgment may be God's preliminary activity, whose sole purpose, as in the case of the infliction of pain by the doctor, is to make possible the subsequent saving activity.[1]

Origen sees clearly that the idea of judgment is closely related to the cross. The emphatic 'now' of the moment of judgment in John xii. 31 refers to the immediate proximity of the passion. He appears to give three closely allied explanations of this link. First, the cross is the crucial factor in determining the judgment of every living being. Secondly, it is the occasion of the overcoming of the principalities and powers, and even of the destruction of their leader. Thirdly, it is the cross which cleanses the elect and thereby prepares them for their destined role as judges of the world.[2]

It is Theodore who points with the greatest clarity to the surface contradiction to be found within the Gospel itself on the subject of judgment and its relation to the purpose of Christ's coming. He sets out his explanation also with great clarity; the one set of sayings are concerned with the purpose, the other with the result of his coming.[3]

The same point is made by Cyril,[4] but both he and Theodore find it difficult to do full justice to the idea of the judgment as a present fact. If the unbeliever is condemned already, it is because his refusal of the offered way of salvation is a kind of advance vote against himself as deserving punishment.[5] If Jesus says that he judges no man, it is because he is reserving his activity as judge to another occasion.[6] Most striking of all, the insistence that now is the moment of the world's judgment seems to Cyril to be clearly

---

[1] O. Frag. 41 (John iii. 18–19; ix. 39). For the first interpretation see *Philocalia*, 27, 10; for the second see *Con. Cel.* 7. 39. Another excellent early exposition of this theme along the lines of the first and more natural interpretation is to be found in Irenaeus, *Adv. Haer.* 5, 27, 2 (vol. II, p. 399) (John iii. 18 and 21).

[2] O. Frag. 89 and 90.

[3] T. 138, 36–139, 2 (John ix. 39; iii. 17); T. 179, 8–29 (John xii. 47; v. 22; ix. 39).

[4] Cyr. *in* John ix. 39 (II, 204, 1–6).

[5] Cyr. *in* John iii. 18 (I, 230, 3–6).

[6] Cyr. *in* John viii. 15 (I, 720, 13–15).

false. It is only Satan who is being judged, in the sense of being condemned, now; the present judgment of the world is not a condemnation at all but a vindication for the wrong done to it by Satan in the past.[1]

The two writers who do most justice to the concept of judgment as a present fact in their interpretation of the Gospel are Chrysostom and Didymus, though even so neither of them is entirely at home with the idea. Chrysostom gives two alternative interpretations of the idea. We may think of the sentence having been passed in advance, while the actual punishment awaits Christ's future coming. This interpretation is very close to those of Theodore and Cyril. Or alternatively (and Chrysostom gives this alternative as his first suggestion) we may regard unbelief as being itself the punishment, on the ground that no punishment could be greater than the exclusion from the light, which is already involved in unbelief.[2] Didymus appears to have accepted the idea of the present judgment of unbelievers so completely that, when the Gospel speaks later of a twofold resurrection to life and judgment, he insists that the resurrection to judgment cannot refer to unbelievers, who have already been judged, but must refer to believers who have sinned after believing.[3]

Augustine gives a different solution to the apparent conflict of ideas within the Gospel on the question of judgment. There is a good sense to the word judgment, according to which it means simply discrimination; in this sense judgment was a part of the purpose of Christ's coming, but it must be carefully distinguished from the sense of punishment or condemnation, which is also present in other statements in the Gospel.[4]

7. GLORY

In the course of commenting on John xiii. 31 Origen gives a full investigation of the meaning of this term. Its normal Greek meaning is the praise of the many, but there is also a distinct Biblical meaning of the word which is far more important for the understanding of its

---

[1] Cyr. *in* John xii. 31 (II, 322–3).
[2] Chr. 28, 1 (John iii. 18).
[3] Didymus *in* John v. 29 (*P.G.* 39, 1645 c); *in* Ps. i. 5 (*P.G.* 39, 1160B).
[4] *Tract. Joh.* 22, 5; 44, 17 (John ix. 39).

significance in the Gospel. In the Bible the word is frequently associated with a physical brightness, whose deeper meaning is that knowledge or vision of God which transforms man into the likeness of God.[1] This provides the key to an understanding of the difficult conception of the mutual glorifying of the Father and the Son. Origen develops four distinguishable ideas:

(*a*) The glorification of the Son. The Son is glorified by the mere fact of his perfect knowledge of the Father.

(*b*) The glorification of God in himself. (This idea does not receive direct expression in the Gospel, but is the implied contrast to God's glorification in the Son.) This refers to something utterly beyond the range with which human language is equipped to deal. It refers to the inexpressible joy of God's perfect self-knowledge and self-contemplation.

(*c*) The glorification of God in the Son. This is the fruit of the incarnation. Jesus in his sinless perfection is the perfect image of God, and reveals him to men. Therefore those who truly know or see Jesus are being enabled to know or see God. Thus, in the deep Biblical sense of the word, God is glorified in the world in Jesus.

(*d*) The glorification of the Son in God. As the Son has glorified God, God repays him with an even greater kind of glory—the glory that he has in himself, which must of necessity be greater, as the Father is greater than the Son. Here again we are being taken up into a realm where human language is hopelessly inadequate. This glory is spoken of in the Gospel in the future tense (John xiii. 32).[2]

Origen thus believes that the Gospel speaks of two kinds of glory in relation to the Son. He finds this clearly expressed in John xii. 28.[3] There is a 'humble glory' which is to be seen even in Christ's death as John xiii. 31 and xvii. 1 emphatically show.[4] The term 'glory' is applied to the cross because of its central place in achieving the glory of man's salvation.[5] In addition there is a 'glorious glory' which is added to the other at the resurrection.[6] This final glory is, as we have seen, one which in Origen's estimation far outpasses the power

---

[1] O. 32, 26–7. [2] O. 32, 28–9.
[3] Sel. *in* Ps. xx (xxi). 6 (*P.G.* 12, 1249 C).
[4] *Ex. Hom.* 6, 1; O. 32, 25.
[5] *In Can. Can.* bk. 3 (*P.G.* 13, 163 D: *G.C.S.* ed. Baehrens, p. 196).
[6] *Ex. Hom.* 6, 1; Sel. *in* Ps. xx (xxi). 6 (*P.G.* 12, 1249 C).

of human telling. In so far as he does attempt any analysis of it, he claims that it must refer to the human element in Jesus, which after its utter obedience to the point of death is glorified in God by the final completion of its identification with the Logos. His exegetical ground for such an interpretation lies in the fact that according to John xiii. 31 this glorification is specifically predicated of the Son of Man.[1]

For Theodore the glorifying of Jesus is centred in his resurrection and ascension. It consists in the removal of the limitation of his human life, and the recognition by mankind of his true nature, so that he is no longer judged only by appearance as no more than an example of suffering humanity. As with Origen the use of the title 'Son of Man' in this context suggests that for the human element in Jesus the universal adoration is newly attained through the process of resurrection and ascension.[2] The connection between glory and the cross is reduced almost to a minimum. The reference of John xiii. 31 to the cross is admitted but the element of glory is found only in the attendant portents.[3] In John xvii. 1 a rather closer link between the two is recognised. The prayer that the Father will glorify the Son is a prayer that, at the time of his passion, God will make plain to all 'through what will happen on the cross' both the greatness of his true honour and the voluntary nature of his death. But even here the similarity of the language used to that used in the comment on John xiii. 31 suggests that the glory is really associated with the attendant circumstances rather than with the cross itself.[4]

For Cyril the essence of Christ's glory is the fact of his being ὁμοούσιος with the Father.[5] As this is an eternal truth, the main problem for him is the implication of the Gospel that there are special moments of glorification and any enhancement of God's glory. The problem is met by insisting that both the newness and the 'nowness' of glorification refer to the effective revelation of that glory to mankind.[6] It is primarily in this sense that the cross may be

[1] O. 32, 25.
[2] T. 171 (John xii. 23); T. 222, 1–20 (John xvii. 5). Cf. Chr. 80, 2.
[3] T. 186–7 (cf. p. 39 above).   [4] T. 220, 2–12.
[5] Cyr. *in* John xvii. 1 (II. 661, 23–662, 7).
[6] John xvii. 5 remains a difficult verse for Cyril and he has to admit that the incarnation, while not diminishing the Son's divine glory, did involve the assumption

said to be the glory. The cross (or rather the cross and resurrection together, for Cyril sees them essentially as one action) are the starting-point of the true glorification of God throughout the world.[1] In one passage, however, Cyril does suggest an even closer link between the glory and the cross; by this interpretation the cross is the glory of God because it shows the extent of Christ's voluntary suffering for others, and in that very fact shows forth the true character of God.[2]

Chrysostom is the writer who most clearly emphasises the Gospel's direct identification of the cross itself as glory. It is true that, like Theodore, he finds a reference in John xiii. 31 to the accompanying portents.[3] It is true also that, like Cyril, he recognises the existence of a greater glory which is natural to Christ's heavenly existence.[4] Yet he insists frequently and firmly that, within the sphere of earth, the cross for all its seeming shame is in reality the glory. It deserves that title because it is not only an act of love, but an act of death-destroying power.[5]

8. KNOWLEDGE

For Origen, as we have just seen, the idea of glory was closely bound up with the idea of the knowledge of God. And just as he insists on the importance of the Biblical rather than the ordinary Greek meaning of the word glory, so also in the case of knowledge there is a distinctive Biblical usage. The fact that Jesus can speak of knowing those whom he has chosen shows that the word is being used not with its ordinary meaning but with its special Biblical force.[6] Failure to recognise this is one reason for the misinterpretation of Scripture by the heretics. Origen, therefore, in commenting on

of an ἀδοξότατον σῶμα (Cyr. *in* John xvii. 5; II, 677, 3–8). For the insistence that the glorifying of the Son refers entirely to human estimation, cf. Apollinarius *in* John xii. 28 (Corderius, p. 314); Didymus *in* John xvii. 2 (*P.G.* 39, 1653 B).

[1] Cyr. *in* John. xii. 23 (II, 311, 13–24); *in* John xii. 28 (II, 319, 13–15); *in* John xii. 16 (II, 306–7).

[2] Cyr. *in* John xiii. 31 (II, 378–9). Cf. Cyril's penetrating comment on John iii. 16 that unless the Son is fully of the essence of the Father, then the giving of the Son for us does not display any remarkable love on the part of the Father (I, 227, 6–228, 2).

[3] Chr. 72, 2.   [4] Chr. 80, 2 (John xvii. 4).

[5] Chr. 12, 3 (John i. 14); 51, 2 (John vii. 39); 77, 4.

[6] O. 32, 14 (John xiii. 18).

John viii. 19 gives a careful account of the Biblical meaning of the term. Four points emerge from his analysis:

(a) The scriptural usage of the term has a specifically moral connotation. In the Old Testament, it is a regular description of the sinner that he does not know the Lord.

(b) The word is not identical in meaning with belief, but represents a distinct and more advanced stage.[1]

(c) Knowledge is used in the Old Testament of sexual intercourse and implies the closest possible kind of union with the object of knowledge. Knowledge of God, therefore, implies a participation in his divinity.

(d) Knowledge of God as Father is distinct from knowledge of him simply as God. This is implied by the words of Jesus to Mary Magdalene in John xx. 17. It is also the germ of truth which gives rise to the heretical error of distinguishing between the Father and the Creator. It was the same God whom the men of the Old Testament dispensation knew, but they did not know him as Father. The only possible exception to this statement would be any pre-incarnate visitation (νοητὴ ἐπιδημία) of Christ to them, which could reveal God as Father, but the exception may be ignored as any such revelation would have remained unproclaimed and unrecorded.[2]

Theodore gives no special attention to the idea. He recognises that in John x. 14–15 the word must bear the meaning of intimate relationship,[3] but he does not carry this meaning over into other occurrences of the word in the Gospel and in general his interpretation of the term remains at the intellectualist level. The most notable example of this is his interpretation of John xvii. 3 as teaching that eternal life will be awarded on the basis of an accurate and unerring knowledge of the divine nature.[4]

Cyril is far more alive to the depth of meaning implicit in the term. Clearly the word at its lowest level is intended to imply more than a mere knowledge of the existence of God, but carries with it also

[1] This point is developed in the next section on Faith—see p. 87 below. Augustine claims that knowledge is used in two different senses in the Gospel. In one (which is eschatological in reference) it is a stage beyond faith (e.g. John xiv. 20; xvii. 23); in the other it is identical with faith (e.g. John xvii. 8). (Augustine, Tract. Joh. 75, 4; 110, 4.)

[2] O. 19, 3–5.   [3] T. 145, 1–2.   [4] T. 220–1.

the idea of the adoption of an attitude of mind appropriate to that knowledge. This meaning would also serve when Jesus goes on to speak of his own knowledge of the Father, if he is here speaking in his human capacity. But Cyril suspects that the idea may go deeper and imply a unique knowledge of God's essence, which could only conceivably be asserted of the Son, because he alone (with the Spirit) is of the Father's essence and therefore quite literally 'knows' it from firsthand experience.[1]

The main difficulty for Cyril about this interpretation is that there are other passages of the Gospel which are clearly of a similar character and yet where this interpretation will not serve. John x. 14–15 speaks in similar vein of the Son's knowledge of the Father, and goes on to assert that this same knowledge can be mediated to us. This knowledge therefore cannot be an understanding of the essential nature of God. Cyril therefore, like Theodore, here defines knowledge as intimate relationship, and states that this is in accord with general Biblical usage. This intimate relationship is so close that when mediated to us it constitutes us partakers of the divine nature.[2]

Yet another important idea enters into his discussion of the term in John xvii. 3. If the word, he says, carried no more meaning than its everyday intellectualist sense, the definition of 'eternal life' as being the knowledge of God and of Christ would be plainly false. The saying is only true because the word 'knowledge' has a greater existential depth. But here that greater depth is defined as the 'inclusion in itself of the whole power of the mystery and a participation in the mystic blessing, whereby we are united to the living and life-giving word'. Here, therefore, it is clearly implied that the word has a specifically sacramental significance.[3]

[1] Cyr. *in* John viii. 55 (II, 124–9). The words on which Cyril is commenting are 'I know Him and keep His word'. He supports his interpretation of the first half of the phrase by interpreting λόγος in the second half as equivalent to ὅρος, and translating it as 'I contain within myself the limit of his essence'.

[2] Cyr. *in* John x. 14–15 (II, 230, 1–233, 3).

[3] Cyr. *in* John xvii. 3 (II, 668, 21–669, 27).

9. FAITH

Origen returns at frequent intervals to a consideration of the fundamental concept of faith. Two main points receive emphasis in his
treatment of it. The first (which we have already noticed) is the
inferiority of faith to knowledge. The second is the existence of
differing grades within the concept of faith itself.

The inferiority of faith to knowledge is supported by a variety
of Biblical evidence. His support for this distinction within the
Johannine record is John viii. 31, 32, where it is said to those who
believe Jesus that if they abide in his word, then they shall know
the truth.[1] The same point is repeated in a fragment on John xii. 44,
when the superiority not only of the knowledge of God but also
of the vision of God is asserted.[2] Other passages suggest that it is
possible to regard the concept of hearing the words of God as a kind
of middle term between faith and knowledge. Those who only
believe remain at the stage of being the servants of God, and include
the ψυχικοί who may later fall away. Those who hear the words of
God are those who have a real understanding and clear-sighted grasp
of the divine message. They are described in the Gospel as being
'of God', and enjoy the status of children. Knowledge, on the other
hand, implies a measure of assent that goes beyond the level simply
of the understanding.[3] It would be a mistake, however, to regard
this as a fixed hierarchical scheme. Origen's thought is fluid, and he
makes such distinctions as seem necessary for the elucidation of the
particular text which he is being called upon to interpret. What
however is quite clear is that faith is the term used to represent the
lowest conceivable level of positive response to God or to Christ.

Three passages of the Gospel provide Origen with firm ground
for the drawing of distinctions within the concept of faith itself.

(a) John ii. 23–4. Here the Evangelist declares that 'many
believed on His name beholding His signs which He did, but Jesus
did not trust Himself unto them'. Origen argues that this belief on

[1] O. 19, 3. Cf. also Origen, Frag. *in* Ps. iv. 4 (Pitra, *Analecta Sacra*, vol. II, p. 453);
in Ps. cxviii (cxix). 75 (*ibid.* vol. III, p. 280).
[2] O. Frag. 93.
[3] O. 20, 33 (John viii. 47); O. 20, 20 (John viii. 43).

the name of Jesus must be inferior to that full belief in his person of which it is said that 'He that believeth on Him is not judged'. After all the person himself is obviously greater than his name. Those who believe on the name are however to be numbered among the saved and will find their place in one of the many mansions in the Kingdom of Heaven.[1] The distinction appears to be a valid deduction from the passage, although elsewhere the Evangelist uses faith in the name of Jesus to express the full range of faith, thus invalidating the detail of Origen's exegesis.[2] In a fragment dealing with the same passage, Origen writes: 'They believed not on Him, but on His name. They had no firm or complete knowledge.'[3] This statement appears to equate the higher sense of faith with knowledge, and thus renders his first distinction between faith and knowledge logically unnecessary.

(b) John viii. 31 and 45. John viii. 31 is the one text which provided Origen with an exegetical ground in the Gospel itself for his distinction between faith and knowledge; as he also uses it for drawing a distinction between faith and faith, we have further evidence that it is the lower kind of faith that is to be distinguished from knowledge. The distinction between faith and faith here arises from the fact that, in the course of conversation with people who are described as 'those Jews which had believed Him', Jesus says 'Because I say the truth, ye believe me not'. Origen therefore asserts that we are forced to choose between admitting that the Evangelist has overlooked a gross contradiction on the one hand and allowing that there are differences of faith, even though the identical phrase is used, on the other. Origen declares that it is clearly possible to believe in one respect and not in another. We might believe in Jesus as being crucified under Pontius Pilate, but not as being born of the Virgin Mary; we might believe in him as a worker of miracles, but not as Son of the Creator of heaven and earth. Similarly we might believe in God as the Father of Jesus Christ, but not as the Creator of all that is or vice versa. Here he suggests that the relevant distinction

---

[1] O. 10, 44.

[2] John i. 12; iii. 18. Origen does, however, apply his principle to the exegesis of John i. 12. Belief in the name gives the ἐξουσία or δύναμις to become children of God; further progress may lead to belief in him which gives the ἐνέργεια to become children of God (O. Frag. 7). Cf. also O. 20, 33.   [3] O. Frag. 33.

is between faith in Jesus as a worker of visible miracles and disbelief in him as a purveyor of deeper truth.[1]

Elsewhere he gives a comparable though different analysis of faith in Christ. Christ is righteousness, wisdom, Logos, peace, the power of God, hope and strength. Faith in him therefore involves a complete disassociation from the opposites of these various attributes. This analysis is not in fact used to illustrate the possibility of degrees of faith (though clearly it might well have been so used), but to show how faith in Christ is a logical and not a mere arbitrary requirement for salvation from the death of sin.[2]

(c) John xiii. 19. Here, at the very end of his ministry, Jesus says to his disciples that he has warned them of what will happen so that, 'when it is come to pass, ye may believe that I am He'. Yet it seems impossible to assert that the disciples at this point had no faith in Jesus. Clearly faith, like any other virtue, is a continuously developing thing. By a permissible but not strictly accurate use of language, we employ the name of the virtue without qualification to describe its presence even in a still incomplete state.[3] Elsewhere the Gospel speaks of the disciples believing the Scripture and the word of Jesus after his resurrection. This serves to show that completeness of faith will be attained only at the final resurrection of the whole body of Christ. Here once again faith is treated on an exact parallel with knowledge; that also is at present partial and awaits a future perfection.[4]

Theodore also finds evidence in the Gospel that the idea of 'faith' is used to represent differing degrees of faith. The author, he says, 'frequently uses faith in place of confirmation'.[5] This appears most

[1] O. 20, 30 (cf. also O. 32, 16).

[2] O. 19, 23 (John viii. 24). Elsewhere this same analysis is applied to the thought of St Paul to suggest that the ideas of being in Christ and of Christ indwelling the believer are ones which are capable only of a gradual fulfilment, and which may therefore be true in varying degrees (*Comm. Rom.* 6. 11; *De Principiis*, 4, 4, 2). For Origen's insistence on the logical necessity of faith cf. his treatment of John viii. 51, where it is stated that if a man keeps Christ's word, he will never see death. Christ's word is the pre-existent Logos, in which was life. Keeping Christ's word therefore logically excludes the presence of death (O. 20, 39).

[3] O. 32, 15.   [4] O. 10, 43 (John ii. 22). Cf. also O. 10, 37.

[5] T. 41, 22–3. The same point is made by Origen in commenting on the same text (O. Frag. 30).

clearly in cases where it is stated that the purpose or result of Christ's action was the faith of the disciples, when in fact they already had some measure of faith.[1] The nobleman passes through a preliminary stage of the trusting acceptance of Christ's word on the road to a full faith.[2] The reserve of Jesus towards those who are said to have believed on his name can only be explained on the ground that their faith consisted merely of admiration for him as a wonder-worker, and did not amount to accepting him as an undoubted teacher of the truth, which is the measure of true faith.[3]

Cyril, however, makes little use of the idea of partial faith. The reserve that Christ shows in some instances towards those who have faith in him is not because their faith is partial, but because a new-found faith has always an element of instability about it. The faith of those described in John ii. 23 was a full faith in his essential divinity, and the reserve of Jesus is a valuable warning to the ecclesiastical administrator of the danger of promoting neophytes too rapidly.[4]

As Cyril's comment on John ii. 23 suggests, for him the essence of faith is the recognition of Christ's substantial divinity. This interpretation of faith is in line with Cyril's understanding of the purpose of the Gospel as a whole, and has a firm exegetical basis in the text of the Gospel itself. It is the faith to which Thomas ultimately attains, and it is the reason which enables Jesus to equate faith in himself with faith in the Father who sent him.[5] It is also regularly understood to be the implicit meaning of the concept of faith, even though it may not be absolutely demanded by the immediate context.[6]

---

[1] T. 41, 20–3 (John ii. 11); T. 158, 26–33 (John xi. 15).

[2] T. 68–9 (John iv. 46–53).

[3] T. 45, 19–29 (John ii. 23–4). Theodore regards Nicodemus as an example of this kind of faith, and Jesus refuses to trust himself to such people. The story of iii thus illustrates the principle asserted at the end of ii (T. 46, 1–8).

[4] Cyr. *in* John ii. 23–4 (I, 213–14).

[5] Cyr. *in* John xx. 28 (III, 151, 11–152, 12); *in* John xii. 44 (II, 329–30).

[6] E.g. Cyr. *in* John viii. 24 (II, 19, 25–20, 1); *in* John viii. 45 (II, 101, 23–30); *in* John xiv. 1 (II, 400–2). It is interesting to note that, although it would admirably have suited his purpose, Cyril does not interpret the words 'Unless ye believe that I am' in John viii. 24 as involving a claim to the divine name of Exod. iii. 14, but simply as the assertion of fulfilling in his person a variety of Old Testament prophecies.

One other passage included in Pusey's edition of Cyril's commentary draws a distinction between two kinds of faith. The primary sense is the 'dogmatic' and involves the assent of the soul; it is necessary for salvation and is the normal meaning of the word in the Gospel. The second is a particular gift, of which St Paul speaks in his epistles, and which makes possible the working of super-human achievements. This is the faith which is demanded as Martha's part in bringing about the raising of Lazarus. The attribution of the passage is, however, doubtful and in view of the uncharacteristic nature of its contents it is unlikely that it is a genuine part of the commentary.[1]

10. VISION OF GOD

The vision of God clearly involves a figurative use of the notion of seeing. The distinction between the literal and the metaphorical meanings is clearly enunciated by Origen. There are two senses of the word—the αἰσθητικός and the νοητικός—the first of which is applicable to bodily substances, the second to the non-physical realm.[2] The proper sense of the word refers to the illumination of the eyes of the mind or of the soul.[3] This deeper sense of the word, as we have already seen, is, like the knowledge of God, one with a fuller content than the range of faith.[4] The two concepts of knowledge and vision are exact equivalents for Origen, although the term which he normally uses to express the idea of vision in less metaphorical language is neither εἰδέναι nor γινώσκειν but νοεῖν.[5]

Celsus regards this double sense to the concept of seeing as something of Greek origin, but Origen declares that it is a fundamental Biblical notion and has its roots in Old Testament usage.[6]

---

[1] Cyr. in John xi. 40 (II, 284, 15–285, 14).

[2] O. Frag. 13 (John i. 18).

[3] O. Frag. 73 (John ix. 37; xiv. 9).

[4] O. Frag. 93 (John xii. 45; xiv. 9); O. 13, 53 (John iv. 42).

[5] O. 19, 6 (John viii. 19; xiv. 9); O. 6, 4 (John xiv. 9). Origen, however, is not altogether happy that the idea of vision is entirely free of material associations. He insists that it is the less material word 'knowledge' which is the most characteristically Biblical word for describing the interrelations of the Trinity (De Principiis, 1, 1, 8; 2, 4, 3).

[6] Con. Cel. 7, 39. With the judgment of Celsus cf. Dodd, p. 167, 'This identification of knowing with seeing is...characteristically Greek'.

Both the literal and the metaphorical uses are to be found in the Gospel, and the sense may require moving from one to the other within a single saying.[1]

In the literal physical sense one cannot see God at all, and this is not a mere empirical truth, but follows logically from the fact of God's incorporeal nature.[2] Men could and did see Christ in the literal sense without thereby doing so in a deeper sense.[3] In the case of the healing of the man born blind, however, there is a double gift both of physical and of spiritual vision.[4]

To see Christ in this deeper sense is to see or to know God, because Christ is the image of God.[5] In two passages this mediating role of the vision of Christ is subjected to a more detailed analysis. In the first, Christ's role as the image is explained in terms of identity of will, though this does not detract from the assertion that there is a divinity in Christ, which is the image of the ultimate (ἀληθινός) divinity.[6] The analysis in the second passage is similar to that given of faith in commenting upon John viii. 24.[7] Christ is Logos, wisdom and truth. The vision of these things is the essential preliminary to the actual vision of the οὐσία of God or of the power or nature of God which goes beyond classification as οὐσία. Thus it must logically be Christ who is the way to the vision of God and never the other way round.[8]

As long as we remain within this temporal finite existence, this vision of God remains imperfect. Origen suggests that the πώποτε in John i. 18 is to be interpreted as meaning that no one sees God as long as his mind remains embroiled in this material life.[9] Elsewhere he suggests that in the final consummation the image will

---

[1] E.g. Origen's peculiar views about judgment require him to interpret John ix. 39 ('For judgment came I into the world, that those who do not see may see and that those who see may become blind') as referring to the eyes of the soul in its first clause and to the eyes of the senses in its second (*Con. Cel.* 7, 39). Both Theodore and Cyril, approaching the text without Origen's presuppositions about judgment, are able to give a more satisfactory exegesis which recognises a double meaning throughout rather than an alternation of meanings (T. 139, 7–13; Cyr. *in* John ix. 39; II, 203–5).

[2] O. Frag. 13 (John i. 18).   [3] O. Frag. 73; *Con. Cel.* 7, 43.

[4] O. Frag. 73 (John ix. 38).   [5] *Con. Cel.* 7, 43; 8, 12 (John xiv. 9).

[6] O. 13, 36 (John iv. 34; v. 19–20; xii. 45).

[7] Cf. p. 89 above.

[8] O. 19, 6 (John viii. 19; xiv. 9).   [9] O. Frag. 13.

be no longer needed; then there will be open to man the same direct vision of the Father which is already enjoyed by the Son.[1]

Theodore gives no special treatment of the theme. Cyril treats it in a way closely parallel to his treatment of the idea of knowledge. The Son's vision of the Father is something which human language cannot possibly describe, but it is a knowledge of the divine nature, which is open to the Son only because of that interpenetration of essence which exists between them.[2] He can mediate to us the vision of God, because he is the image of God and fully of his essence.[3] The vision that is mediated to us is, however, less direct or complete than that enjoyed by the Son—it is the most complete conceivable for man, but it remains of his glory rather than of his essence.[4]

At one point he suggests a distinction between the ideas of knowledge and of vision, but it is related to their source rather than to their essential character. The source of the one is to be found in the words of Christ, the source of the other in his works. But both have led to a common goal, the recognition of the Son's divinity.[5]

II. LOGOS

In deference to Origen's methodological principle, we come last to the term with which the Gospel begins—Logos, word or reason. The advantage of this procedure, according to Origen, is that we are then less likely to make the mistake of treating it as if it were a literal non-figurative title.[6] We need, he says, to treat it strictly on the analogy of the other titles, such as light and life. Christ is called

[1] O. 20, 7 (John viii. 38).

[2] Cyr. *in* John i. 18 (I, 155, 26–156, 4); *in* John vi. 46 (I, 510–12); *in* John viii. 38 (II, 75, 15–18).

[3] Cyr. *in* John v. 37 (I, 383, 12–19); *in* John xiv. 7 (II, 412, 14–413, 17); *in* John xiv. 11 (II, 437, 9–16; 455, 11–25); *in* John xvii. 6–8 (II, 682, 29–683, 2).

[4] Cyr. *in* John xiii. 23 (II, 366, 17–367, 12).

[5] Cyr. *in* John xiv. 7 (II, 416, 15–30).

[6] O. 1, 21. Hippolytus (*Con. Noet.* 15) gives evidence of a contemporary tendency in exegesis diametrically opposed to that here attacked by Origen. He quotes a hypothetical objector saying: 'You are importing an idea which is strange to me in calling the Logos Son. John indeed speaks of the Logos, but he is merely allegorising.' Thus while Origen opposes those who took the term so literally as to regard it as a more or less literal description of the Son, Hippolytus opposes those who took it so figuratively as to deny its applicability as a title to the Son at all.

light and life because he gives light and life to men. Similarly he is called λόγος because he makes men λογικός, or in other words because he is the principle of rationality in men. In fact there are claims made by Jesus within the body of the Gospel which are only true on this understanding of his person.[1] Thus Origen's primary understanding of the word is in terms of reason, but he also acknowledges its meaning as word. As in human experience a word is the expression of the hidden content of the mind, so Christ is the perfect revelation of the Father.[2]

He does not distinguish it from Christ's other titles as one more properly descriptive of his own intrinsic nature. He does draw a distinction between those titles which would have been true of Christ even if man had never sinned, and those which he has come to possess on account of human sin. But this is a distinction between revelatory and redemptive titles rather than between intrinsic and revelatory ones. And Logos does not stand alone in the more permanent class; wisdom, truth and life fall within the same category.[3]

Origen's interpretation of the term, therefore, is essentially revelatory. He pours scorn on any purely literal understanding of the concept as if the Logos were a syllabic utterance of the Father without substantial existence of its own, and he regards that as a sufficient safeguard against the drawing of any derogatory conclusions about the nature of the Son from the title.[4] But later orthodoxy was not satisfied with such safeguards. Theodore's comments provide an illuminating contrast to those of Origen.

Theodore is a writer with whom we might expect to find the revelatory significance of the term well to the fore, but in fact he most studiously avoids it. He disobeys the injunction of Origen in that this is the one term in the Gospel to which he devotes any thorough or extended investigation. None the less he remains fully aware of the analogical character of the title. But its significance is emphatically not revelatory. If we say that the Son is called Logos

[1] O. 1, 37. Origen's primary examples of this are John xv. 22 and John x. 8 (for the latter, see p. 102 below). It might also be added that this understanding of the idea of Logos is also essential to a full appreciation of the irony of some of the sayings in the main body of the Gospel—cf. Theodore of Heraclea *in* John vii. 15 (Corderius, p. 207).

[2] O. 1, 38.   [3] O. 1, 20.   [4] O. 1, 24.

because he is the perfect expression in word and act of the will of God, such an interpretation fails to differentiate him in any way from the angels. The Evangelist has been careful to call him Logos absolutely and without such qualification as 'word of God', or 'word of the Lord'; those phrases have a lesser revelatory meaning as terms to describe the κήρυγμα. 'Word' is used in two ways—either of the word spoken or of the word in the mind, which is distinguishable from the mind though inseparable from it. It is this second concept which lies behind the use of the term Logos, and its purpose is to express the timeless relation of unity between the Father and the Son.[1] The sounder exegetical approach of Origen had to give way before the requirements of a more developed doctrinal approach. Between the two stand the doctrinal controversies of the fourth century.[2]

[1] T. 11–14.
[2] For the use of the text John i. 1, and discussions of the significance of the concept of the Logos in the controversies of the fourth century, see G. Bardy, *Recherches sur Saint Lucien d'Antioche et son École*, pp. 288–92.

CHAPTER VI

THE FOURTH GOSPEL AND
THE GNOSTICS

Our earliest commentary on the Gospel comes, as we have seen, from the pen of Heracleon, a Valentinian Gnostic. This is no accident. At first the Gospel appears to have received a wider circulation amongst the Gnostics than amongst the orthodox.[1] Before long, however, despite slight misgivings it was receiving an equally general acceptance among the orthodox as the final strand of the fourfold Gospel. It was, therefore, a natural battle ground for the struggle between Gnosticism and orthodoxy. Both sides accepted its authority, but interpreted it differently. An essential element, therefore, in the struggle with Gnosticism was the question of the right exegesis of the Gospel.[2]

In this struggle Irenaeus was the principal contestant on the side of orthodoxy. A good deal of so-called Gnostic exegesis could be dismissed with comparative ease as not really exegesis at all. Irenaeus recounts Ptolemaeus' interpretation of the prologue as demonstrating the first Ogdoad in the Valentinian system—Pater, Charis, Monogenes, and Aletheia, Logos, Zoe, Anthropos and Ecclesia. To this Irenaeus can reply quite simply that if it were the author's intention to indicate this Ogdoad, he has set about it in a very surprising manner. The terms do not appear in anything like the order that they are supposed to hold in the Valentinian system, and in fact one of them, Ecclesia, does not figure in the passage at all. Moreover the interpretation appears to involve giving the word 'Logos' in *v*. 1 a different reference from that given to the same word in *v*. 14.[3] In fact, the interpretation can be summarily dismissed

---

[1] J. N. Sanders, *The Fourth Gospel in the Early Church*, pp. 47–66.

[2] W. von Loewenich, *Das Johannes–Verständnis im zweiten Jahrhundert*, p. 4.

[3] Irenaeus, *Adv. Haer.* 1, 9, 1–2 (vol. 1, pp. 80–3); cf. Loewenich, *op. cit.* p. 78. This second point is not quite so impossible exegetically as the first. The idea of the two 'Logoi' seems to have had fairly wide currency in the second century (see

as not being an example of exegesis at all, but rather of eisegesis.
As Loewenich suggests, Ptolemaeus has probably not derived his
Ogdoad from the prologue at all in the first instance, but merely
made some minor modifications to an already existing Ogdoad so as
to bring it more or less into line with the language of the prologue.[1]

But not all Gnostic exegesis of the Gospel could be dismissed so
lightly. It was not sheer chance which prompted the early popularity
of the Gospel in Gnostic circles, nor was it sheer irrationality which
moved the Alogoi to attribute its authorship to Cerinthus. There is
a certain affinity between the thought of the Gospel and that of
Gnosticism, which lends some plausibility to a Gnostic interpretation of it. The newly published 'Gospel of Truth' may be cited by way
of example as an early Gnostic work which appears to incorporate
amongst other features a real grasp of some of the central themes
of the Gospel.[2] For the author the essence of sin is ignorance of the
Father;[3] the darkness of this ignorance is enlightened by Jesus.[4]
This process may also be described as the Father's revealing of his
bosom, that hidden part of him which was his Son,[5] or as the
appearance of the Word, not merely as a sound but as having a body.[6]
As the root of sin was ignorance of the Father, it is automatically
dispelled by this act of revelation.[7] The same is true if we use the
imagery of light or life.[8] Those in error were translated into knowledge; those who claimed to be wise were shown to be meaningless.[9]
This was the judgment which came.[10] The saved become what Christ
is—'beings from on high';[11] 'they are themselves the Truth, and
the Father is in them and they are in the Father, being perfect and

R. P. Casey, 'Clement and the Two Divine Logoi'; Clement, *Excerpta ex Theodoto*,
19, 4). *Excerpta ex Theodoto*, 7, 3 quotes the difference between μονογενής in John i.
18 and ὡς μονογενής in John i. 14 as exegetical ground for this kind of distinction.
[1] Loewenich, *op. cit.* p. 80.
[2] *Evangelium Veritatis*, ed. M. Malinine, H. C. Puech and G. Quispel. The work
is clearly of Valentinian origin and to be dated before A.D. 180 (Introduction,
p. xii).
[3] *Ibid.* p. 18, 8–9 (cf. John xvi. 3).
[4] *Ibid.* p. 18, 16–17 (cf. John i. 5; viii. 12; xii. 35; xii. 46).
[5] *Ibid.* p. 24, 9–14; 27, 7–8 (cf. John i. 18).
[6] *Ibid.* p. 26, 4–8 (cf. John i. 14).   [7] *Ibid.* p. 24, 28–25, 3.
[8] *Ibid.* p. 25, 17–19.   [9] *Ibid.* p. 19, 21–5.
[10] *Ibid.* p. 25, 36 (cf. John iii. 19).
[11] *Ibid.* p. 22, 2–3 (cf. John iii. 13; viii. 23).

inseparable from that truly good Being.'[1] It is true that there are other elements in the 'Gospel of Truth' which are far less akin to the Fourth Gospel, but there is sufficient community of ideas between them to suggest that one source at least of the 'Gospel of Truth' is a serious attempt to understand the meaning of the Fourth Gospel.

In particular there are four important respects in which the Gnostic could find grounds within the Gospel itself appearing to support an intepretation along lines characteristic of his own peculiar way of thought. These four issues are of interest not only for the immediate struggle between Gnosticism and orthodoxy around the close of the second century, but are of permanent significance in determining a true exegesis of the gospel.

I. THE PHILOSOPHICAL CHARACTER OF THE PROLOGUE

We have already seen that much Gnostic use of the prologue was obviously invalid as exegesis. Gnostic interpreters claimed to find their developed systems of Aeons there, when in fact they were simply imposing their systems upon the text. Nevertheless the term Logos was an established philosophical term and the passage as a whole appears to have a broad cosmological reference. It is therefore possible to assert that the passage does demand a philosophical and cosmological interpretation, far more restrained than the fully developed Gnostic systems but not altogether different in kind from them.

The earliest use of the Gospel in orthodox circles in the second century certainly appears to suggest this kind of interpretation of its thought. Thus Loewenich declares that Justin knew St John's Gospel and treated it as a fully philosophical Gospel, developing the concept of the Logos along markedly philosophical lines; Tatian, he says, gives an anthropological interpretation of the prologue, in which the relationship between darkness and light is understood of the soul and spirit of man; Theophilus definitely bases his Logos speculation on St John's prologue.[2] But this account is somewhat

[1] *Evangelium Veritatis*, p. 42, 25–30 (cf. John xiv. 10–11; xvii. 22).
[2] Loewenich, *op. cit.* pp. 50–4.

misleading. Justin's knowledge of St John's Gospel may be accepted as at least highly probable,[1] yet that only makes it the more significant that in the development of his Logos theology there are no direct allusions to the Gospel prologue. It seems probable that his thought about the Logos is of independent origin and not derived from the Gospel.[2] Both Tatian and Theophilus do make explicit reference to the prologue, but even so we need to beware of thinking of them as setting out to interpret the Gospel. Once again it is more probable that the real derivation of their thought is independent, and that they were simply attempting to link up their own conceptions with similar ideas in the Fourth Gospel, whose prestige and recognition as an authoritative scripture was steadily growing.

With Irenaeus the case is different. There is no question but that his purpose is to expound the prologue of the Gospel. He has no desire to deny the cosmological significance of the prologue; it is concerned with the Word of God, 'who in an invisible manner contains all things created, and is inherent in the entire creation' and who 'governs and arranges all things'.[3] The concept, in fact, is one of which Irenaeus makes considerable use in the development of his own theology. What he emphasises against the Gnostics is that the passage is concerned only with one being, not a number of aeons, and that this one being became fully incarnate in the historic person of Jesus of Nazareth.[4] The difference between Irenaeus and the Gnostics is not the difference between a soteriological and cosmological concern; both these concerns are common to both sides. The real difference is between an approach which is under the strict control of historical fact and one which allows free rein to the speculative imagination.[5]

We may therefore conclude that while we ought not to regard every form of 'Logos' theology as a definite interpretation of the Gospel prologue, yet even the most anti-Gnostic writers do not doubt that the prologue has a philosophical and cosmological character. But within such a general measure of agreement amongst

[1] Barrett, p. 94.
[2] J. N. Sanders, op. cit. pp. 20–7; Barrett, p. 54.
[3] Irenaeus, Adv. Haer. 5, 18, 2–3 (vol. II, p. 374).
[4] Ibid. 1, 9, 3; 5, 18, 3 (vol. I, p. 84; vol. II, p. 374).
[5] Loewenich, op. cit. p. 120.

orthodox interpreters there was still room for considerable variation of interpretation. It was possible for some writers to find the primary meaning of the passage in its philosophical significance, while others placed the main emphasis on the incarnational reference. This contrast can clearly be seen in a comparison of the interpretations of Cyril and of Theodore, as representatives respectively of the more philosophical school of Alexandria and of the more historical school of Antioch. According to Cyril, the light that shines in the darkness is the light of rationality shining in the darkness which is characteristic of created nature as such.[1] In John i. 9 the words 'coming into the world' are to be taken with 'man' and not with 'light'. This exegesis is supported by the fact that if they were taken with 'light', they would represent a contradiction of the immediately succeeding words that the light was in the world. This verse also, therefore, is speaking of the universal activity of the divine gift of reason.[2] In continuation of this line of interpretation, he has to minimise the force of the words that 'the world knew him not'. The world in its blindness fails to benefit as it should from the gift of God, but not completely so. For to some degree at least the God-given gift of reason has been preserved in our ordinary human nature.[3] So far, therefore, Cyril's interpretation of the prologue is a philosophical account of God's dealings with man as a whole. It is at John i. 11, so he declares, that the Evangelist moves on to the subject of the incarnation.[4]

Theodore is equally clear that there is a point of transition from the theme of the Son's eternal relationship with the Father and his part in the creation and general endowment of nature and of man, on to the theme of his redemptive incarnation. But this transition he finds at v. 5.[5] In v. 9 he takes 'coming into the world' with 'light' rather than with 'man', thus interpreting this verse also as

[1] Cyr. *in* John i. 5 (1, 87–9).

[2] Cyr. *in* John i. 9 (1, 112, 15–113, 23). The ambiguity of the Greek is recognised by Origen (O. Frag. 3). It is clear from *Jer. Hom.* 14, 10 that his own preference is to take the words with 'man' and interpret them in the same way as Cyril.

[3] Cyr. *in* John i. 10 (1, 129, 13–16).

[4] Cyr. *in* John i. 11 (1, 130, 9–17).

[5] T. 20, 22–9. Cf. Chr. 5, 3 where the incarnational reference of this verse is made still more emphatic by interpreting it specifically of the preaching of Christ.

a specific reference to the incarnation. For the sake of this interpretation, he in his turn has to minimise the natural force of the Evangelist's words. When John asserts that he enlightens every man by his coming into the world, this must not be taken to imply a universal salvation. 'Every' must be interpreted to mean everyone who is willing.[1]

2. DUALISM

Gnosticism is essentially a dualistic system. The Fourth Gospel also has its radical antitheses which lend themselves to a dualistic interpretation. Gnostic writers, therefore, did not have far to seek to find ground for interpreting the Gospel in terms of a radical cosmological dualism. John xv. 19, which speaks of Christ's salvation as choosing people out of the world, was used to suggest that he must be in opposition to the creator God.[2] This distinction between the demiurge and the Father of Jesus led also to a historical dualism, in which the Old Testament was associated entirely with the demiurge and the New was regarded as in radical opposition to it. This dualism is a less plausible interpretation of the Gospel than the cosmological one, but none the less evidence was found there to support it also. The most striking example is the interpretation of the words of Jesus 'All that came before me are thieves and robbers' as referring to the Law and the prophets.[3] Similarly Heracleon, as we have already seen, could find in the story of the woman at the well of Samaria two illustrations of this radical contrast in the two kinds of water and in the two kinds of worship.[4]

In all these cases the orthodox were ready to offer an alternative exegesis which does not involve any such ultimate dualism. The disparaging references to this world can be interpreted without recourse to the concept of an inferior creator God.[5] The Law is described in the Gospel as 'given through Moses', and thus leaves room for the assertion that its ultimate source is the Father or the Word and therefore identical with the source of the succeeding

[1] T. 21, 22–9 (John i. 9). Cf. Chr. 8, 1.
[2] Adamantius, *Dialogos*, 2, 20.
[3] Hippolytus, *Elenchos*, 6, 35, 1.
[4] Cf. pp. 46–7 above.   [5] Cf. pp. 76–9 above.

grace and truth.[1] The truth which came through Jesus Christ is to
be contrasted with the Law, not as falsehood but as type.[2] John x. 8
was more of a problem. It is normally employed by the second- and
third-century writers to describe the schismatics or false teachers
of their own day, but this is clearly of no value as an alternative
exegesis.[3] Clement of Alexandria, in conscious opposition to a more
literal exegesis which would include the prophets, interprets the
saying of the Greek philosophers, who, according to his theory, had
'stolen' their ideas from Hebrew prophecy.[4] While this is not ruled
out immediately as exegesis on the ground that as such it would be
pure anachronism, yet it is perfectly clear that as exegesis it cannot
possibly stand. Origen solves the problem by interpreting the
saying not of the incarnation at all, but of the complete coming of
the Logos to the fully mature human soul.[5] Theodore of Heraclea
interprets it of false prophets, emphasising that it is stated that they
'came' and not that they were sent.[6] Chrysostom applies it to such
figures as Theudas and Judas, leaders who supported a policy of
political rebellion.[7]

But this was not the principal means by which such a dualist
interpretation of the Gospel was met. More important was the
demonstration of positive teaching in the Gospel, which showed
Jesus to be utterly at one both with the God of creation and with the
God of the Old Testament. In this task it was the prologue which
provided the most important evidence. John i. 3 declared of the
Logos that 'all things were made through Him and without Him was

[1] Clement, *Paidagogos*, 1, 7, 60; O. 6, 6. Clement emphasises the use of the word
διά as showing the subordinate role of Moses; Origen points to the contrast of the
use of the word ἐδόθη of the law and ἐγένετο of grace and truth. Origen is not afraid
of pressing the subordinate role implied by the preposition διά even in relation to
John i. 3 (ἡ διὰ πρόθεσις τὸ ὑπηρετικὸν ἐμφαίνει: Frag. *in* Eph. i. 1, *J.T.S.* vol. III,
1902, p. 234). He protests that Heracleon is guilty of a gross abuse of language when
he interprets John i. 3 of the Logos as the ultimate source of creation and says that the
demiurge is the immediate agent (O. 2, 14).

[2] Cf. pp. 68–9 above.

[3] E.g. Irenaeus, *Adv. Haer.* 3, 4, 1 (vol. II, p. 15); ps-Cyprian, *Ep. ad Nov.* 2;
Origen, Sel. *in* Jer. xxiii. 30.

[4] Clement, *Stromateis*, 1, 17, 81.

[5] O. 1, 37 (cf. p. 94 above).

[6] Corderius, p. 265.

[7] Chr. 59, 3.

not anything made'. Orthodox writers emphasised the full meaning of the word 'all'. The majority of Gnostics interpreted it as referring only to the supra-cosmic Pleroma and denied any reference to our created world. Against them Irenaeus insists with great force that 'all things' must include this world of ours.[1] Heracleon, on the other hand, allowed the reference to be to the created world, but excluded the Aeons from its scope.[2] Here again the orthodox insisted that the text gave no justification whatever for such an exception, and in fact the words of St Paul in Col. i. 16 expressly include such supra-human spiritual powers.[3] The strength of the orthodox case, therefore, lay in insisting on the fullest possible meaning for the word 'all'. This Origen is prepared to do fearlessly. He avoids having to include evil and sin in that which was created through the Logos by claiming that evil has no substantial existence; it is neither an original nor a permanent element in the creation and, in contradistinction to the good, it is to be classed among 'the things that are not'; it is therefore by definition excluded from the category of 'all things'.[4] He does, however, include the Holy Spirit amongst the 'all things' created through the Logos.[5] This assertion is regularly refuted by later writers. The horror of any suggestion of such an interpretation seems to have been largely influential in determining the punctuation finally adopted in the text of the Gospel itself.[6] 'Without Him was not anything made that was made' seemed a better safeguard against such interpretations than the more unqualified assertion. It made clear that the passage was concerned with all created things and not with all things absolutely. Later orthodoxy is, therefore, inclined to emphasise the limitation of the

---

[1] Irenaeus, *Adv. Haer.* 2, 2, 5; 3, 11, 1; 5, 18, 2 (vol. I, p. 256; vol. II, p. 41; *ibid.* p. 374). [2] O. 2, 14.
[3] O. 2, 14; *De Principiis,* 1, 7, 1. Cf. also Irenaeus, *Adv. Haer.* 1, 22, 1; 3, 8, 3 (vol. I, pp. 188–9; vol. II, p. 29).
[4] O. 2, 13. [5] O. 2, 10.
[6] Both Chrysostom (Chr. 5, 1–2) and Epiphanius (*Ancoratus,* 75) discuss the punctuation of the passage with direct relation to the question of heresy. For a full discussion of the evidence, see Westcott, Additional Note on ch. 1 (vol. I, pp. 59–63). This explanation of the change in punctuation is accepted by Hoskyns (pp. 142–3), but surprisingly rejected by Barrett (pp. 130–1). See also J. Mehlmann, 'A note on John i. 3', for evidence suggesting that it was early Gnostic rather than Arian misunderstanding of the passage that prompted the change.

term 'all things', where earlier orthodoxy had needed to stress its all-inclusiveness.[1]

John i. 3, then, provided a sound basis for the rejection of all Gnostic interpretations which dissociated Christ from the God of the creation. Subsidiary evidence was found in Christ's use of material things in the performance of his signs,[2] but John i. 3 remained the primary plank in the orthodox case. It was capable of further extension to counter the historical form of the dualist argument also. The 'all things' created through the Logos must include the Law and prophets,[3] yet in this case it was an incidental rather than a primary form of the answer. Other texts could easily be found which related more specifically to the theme of the Old Testament, such as the fact that Jesus was greeted as King of Israel[4] or his declaration that Moses wrote of him.[5] But the main text on which the orthodox relied is once again to be found in the prologue; at first sight it appears to be a rather surprising choice, but it is not without considerable force. Embedded in the very heart of the prologue stands an assertion about John the Baptist and his function as witness to Christ. Yet John the Baptist comes in the spirit and power of Elijah, and is a typical representative of the Old Testament prophetic tradition. He is, therefore, an effective witness to the identity of the God of the Old Testament and the God of Jesus, which undermines the whole Gnostic position on this score.[6]

One last example may be given in which Origen finds evidence in the Gospel which refutes with precision the exact form in which the Gnostic duality of gods was commonly presented. On the one hand stood the benevolent God, unknown to the world but Father of Jesus; on the other hand stood the just God, known to the world

---

[1] The comment of Theodore (T. 18, 1–14) is of especial interest. In arguing that scriptural custom does not always require the fullest interpretation of the word 'all', he uses as his illustration John x. 8, where, he says, the 'all' who came before Jesus and were thieves and robbers cannot include Moses, Samuel and the prophets. This, as we have seen, is a point of exegetical importance which belongs to the same area of discussion. [2] Cf. pp. 42, 54 above.

[3] Origen, from bk. 3 *in Ep. ad Col.*, quoted in Pamphilus, *Apologia*, 5 (p. 6, 17, 589 B).

[4] Irenaeus, *Adv. Haer.* 3, 11, 6 (vol. II, p. 44) (John i. 49).

[5] *Ibid.* 4, 2, 3 (vol. II, p. 148) (John v. 46).

[6] *Ibid.* 3, 11, 4 (vol. II, p. 43) (John i. 6–7). Cf. also O. 2, 34.

because he is its creator and proclaimed by the Law and the prophets. Yet Jesus addresses God in his prayer with the words: 'O Righteous Father, the world hath not known thee.' The righteous God is clearly identical with the Father of Jesus, whom the world has not fully known.[1]

3. DOCETISM

When Gnostic dualist ideas were applied to the concept of the person of Christ, they gave rise either to a docetic view of his person, according to which he was an appearance rather than an incarnation, or else to a dualist view in which the divine Christ was rigidly differentiated from the human Jesus. The basis of such views was dogmatic rather than exegetical. They were desperate expedients to square the Gospel story with a belief that matter is inherently evil. It was open therefore to the orthodox to fall back once more upon the evidence of John i. 3, and to undermine the belief which prompted such theories by insisting that 'flesh' must be included in the 'all things' created through the Logos.[2] But a still clearer answer to such theories was to be found in yet another verse of the prologue— 'The word was made flesh'—and it is upon this assertion that the orthodox case is mainly based.[3] In addition Irenaeus could even insist that the express purpose of the Gospel—'that ye might believe that Jesus is the Christ, the Son of God'—was to counteract all dualistic interpretations of Christ's person.[4] Moreover there are several individual touches in the Gospel, such as his weariness at the well of Sychar, his weeping at the tomb of Lazarus, or the issue of blood and water from his side, which show conclusively that this one Son of God was no mere appearance, but had a fully human, in fact a fully fleshly, existence.[5]

Exegetical support for the docetic or dualist view of the person of Christ seems to have been found mainly in a combination of the fact that the Gospel has no explicit reference to Christ's birth and

[1] *De Principiis*, 2, 5, 4 (John xvii. 25).
[2] Tertullian, *De Resurrectione Mortuorum*, 5, 6.
[3] Irenaeus, *Adv. Haer.* 3, 11, 3; 3, 16, 8 (vol. II, p. 42; *ibid.* p. 90) (John i. 14).
[4] *Ibid.* 3, 16, 5 (vol. II, p. 86) (John xx. 31).
[5] *Ibid.* 3, 22, 2; 4, 33, 2 (vol. II, p. 122; *ibid.* p. 258) (John iv. 6; xi. 35; xix. 34).

the manner in which Christ speaks of his being 'sent' and 'coming from heaven'.[1] Once again the orthodox controversialists have looked to the prologue to supply this lack of any clear reference to Christ's birth. Irenaeus and Tertullian find their answer in John i. 13. Irenaeus appears to know the verse in its singular form and regularly interprets it of the birth of Christ.[2] Tertullian not merely accepts the reading 'who was born', making the verse apply directly to Jesus, but explains the plural form as due to a Gnostic tampering with the text.[3] Nevertheless it is more probable that it is the singular reading which has been evolved in orthodox circles in the search for a clear answer to this particular Gnostic argument. Some modern commentators have suggested that, even though the plural form must be accepted as the original, it was probably intended to convey an allusion to the birth of Christ.[4] This does not seem very likely. In any case the allusion, if it be there at all, is of such a kind that it is of very little value as evidence with which to oppose a Gnostic Christology.[5] Origen, who, like all the Greeks, has the plural form of the text, expressly differentiates the Christian birth of which it speaks from that of Christ himself.[6] He does see an allusion to Christ's virgin birth in John viii. 41, but does not find any particular controversial significance in it.[7]

[1] Hegemonius, *Acta Archelaii*, 54 (47).
[2] Irenaeus, *Adv. Haer.* 3, 16, 2; 3, 19, 2 (vol. II, p. 83; *ibid.* p. 103).
[3] Tertullian, *De Carne Christi*, 19, 1; 24, 2.
[4] Hoskyns, pp. 165–6; Barrett, pp. 137–8. For recent statements of the case for the originality of the singular text, see F. M. Braun, 'Qui ex Deo natus est', and M. E. Boismard, 'Critique Textuelle et Citations Patristiques'.
[5] Cf. the argument of Braun (*op. cit.* p. 17) in favour of Irenaeus' knowledge of the singular reading, 'Si...Irénée s'était permis d'appliquer au Christ ce qui de fait était affirmé de tous les croyants, ses arguments auraient croulé par la base; il se serait exposé aux pires malentendus'.
[6] Pamphilus, *Apologia*, 5, quoting from the lost fifth book of Origen's commentary on St John (A. E. Brooke, vol. II, p. 311). The comparison is between the spiritual birth of Christians as sons of God and the eternal begetting of the only Son rather than the virgin-birth of Jesus. Nevertheless it clearly suggests that Origen believed these words to apply only to Christians and not at all to Christ himself.
[7] O. 20, 16.

4. DETERMINISM

If the Gnostics did not always find it easy to derive their docetism from the text of the Gospel, their position with regard to the concept of determinism was a very much stronger one. Gnostic determinism involved a belief in fixed times when certain events must happen, and in fixed natures according to which particular people are created either good or bad, either capable or incapable of spiritual response. There is much within the Gospel that appears to reinforce Gnostic beliefs on both these scores, and it was possible to make out a strong case for the claim that the Gospel requires an interpretation along determinist lines.

The Gospel speaks frequently of Christ's hour. The fact that 'His hour was not yet come' is given as a reason determining both the actions of Christ himself and also the failure of his enemies to arrest him. This expression comes not only in the explanations of the Evangelist but also from the lips of Christ. Basilides therefore claims that Jesus himself is witness to the truth of the conception of fixed times for particular events.[1] The orthodox reply is that the language of Christ's hour is to be interpreted not in terms of fatalism, but in terms of foreknowledge and fittingness. Christ always acted at the appropriate moment, in complete conformity with the Father's will; and, in view of the omniscience of God, such actions were also in exact concordance with the Father's complete foreknowledge.[2]

The main passage in the Gospel lending itself to an interpretation in terms of fixed natures is the discussion between Jesus and the Jews on the subject of the fatherhood of Abraham, of the devil and of God (John viii. 33–47). We have Origen's commentary on the greater part of this section, and in it he makes frequent references to the interpretation of Heracleon. Heracleon's view is not an extreme example of the fixed-nature theory. He believed that there were three types of people—the χοϊκοί, the ψυχικοί and the πνευματικοί.

---

[1] Hippolytus, *Elenchos*, 7, 27, 5 (John ii. 4).
[2] Irenaeus, *Adv. Haer.* 3, 16, 7 (vol. II, p. 88) (John ii. 4; vii. 30). The 'hour' in John ii. 4 is normally assumed to refer to the hour of his death (e.g. Origen, *Matt. Comm. Ser.* 97). Elsewhere, however, Origen (cf. p. 41 above) and also Apollinarius (Corderius, p. 70) interpret it as meaning the hour appropriate for beginning his signs.

While the first and last groups are completely fixed in nature by their parentage, the middle group can become by adoption either children of the devil or children of God. This factor complicates the whole discussion considerably. At one point he apparently asserts that Jesus is addressing the ψυχικοί and not the χοϊκοί,[1] but for the most part his interpretation requires that the Jews are to be understood as χοϊκοί. Certainly it is this conception of people as χοϊκοί, fixed irrevocably by their created nature in the ways of evil, that Origen is primarily concerned to refute. The issue at stake is whether or not the concept of sonship implies derivation from the οὐσία of the father, that is to say the permanent inheritance of the father's essential nature.[2] Origen, as we would expect, argues with great emphasis that sonship is always a matter of a freely chosen pattern of behaviour. The wording of John viii. 44, 'When one speaketh a lie, he speaketh of his own', is even said to imply that every lying spirit acts so not by virtue of his already fixed nature but by his deliberate choice of the way of lying.[3] Even the devil himself cannot be of a fixed evil nature (in spite of what the reference to his desires rather than his will in *v.* 44 might suggest), or else he would deserve to be pitied rather than to be blamed.[4] In countering the interpretation of Heracleon, Origen is forced back on some rather doubtful exegesis. In John viii. 37, 38 his whole argument turns on the questionable assertion that 'the Father' in the second half of *v.* 38 refers to God and not to the devil.[5] In John viii. 47 he has to claim that being 'of God' is a kind of intermediate stage between being 'not of God' and being a 'son of God'.[6] He is on stronger ground when he claims that the positive assertions of the Gospel elsewhere show that the possibility of moving from one class to the other is

[1] O. 20, 24. The Valentinians, whom Hippolytus describes, certainly appear to have identified the children of Abraham of whom this passage speaks as the ψυχικοί (*Elenchos*, 6, 34, 4).

[2] The whole argument in a simpler, compressed form can be found also in Irenaeus, *Adv. Haer.* 4, 41, 2 (vol. II, pp. 304–5).

[3] O. 20, 29.

[4] O. 20, 24, 28.

[5] O. 20, 8, 9. But cf. J. H. Moulton, *A Grammar of New Testament Greek*, vol. I, p. 85, who prefers the rendering 'the Father' to that of 'your father'.

[6] O. 20, 33.

absolutely esssential to the whole purpose of the Gospel.[1] Irenaeus uses John iii. 36, with its reference to the crucial significance of belief, as evidence of this same point, but as it contains no direct reference to the possibility of transition it is not as good an illustration as those adduced by Origen.[2]

One other passage is of particular difficulty for a non-determinist interpretation of the Gospel. John xii. 39–40 accounts for the failure of the Jews to believe on the ground that they were inflicted with spiritual blindness. Origen readily accepts this statement, interpreting it of the activity of the devil. But he goes on to assert, on the analogy of the physical healings of the Gospel, that all blindness is capable of being cured by Christ. The blindness of the Jews, therefore, is a fair explanation of the fact that they could not then and there believe. But it does not amount to an assertion of an absolute impossibility of belief for them. They could have been healed of their blindness by Christ, and then belief would have been open to them.[3]

Both forms of determinism—the belief in fixed times and the belief in fixed natures—converge in the enigma of the person of Judas. His treachery had been foretold and he, if anybody, was a son of the devil by very nature. Origen vigorously refutes the necessity of a determinist interpretation on either score. He is entirely convinced that the kind of foreknowledge implied by prophecy is compatible with freedom of the will.[4] Jesus also could foretell Judas' act at an early stage of the Ministry, because 'He knew what was in man'; and this means that Jesus could read perfectly the state of his mind, and not, as the Naassenes appear to have interpreted it, that he knew the fixed nature of each person.[5] Origen finds further specific signs that Judas was not wholly and irrevocably evil in certain details of the text. It is implied by the very form of the prophecies of his treachery themselves, when they speak of him as 'man of

[1] *Ibid.* (John i. 12). See also O. 19, 20 (John xv. 19; cf. p. 76 above); O. 28, 21 (John xi. 51). Origen's objection to Heracleon's interpretation of the woman of Samaria as an example of Christ's dealings with a πνευματικός rests on the same principle. The story is a conversion story. She had been an adulteress. She cannot therefore have been always πνευματικός (O. 13, 11).
[2] Irenaeus, *Adv. Haer.* 4, 37, 5 (vol. II, p. 289). [3] O. Frag. 92.
[4] Origen, *De Oratione*, 6, 3; *Comm. Rom.* 7, 9.
[5] Origen, *Con. Cel.* 2, 20; Hippolytus, *Elenchos*, 5, 8, 12 (John ii. 25).

peace in whom I hoped' and 'my equal, companion and familiar friend'. Nor would Judas have been entrusted with the money-bag if he had been a thief from the start; that in itself is evidence that he was at one stage a man worthy of trust.[1] Judas is, therefore, entirely responsible for his own sin. This does not imply any denial of the agency of the devil in prompting the act of treachery. The responsibility of Judas lies in his unpreparedness to resist the assault of the devil.[2] Elsewhere, in fact, Origen declares that the belief, common among the learned, that sin arises simply from man's own evil thoughts and not from the external assault of evil spirits is in direct contradiction to the teaching of Scripture as a whole.[3]

These themes continue to recur in the later commentators, who could not but recognise that there were a number of texts in the Gospel which demanded careful exegesis if they were to be reconciled with the prevailing belief in the freedom of man's will.[4] Cyril finds it necessary to include a considerable excursus attacking heretical notions of the power of hours, days and seasons over the affairs of human life.[5] Theodore with his usual brevity asserts simply but firmly that if men cannot hear the word of Jesus, the cause lies in their will and not in their nature.[6] Chrysostom insists that when the Gospel speaks of the Father giving men to Christ or of the necessity of being drawn by him to Christ, this does not deny the doctrine of free will. It only shows our need of divine help; faith results from the meeting of divine revelation and a soul ready to receive it. Both are equally essential.[7] All three repeat the regular assurance that

---

[1] O. 32, 14, 19 (John xiii. 18). But contrast the interpretation of Apollinarius, who says that it was not a sign of special trust, but a lower form of ministry as shown by the record of the appointment of the deacons in Acts vi (Cramer, p. 324). Augustine has no hesitation in insisting that the Gospel presents Judas as a faithless apostle throughout (*Tract. Joh.* 50, 10).

[2] O. 32, 2 (John xiii. 2). See also Origen, Frag. *in* Eph. iv. 27 (*J.T.S.* vol. III, 1902, pp. 554–5); O. 10, 45 (John xiii. 27).

[3] O. 20, 40. See also *De Principiis*, 3, 2, 4 (John xiii. 2).

[4] Numerous examples are to be found in the Catena fragments, e.g. Isidore *in* John x. 29 (Corderius, p. 272); Theodore of Heraclea, Apollinarius and Ammonius *in* John xii. 39 (Corderius, pp. 321–3). The concepts of free will and of merit seem to be especially prominent in the fragments attributed to Theodore of Heraclea (cf. *in* John viii. 37, xiv. 2 and xv. 4; Corderius, pp. 235, 354 and 378).

[5] Cyr. *in* John vii. 30 (I, 663–72). [6] T. 126, 5–10 (John viii. 43).

[7] Chr. 45, 3; 46, 1 (John vi. 37; vi. 44).

prophecy does not destroy free will.[1] It is here, however, that we do find one surprising new development. Although his general views on prophecy and foreknowledge do not demand it, Theodore denies that the so-called prophecy about Judas in John xiii. 18 is really a prophecy at all. He regards the quotation from the Psalm simply as an instance of words of Scripture being applied to Judas because the outcome of events had shown their appropriateness.[2]

[1] Cyr. *in* John xii. 38–40 (ii, 327); *in* John xiii. 18 (ii, 357–60); T. 176, 27–177, 2 (John xii. 37–8); Chr. 81, 2 (John xvii. 13).

[2] T. 184, 21–30. Theodore gives a similar non-prophetic explanation of the quotation from Ps. lxix in John ii. 17 (T. 42); but in the case of John xix. 28, where the reference is to the same Psalm, he is content to accept the obvious meaning of the Gospel and explain the words of Jesus as deliberately designed to fulfil an outstanding prophecy (T. 242, 1–2). R. Devreesse points out that there is a development in Theodore's outlook on this issue; he is more inclined to accept the traditional straightforward interpretation of prophecy in his later works, such as the commentary on St John, than he is in his earlier writings (*Essai sur Théodore de Mopsueste*, p. 279, n. 1).

CHAPTER VII

CHRISTOLOGICAL INTERPRETATION IN THE THIRD AND FOURTH CENTURIES

The struggle with Gnosticism, as we have seen, involved a consideration of the right exegesis of the Fourth Gospel over a broad front. Subsequent heresies, and particularly the Arian controversy, involved a similar consideration of the right exegesis of the Gospel on the narrower front of Christological interpretation. This issue had been one important feature in the arguments with the Gnostics. Irenaeus had even declared the refutation of a dualist Christology to be the very purpose of the writing of the Gospel.[1] But in fact at that stage it was only a single strand among many. In the centuries that followed it became the issue of all-absorbing importance.

The Valentinian Christology (in so far as the very limited and sketchy evidence allows us to judge) had been built up on a one-sided application of such texts as John x. 30 and John xiv. 6.[2] The orthodox had replied with an insistence on those texts which emphasised his real humanity.[3] But they had also to meet the theories of men like Theodotus, who could point to such a text as John viii. 40 and claim that it proved Jesus to be a mere man and no more.[4] Origen clearly recognised that the fundamental fault in both these types of heresy was the arbitrary exclusion of a part of the evidence in the interests of an apparently more consistent picture of Christ, either as straightforwardly divine or entirely if superlatively human.[5] It was evident that what was needed was a more careful statement of the divine and human elements in the person of Christ.

[1] Irenaeus, *Adv. Haer.* 3, 16, 5 (vol. II, p. 86) (cf. p. 105 above).
[2] Clement, *Excerpta ex Theodoto*, 61, 1 (Loewenich, *op. cit.* pp. 99–100).
[3] See p. 105 above.
[4] This at least is what the orthodox accused him of saying (Epiphanius, *Pan. Haer.* 54; ps-Tertullian, *Adversus Omnes Haereses*, 8). It is more probable that his true belief, while stressing the humanity of Jesus, was not quite so straightforward a psilanthropism (cf. Bethune-Baker, *Early History of Christian Doctrine*, p. 98, n. 2).
[5] O. 10, 6.

The necessary principle is clearly enunciated by Origen in his commentary. Origen is faced with the apparent conflict between the statements of Jesus in John vii. 28 and John viii. 19. 'Ye both know me and ye know whence I am...but He that sent me is true, whom ye know not.' 'If ye knew me, ye would know my Father also.' This is to be explained in the light of the general principle that the Saviour sometimes speaks of himself as man, and sometimes as a more divine nature and united to the uncreated nature of the Father. He illustrates this principle from the very texts which we know were used by the heretical teaching on each side. In John viii. 40, when he is speaking of their attempts to kill him, he is obviously speaking of himself as man;[1] in John x. 30, xiv. 6, xi. 25 and such like texts, it is not the man whom they were trying to kill about whom he is teaching, but the divine element in him. Finally the whole surrounding contexts of the two sayings, vii. 28 and viii. 19, show that he is speaking of his humanity in the one instance and of his divinity in the other.[2]

The principle is frequently employed by Origen and other writers of the period in exegetical work. The variety of Christ's actions was intended to make both aspects of his nature clear. So on one occasion he sends his disciples to buy bread, while on another he multiplies loaves in the wilderness.[3] His opponents cannot take him before the time because of his divinity; nevertheless he withdraws from them, lest his continued immunity from arrest should destroy the proper balance of his human station.[4] Moreover this twofold character can be seen in the different aspects of a single action. He performs the miracle of the loaves that he may be acknowledged as God; he says grace as he does so that he may be acknowledged as man.[5] There is a difference between the human life which is laid down and taken again, and the divinity which does the laying down and the taking again.[6]

---

[1] Cf. also the use of the word 'man' in John xi. 50, on which Origen comments that it is the man who dies for the people and not the Divine Word, who as image of the invisible God and first-born of all creation is incapable of death (O. 28, 18).

[2] O. 19, 1–2. Cf. also Con. Cel. 1, 66; 2, 25; 7, 16–17.

[3] O. Frag. 53 (John iv. 8).   [4] O. Frag. 75 (John x. 39).

[5] Origen, Possinus' Catena in Matt. xiv. 19 (John vi. 11).

[6] Dionysius of Alexandria, 'Exegetical Fragments', p. 242 (cf. Origen, De Principiis, 4, 4, 4; John x. 18). One even earlier example of a similar piece of exegesis

The same principle had already been expressed by Tertullian in the course of his more explicitly doctrinal work. The terms which he uses to describe the two aspects of Christ's nature are Spirit and Flesh; the former is responsible for the miracles, the latter is seen in his hunger, thirst, weeping, anxiety and death. These two natures correspond to the two titles Son of God and Son of Man.[1]

This last point—the identification of the title Son of Man with the human aspect of Christ's nature—was a natural one to make, and one that must have flowed with particular ease from the pen of Tertullian with his love of balanced phrases and antitheses. Nor does Tertullian stand alone. Precisely the same point is made by Origen when he explicitly identifies the significance of the title 'Son of Man' with that of 'man' in John viii. 40.[2] Yet it was one fraught with difficulty and with consequences of extreme importance for the whole pattern of later exegesis. Hippolytus is clearly aware of the difficulty in his quotation of John iii. 13, which speaks of 'He that came down from heaven, even the Son of Man, which is in heaven'. For him this is a curious example of imprecise usage, for which he has no specific explanation to give.[3] Despite an occasional protest that the real significance of the title ought to be seen not in its assertion of humanity but as a title for the heavenly eschatological judge,[4] the

is to be found in Heracleon's interpretation of the words of John i. 29 'The lamb of God, which taketh away the sin of the world' (O. 6, 60). 'The lamb of God' is the declaration of John as a prophet and must refer to Christ's body because a lamb is an ἀτελής example of the genus sheep. 'Which taketh away the sin of the world' is the declaration of one who is more than a prophet and refers to him who indwells the body. This is scornfully dismissed by Origen, no doubt because it was developed too much in the interests of a fully dualist Christology, but in the principle of its reasoning it is exactly akin to the orthodox two-nature exegesis of the third century.

[1] Tertullian, *Adv. Prax.* 27.

[2] O. 32, 25 (John xiii. 31). Cf. also Origen, *Comm. Matt.* 15, 24.

[3] Hippolytus, *Con. Noet.* 4.

[4] E.g. Cyril of Jerusalem, *Catecheses*, 10, 4. The relation of the function of judgment to the title Son of Man in John v. 27 presented a problem to the orthodox commentators. The ante-Nicene writers regularly take the words 'because he is the Son of Man' with the preceding statement about judgment (e.g. Tertullian, *Adv. Prax.* 21, 12; O. 1, 35). Chrysostom, however, takes the words with the phrase following and attacks the other rendering as untrue and characteristic of Paul of Samosata (Chr. 39, 3). Cyril accepts the ancient and natural phrasing but insists that the title Son of Man is used not in relation to the function of judging but to the language of

underlying principle remained generally unquestioned. Son of Man was clearly a title appropriate to Christ's humanity, and if it was sometimes used in apparently inappropriate contexts, some good reason for that fact must be found. Origen suggests a reason which was to be greatly developed at a later period.[1] He was fully conscious that Scripture spoke frequently of the dying of the Son of God and of the coming of the Son of Man in the glory of his Father. This, he says, is expressive of the indissoluble unity between the divine Word and the human soul or flesh.[2] This answer turned an apparent difficulty, which might have seemed to obscure the difference of the two natures, into valuable positive evidence for the unity of Christ's person.

As yet, however, this issue was not the important one. At this stage the orthodox were concerned for the most part simply to assert that human and divine must both be predicated of the one Christ Jesus. The nature of their union in the one person was a problem that lay still in the future. And so the third-century writers are concerned simply to show that both elements stand there inescapably side by side. In this task St John's Gospel, with its exalted teaching on the one hand and its picture of Christ accepting the ordinary privations of human life on the other, was an invaluable instrument. But it could well be argued that the Gospel does not really maintain what Origen calls 'the proper balance of his human station'. It was the docetic or modalist heresies that had turned most naturally to the Fourth Gospel for their support. While Theodotus could quote John viii. 40 in the argument of his case, yet he, and those who thought like him, clearly found their true spiritual home rather in the Synoptic records. Whatever be the implications of the incidents recorded about Christ in the Gospel, there can be no question that the specifically Christological teaching of the Gospel

---

being given authority (Cyr. *in* John v. 27; I, 347, 19–21). Theodore follows Chrysostom's punctuation (T. 85, 4–5), although elsewhere he emphatically relates the function of judging to Christ's humanity, on the ground that the judge should be visible (T. 82, 33–5; John v. 22).

[1] See pp. 134–6 below.

[2] *De Principiis*, 2, 6, 3. He does not appear to appeal to this precise principle in his commentary on St John, though O. 1, 28 contains a strong assertion of the unity of the person of Christ in a similar context.

is heavily weighted on the side of his divinity. This fact requires some explanation. Novatian affirms that the apparent disproportion is due to the fact that the Jews fully recognised his humanity; there was, therefore, no need for Christ to speak about it. He needed to lead them on to a belief also in his divinity, and it was therefore appropriate for him to speak of his divinity alone.[1] This principle also, in a somewhat modified and developed form, came to play an important part in later exegesis.[2]

Thus the principle was clearly laid down that the statements of Jesus in the Gospel cannot be given a simple, uniform and all-embracing interpretation. In the doctrinal controversies of the early fourth century this principle was once again of service on both fronts. On the one hand, Marcellus argued that the great titles used of Christ in the Fourth Gospel—life, way, resurrection, door and bread —were all (with the one exception of the title Logos) used of him after the incarnation. All such titles were therefore to be applied not to the eternal nature of the Logos but to the incarnate Christ. Apart from the incarnation they were without reference or signifi-cance.[3] In order to undermine the exegetical ground of such teaching it was necessary to insist that some of the sayings about the incarnate Christ in his ministry do in fact refer exclusively to his eternal divine nature, while others refer only to his human nature.

Arianism on the other hand, which Basil described as a heresy diametrically opposed to that of Marcellus, emphasised the most human sayings about Jesus in the Gospels and insisted that these did apply to the pre-existent Christ, who could not therefore be absolutely one in essence with the Father.[4] Despite the radical difference between this argument and that of Marcellus, the same basic exegetical method was required for its refutation also. Atha-nasius repeatedly insists that such sayings are applicable only to Christ's human nature or to Christ 'as wearing a body'.[5] The two-nature exegesis was thus an essential feature in the whole case of Athanasius against the Arians. He is, however, extremely careful in

[1] Novatian, *De Trinitate*, 15.
[2] See pp. 140–1 below.
[3] G. Bardy, *Recherches sur St Lucien d'Antioche et son École*, p. 126 n. 3.
[4] Athanasius, *Or. Con. Ar.* 3, 26 (John xi. 34; xii. 27–8; xiii. 21).
[5] *Ibid.* 31–2; 54–6.

his use of it to insist that it must not be understood to imply two distinct sets of actions or experiences. Every act is the act of the one divine Lord, acting sometimes in his purely divine capacity, some-times in accordance with his adopted human status. In fact the two cannot possibly be rigidly separated in practice when even such an exalted utterance as 'I and my Father are one' (John x. 30) has to be uttered with a human tongue.[1]

The third century thus saw a growing emphasis on the twofold nature of Christ and an insistence that this fact must be fully recognised as a methodological principle in the interpretation of the Fourth Gospel. One of the reasons that had made this insistence particularly necessary was that the emphasis of the Gospel teaching on the side of Christ's divinity could easily result in the neglect of his real humanity. This same characteristic of the Gospel gave rise also to the teaching of Praxeas and Noetus, who identified the divine element in Christ with the Father. This challenge could be met in two ways. In the first place, it was necessary to show that the Gospel makes a clear distinction between the persons of the Father and the Son. And secondly, it was necessary to give an alternative exegesis of those texts on which Praxeas and Noetus had sought to base their case. Both tasks involved a more precise definition of the pattern of Christological interpretation demanded by the Fourth Gospel.

The first task was not an unduly difficult one. Tertullian culls a vast array of Johannine texts with which to crush the monstrosity of Praxean heresy.[2] Not all of them hit the mark, but cumulatively they represent a valid case. The Gospel depicts Christ's coming as an act of revelation rather than as an act of direct self-revelation (John i. 14–18). Christ speaks frequently of his having been sent, and expressly differentiates himself and his Father. He and his Father are the two witnesses required by the Law (John viii. 16–19); he on earth prays to the Father in heaven, and the Father speaks from heaven to him on earth. In fact when Jesus describes the voice from heaven as coming 'not for my sake but for your sakes' (John xii. 30), Tertullian interprets this to mean in order that you 'may believe both in the Father and in the Son, severally, in their own names and persons and positions'. In some at least of these instances, it would

---

[1] *Ep. ad Serap.* 4, 14.   [2] *Adv. Prax.* 21–5.

have been open to Praxeas to reply by the application of the principle of the two natures of Christ and the necessity of applying some texts to the one nature and some to the other. Thus Tertullian includes among his evidence John vii. 28, the very verse which provided Origen in his commentary with a starting-point for distinguishing sayings applicable only to the human element in Christ.[1] Later writers, with their anxiety to avoid any kind of apparent derogation of the Son's dignity, would have classed many more of the sayings which concern the sending of the Son or his doing of the Father's will in the same category.[2] Nevertheless, however far such a criticism can be carried, it cannot account for the whole range of Tertullian's evidence. It is obviously inapplicable to such texts as John i. 1, with its assertion that 'the Word was with God'. Tertullian's case, if overstated, is clearly a sound one.

Praxeas apparently based his case on a selection of texts, including especially three assertions of Jesus recorded in St John's Gospel— 'I and my Father are one': 'He that hath seen me hath seen the Father': 'I am in the Father and the Father in me.'[3] The orthodox needed to give an account of these texts which did not involve the assertion of a personal identity of Father and Son. Their first line of answer, as so frequently in dealing with heresy, was the assertion that however reasonable such an interpretation might be of those three texts in isolation, it could not be accepted in the light of the far greater weight of evidence in the Gospel which clearly contradicted such a belief. The few must be interpreted in the light of the many, not the many in the light of the few.[4] But they were prepared to go further than that, and to assert that such an interpretation could not even stand as a valid exegesis of those texts alone. The plural form of the verb and neuter form of the word 'one' in John x. 30 was clear evidence that the saying could not imply personal identity; such a meaning would require a singular verb and a masculine predicate.[5] What then was the nature of the unity that the words are intended to assert? Of this they give different definitions. For Tertullian it is

[1] See p. 113 above.   [2] See pp. 121–4 below.
[3] Tertullian, *Adv. Prax.* 20.
[4] *Ibid.*
[5] Tertullian, *Adv. Prax.* 22, 10; Hippolytus, *Con. Noet.* 7; Novatian, *De Trinitate,* 27.

a 'unity of substance, not singularity of number'; for Hippolytus it is a 'unity of power rather than of substance'; for Novatian it intimates 'social concord, not personal unity'.[1] The conflict between these statements is apparent rather than real. When they come to expand their more epigrammatic expressions of the contrast, we find them using essentially the same language—Tertullian speaks of 'unitas, similitudo, conjunctio, dilectio Patris qui Filium diligit et obsequium Filii qui voluntati Patris obsequitur'; Hippolytus of 'ἡ δύναμις καὶ ἡ διάθεσις τῆς ὁμοφρονίας'; Novatian of 'concordia, eadem sententia, et ipsa caritatis societas' or 'concordia, amor et dilectio'.[2] It is clear that the unity in each case is understood in terms of a perfection of moral and purposive harmony. In this they are at one with Origen, their Greek contemporary, who defines the unity of which the text speaks as one of mental unity, agreement and identity of will.[3]

John xiv. 9 was to be interpreted in terms of Christ as the image of God. He is the visible expression, through whom the invisible God becomes known. This gives an interpretation of the text in line with the main conception of the Gospel, and not involving any identification of Father and Son.[4] Novatian uses the concept of the image, but suggests that we have here, as frequently in prophetic usage, a past tense with future meaning. Those who have seen Christ in the sense of becoming his followers will receive the ultimate reward of being able to see the Father. This makes no difference to the significance of the text in anti-monarchian apologetic, but clearly makes a radical difference to its significance for the meaning of the Gospel as a whole.[5]

John xiv. 11 does not receive the same measure of attention. Tertullian insists that to support the contention of Praxeas the text

[1] Tertullian, *Adv. Prax.* 25, 1 ('substantiae unitas non numeri singularitas'); Hippolytus, *Con. Noet.* 7 ('δύναμις and not οὐσία'); Novatian, *De Trinitate*, 27 ('societatis concordia non unitas personae').

[2] Tertullian, *Adv. Prax.* 22, 11; Hippolytus, *Con. Noet.* 7; Novatian, *De Trinitate*, 27.

[3] *Con. Cel.* 8, 12 (ἐν δὲ τῇ ὁμονοίᾳ καὶ τῇ συμφωνίᾳ καὶ τῇ ταὐτότητι τοῦ βουλήματος). Cf. also O. 13, 36; Prologue *In Can. Can.* (*P.G.* 13, 69A–B: *G.C.S.* ed. Baehrens, p. 69).

[4] Tertullian, *Adv. Prax.* 24; Hippolytus, *Con. Noet.* 7.

[5] Novatian, *De Trinitate*, 28. For Origen's interpretation of the text, see pp. 91–3 above.

would need to read 'that I am the Father'. The real text suggests an indwelling of the Father only in the sense that the Father makes himself known by the mighty works and words of Jesus. Tertullian is clearly on strong ground against an extreme monarchian exegesis, which would identify the Father and the Son altogether. It is less certain that his jibe carries weight against the more refined form of the doctrine which appears to have been held by Callistus, and probably by Praxeas also, according to which it is the divine element in Christ which is to be identified with the Father.[1]

Origen says that the assertion of Christ in John ii. 19 that he would raise up his own body in three days, when compared with other Scriptures which attributed this work explicitly to the Father, has misled some into believing that there was no difference even in number between the Father and the Son. Origen meets the argument by appealing to John v. 19 with its assertion that every activity of the Son derives from a similar activity of the Father.[2]

Thus in addition to its emphasis on the two natures of Christ, the third century laid equal emphasis on the distinction of persons between the Father and the Son. This too, it was shown, is something to be borne constantly in mind in the interpretation of the Fourth Gospel. The unity of Father and Son, of which the Gospel also speaks, was certainly recognised but did not receive the same measure of emphasis. Its nature was not expounded with precision, but rather negatively over against excessive assertions of it. The needs of the Arian controversy, however, soon served to reverse this emphasis completely in a way that had important repercussions on the exegesis of the Gospel.

In controversy with Arianism there was no need to emphasise the difference between the first two persons of the Godhead. John xvii. 3 had been interpreted by Origen as evidence of Christ's divinity against those who regarded him as mere man, but still more importantly as evidence of a clear distinction within the Godhead between him and 'the only true God' to be used against those who denied the separate identity of the Son.[3] In the light of Arian usage

---

[1] Tertullian, *Adv. Prax.* 24, 8. For Callistus' use of the text, see Hippolytus, *Elenchos*, 9, 12, 17.

[2] O. 10, 37.   [3] O. 2, 2.

of the text this latter emphasis was forgotten, and Athanasius insists that it is Christ's oneness with God, not his radical difference, that the text indicates.[1] John i. 18 had been included in Tertullian's catena of passages against Praxeas to emphasise the difference between the revealer and the one revealed; but in the hands of Asterius this difference was so radically drawn that he could even be accused of falsifying the text to suit his purpose, although the reading which he employed was the one which had been regularly known in earlier centuries to Irenaeus, Clement and Origen.[2]

It would be a mistake to regard Arianism as based on nothing more than the forced interpretation of a few isolated texts. It had a far broader exegetical basis than any of the earlier heresies. Its appeal to the Fourth Gospel was a considerable and not unreasonable one. In large measure it built upon the foundation of the anti-monarchian writers of the previous century. Tertullian had appealed to those texts which spoke of the Father's giving of authority to the Son as evidence of the Son's distinct existence; these same texts were used by the Arians to illustrate his inferiority to the Father.[3] Tertullian had put to the same use those texts which spoke of his being sent by the Father; these too were turned to the Arian purpose.[4] To these arguments Athanasius replied that the Gospel itself requires us to understand such texts in a way which does not involve any inferiority but rather an absolute equality between Father and Son. His primary exegetical ground for this assertion was John v. 26 'As the Father has life in himself, so has he given to the Son also to

[1] Athanasius, *Or. Con. Ar.* 3, 9.
[2] G. Bardy, *Recherches...* p. 330. The originality of the reading θεός rather than υἱός is defended by Westcott, Additional Note on John i. 18 (vol. 1, pp. 66–8) and by Hort (*Two Dissertations*, pp. 1–72). Although υἱός is preferred by Hoskyns (p. 154), by Barrett (p. 141), and by Lightfoot (p. 90) on the ground of its greater suitability to the context, yet the combination of the early evidence for θεός and a strong doctrinal reason for the change away from it represent a very strong case in favour of that reading and it ought probably to be accepted. Barrett (*Exp. T.* (March 1957), pp. 174–7) points out that it has recently acquired the additional support of 𝔓66, and thinks that this ought perhaps to sway the balance of judgment in favour of the reading. In any event the usage of Irenaeus, Clement and Origen is in itself sufficient refutation of the charge against Asterius.
[3] Tertullian, *Adv. Prax.* 21; Athanasius, *Or. Con. Ar.* 3, 26 (John iii. 35; v. 19; v. 22; vi. 37).
[4] Tertullian, *Adv. Prax.* 21; Athanasius, *Or. Con. Ar.* 3, 7 (John v. 23; vi. 38).

have life in himself'. If the 'as' and the 'so' are given their proper force, they rule out any idea of inferiority or difference of essence. The language of 'receiving', however, is not altogether without purpose. It is intended (as Tertullian had seen) as a safeguard against any identification of Father and Son—a safeguard still needed in the light of Sabellian teaching.[1] More positively, it is congruent with the whole redemptive purpose of the incarnation that Christ should be said to receive God's gifts not as needing them himself, or for his own sake, but for the sake of mankind.[2]

The most obvious text, however, for emphasising the inferiority of the Son is the saying of Jesus in John xiv. 28, 'My Father is greater than I'. The third-century writers interpreted it in a straightforward manner. It was one of the verses that Tertullian used against Praxeas, and his comment is that 'the Father is the whole substance, the Son an outflow and portion of the whole'.[3] Origen went even further. For him it is evidence that the Son is subordinate;[4] he is transcended by the Father to the same degree or to an even greater one than that by which he and the Holy Spirit transcend all created beings.[5] Such a text was an obvious weapon in the Arian armoury. It does not, however, appear to have played a very prominent part in the earlier stages of the controversy. Its use is ascribed to Arius himself and also to Athanasius of Anazarbus; but Athanasius of Alexandria does not appear to have found it necessary to give the text any thorough discussion in his discourses against the Arians.[6] It is with the emergence of a more radical Arianism about the middle of the century, which was determined to stress to the full the difference

[1] Athanasius, *Or. Con. Ar.* 3, 35–6.
[2] *Ibid.* 37–40. Cf. the Catena fragment on John vii. 39 attributed to Athanasius (Corderius, p. 219). For the very important development of this notion in the writings of Cyril, see chapter ix below.
[3] *Adv. Prax.* 9, 2.
[4] *Con. Cel.* 8, 15. The word used is ὑποδεέστερον.
[5] O. 13, 25. This judgment is modified in *Comm. Matt.* 15, 10 where he says that the transcendence of the Father over his image, the Saviour, is less than the transcendence of the Saviour over all lesser things (see also O. 32, 29; *De Principiis,* 4, 4, 8).
[6] G. Bardy, *Recherches...* pp. 208–10, 281–3. For Arius, see *Praedestinatus,* 3, 13–14 (*P.L.* 53, 652 B). For Athanasius of Anazarbus, see *P.L.* 13, 621 A–B. For Athanasius of Alexandria, see *Or. Con. Ar.* 1, 58 and 3, 7.

between the Father and the Son, that the text begins to play a more prominent role. It is one of the key texts to which appeal is made in the extreme Arian creed of the second council of Sirmium in 357.[1] Constant reference is made to it by way of reply by the orthodox writers of the second half of the century. Two main traditions are to be found. The one tradition interprets the saying of the sole existing distinction between the Father and the Son, that is to say as ascribing a pre-eminence within the Godhead to the Father as ingenerate.[2] The other, which gradually gains precedence over the first, employs the old principle of the two-nature exegesis and refers the saying entirely to the incarnate status of the Son.[3] In general the first exegesis is preferred by the earlier writers, who regarded the second not as false but as inadequate.[4] The second is preferred by the later writers, who regarded the term 'greater' as inadmissible in reference to the distinctions within the Godhead.[5] It is this second line of interpretation which is adopted by Theodore and Cyril in their commentaries; they both claim that the context clearly supports the reference to Christ's incarnate status.[6]

There is thus a gradual but complete change in the main tradition of the exegesis of this and all the other principal texts of an obviously

[1] G. Bardy, Recherches... p. 209 (see Hilary, De Synodis 11: P.L. 10, 489 A).

[2] It is with this interpretation in particular that Eunomius was concerned. He argued that the terms 'greater' and 'less' cannot properly be used of two things which are of the same essence and that therefore the Son could not be of the same essence as the Father. To this the orthodox reply was that the possibility of comparison was in fact positive evidence of consubstantiality (Evagrius, in the work printed as Basil, Ep. 8, 5: P.G. 32, 253 B, C; Isidore, Epp. bk. 1, no. 422: P.G. 78, 417 A, B; Cyril Alex., Thesaurus XI: P.G. 75, 140 C and 144 B, C). If the second type of interpretation is adopted, Eunomius' argument falls to the ground automatically.

[3] For a full account of the patristic exegesis of the text, see Westcott, Additional Note on John xiv. 28 (vol. II, pp. 191–6).

[4] Thus Gregory Nazianzen includes a reference to the text in his comprehensive list of examples in Theol. Or. 3, 17–18, to which the two-nature exegesis is to be applied as the answer to heretical misinterpretation; but when dealing with the particular text in more detail in Theol. Or. 4, 7, he shows a definite preference for the first interpretation.

[5] For a clear statement of this case, see Didymus in John xiv. 28 (P.G. 39, 1652 C–1653 A).

[6] T. 199, 11–26; Cyr. in John xiv. 28 (II, 513–27). In Thesaurus XI, where Cyril discusses the problems raised by this text at length, he does at times countenance the first type of explanation, but even there his preference for the second is evident.

subordinationist character. In the third century they are freely and without apparent embarrassment interpreted of a distinction of rank within the Godhead. Eusebius of Caesarea, standing firmly within the Origenist tradition on this point, goes so far as to complain that the reference of such texts to Christ's σάρξ or human nature is an obviously invalid expedient which Marcellus might wish to adopt but would hardly dare to do. It is obviously invalid, because if we apply the words of John vi. 38 ('I came down not to do mine own will but the will of Him that sent me') to Christ's human nature, then we necessarily imply the absurdity that Christ's σάρξ has descended from heaven.[1] Athanasius, as we have seen, also applies such texts though with more caution to the derivative nature of Christ's Godhead.[2] The second half of the fourth century reveals a gradual process of change. The rapidly developing doctrine of the Trinity did not leave room for the admission of any distinction of operation between the Father and the Son as touching the sphere of their Godhead. So we find Apollinarius insisting that any distinction between the activities of the Father and the Son, even if it depicts a complete parallelism between them, must *qua* distinction be related to the incarnation. This principle he applies not only to texts such as John v. 19, which have a subordinationist air about the manner of their expression, but also to texts such as John v. 17 and v. 21, which lay direct claim to the divine offices of creation and of life-giving.[3] So also Cyril not only prefers an interpretation in terms of the incarnation for all those texts with possible subordinationist implications, but explicitly states the argument of Eusebius against its application to John vi. 38 and dismisses it as the crooked reasoning of 'the enemy of the truth'.[4]

But the Arians were not content to base their case simply on those texts which had an obvious subordinationist ring about them or which had been somewhat unwisely used in anti-monarchian polemic. They were prepared to use the very texts on which Praxeas had

---

[1] *De Eccl. Theol.* 2, 7 (John vi. 38; v. 30; v. 37; xiv. 28).

[2] Cf. pp. 121–2 above.

[3] H. Lietzmann, *Apollinaris von Laodicea und seine Schule*, Frag. 131, p. 239; Frag. 59, p. 217; Frag. 60, p. 218. Cf. also H. de Riedmatten, 'Some Neglected Aspects of Apollinarist Christology', p. 253.

[4] Cyr. *in* John vi. 38 (1, 488, 26–489, 6).

based his case as positive evidence for their teaching. Thus Arius
appears to have classed John x. 30 and John xiv. 11 together with
the more obvious John xiv. 28 as words of the Lord on which his
belief was firmly based.[1] Asterius explains the mutual indwelling
of John xiv. 11 as a means whereby Christ intended to refer the
authority of his words and the power of his works to the Father and
not to himself; similarly he describes the unity of John x. 30 as
implying 'an exact harmony in all words and works' between the
Father and the Son.[2] This argument was further developed by
insisting that the unity among men for which Jesus prays in John
xvii. 20–3 is to be 'as' the unity of Father and Son. Clearly the unity
amongst men is to be one of harmony not of essence; the unity
between Father and Son must therefore be of the same character.[3]
In all this they are clearly continuing the tradition of third-century
exegesis. συμφωνία was the word that Origen himself had used in
expansion of the meaning of John x. 30; Hippolytus had already
made use of John xvii to determine the sense of the unity intended
by John x. 30.[4] These texts received far more thorough treatment
from Athanasius than John xiv. 28. The essence of his answer
is twofold. The Arian exegesis does not show Christ as making
any unique claim; it does not reveal any essential difference between
the Son and the angels, or even the apostles and patriarchs. Moreover the appeal to John xvii is ruled out of court on the ground
that the unity of the Godhead is being held up simply as an example
for, and not as being identical with, the unity which men ought to
achieve.[5] The oneness of which the text speaks must be applied to
the essence of the Son.[6] This became the regular interpretation of the
orthodox writers of the fourth century, and finds clear expression
in Cyril's commentary, where once again the consciously anti-Arian
exegesis claims the support of the context; in the Gospel the Jews
clearly understand it as a claim to equality with the Father and Jesus

---

[1] Bardy, *Recherches...* p. 281 (*Praedestinatus*, 3, 13–14: *P.L.* 53, 652B).
[2] Bardy, *Recherches...* pp. 346 and 353. (Fragments of Asterius, nos. 13, 14 and
32.) The original wording is διὰ τὴν ἐν πᾶσιν λόγοις τε καὶ ἔργοις ἀκριβῆ
συμφωνίαν.   [3] Athanasius, *Or. Con. Ar.* 3, 17.
[4] Origen, *Con. Cel.* 8, 12; Hippolytus, *Con. Noet.* 7. Cf. p. 119 above.
[5] Athanasius, *Or. Con. Ar.* 3, 2; 3, 10; 3, 18–25.
[6] *Ibid.* 3, 11.

does not contradict them.[1] Theodore discusses the arguments of those who would minimise the sense of unity by reference to John xvii; he argues that unity clearly has different meanings in different contexts and that therefore each case must be settled not by appeal to other examples but in terms of its own context. He claims that the context supplied by *vv.* 28 and 29 shows that the reference in this instance is to a unity of power.[2]

The main tradition of Arian exegesis, therefore, clearly insisted on a unity of will between Father and Son, although it stopped short of affirming an absolute unity of essence. There were however those, especially in the later stages of the controversy, who went very much further and pointed to a difference of will between Father and Son. This line of argument also was based in part upon those Johannine texts which speak of Jesus doing not his own will but the Father's. The point is made forcefully in two fragments preserved by Anastasius of Sinaita and attributed to Arius himself.[3] The genuineness of the fragments is open to doubt,[4] but they show clearly the use to which the Gospel could be put in the service of the more radical Arian cause. Even here a certain parallel is to be found in the exegesis of Origen, though his emphasis is clearly different. Origen, as we have seen, interpreted John x. 30 in terms of an absolute harmony of will between the Father and the Son, but elsewhere, when commenting on a passage of similar character to that used in the fragments preserved by Anastasius, he speaks of that absolute harmony as something that is achieved in the practical obedience of the ministry.[5] Exegetically they are agreed in suggesting that the Gospel's contrast between the will of the Father and that of the Son points to some difference of will between them, but Origen's emphasis remains not on the difference but on the harmony. The later orthodox rejoinder was to claim that such words of Jesus were

[1] Cyr. *in* John x. 30 (II, 254, 7–255, 2).

[2] T. 152, 10–153, 25. Chrysostom gives a similar exposition in Chr. 61, 2; the word there used is δύναμις.

[3] Anastasius, *Contra Monophysitas* (*P.G.* 89, 1180 c). The crucial words of comment are οὐ πάντη ἐφεπομένου καὶ συναινοῦντος τῇ πατρικῇ βουλῇ τοῦ θελήματος τοῦ υἱοῦ. The Johannine texts are John v. 30 and vi. 38.

[4] G. Bardy, *Recherches*... pp. 292–5.

[5] O. 13, 36 (John iv. 34).

deliberately chosen to allay the anxieties of the Jews who thought that he was acting in opposition to God the Father.[1]

One further issue came to hold a place of crucial importance in the Christological controversies of the latter part of the fourth century—the question of Jesus' possession of a human soul. Origen had spoken freely of Christ's human soul, and Pamphilus, who appears to feel that this presents a more reasonable ground for offence than most of the accusations levelled against Origen, defends him on the ground that Scripture does the same.[2] The existence of a human soul in Christ does not seem to have been central to the thought of any of the writers of the early part of the fourth century. The basic pattern of their thought about the incarnation was in terms of a union of λόγος and σάρξ; yet Scripture spoke of Christ's soul, and so they were prepared to do so when referring to the appropriate Scriptures.[3] But the issue was not at that stage one of central importance, and it seems unlikely that the insertion of the words 'and was made man' in the creed adopted at Nicaea was deliberately intended to insist upon the fact of Christ's assumption of a human soul.[4] With the coming of Apollinarius the whole question was raised to a new level of theological importance. Once again the issue was in part a matter of the correct exegesis of Johannine texts. Epiphanius has recorded the basic pattern of argumentation between the heretics and the orthodox on this issue. The heretics insisted that the great Johannine formula for the incarnation was that the Word became flesh, not that it became flesh and soul. When the orthodox argued that John x. 17 and xii. 27 spoke

[1] This argument is found in another fragment in the same collection of Anastasius (*P.G.* 89, 1181 C, D), attributed to Eustathius of Antioch and described as coming from his ἀνατροπὴ τοῦ Κελσοῦ ἐκ τοῦ λόγου τοῦ κατὰ ᾿Ιωάννην. The fragment is printed as no. 82 in M. Spanneut, *Recherches sur les écrits d'Eustathe d'Antioche*, but is almost certainly not genuine (*ibid.* p. 82). The argument is used with reference to the same two Johannine texts by Theodore (T. 85, 30–86, 34; 103, 7–12). See also Chr. 39, 4 (John v. 30). For the wider application of this argument, cf. pp. 139–41 below.

[2] Pamphilus, *Apologia pro Origene*, 5 (*P.G.* 17, 590A, B) (John x. 18 and xii. 27).

[3] See H. de Riedmatten, *Les actes du procès de Paul de Samosate*, pp. 72–80 on Eusebius of Caesarea (note especially p. 78 n. 75 with references to John x. 11, x. 17 and xii. 27). See A. Grillmeier, *Das Konzil von Chalkedon*, vol. 1, pp. 77–102 on Athanasius.

[4] A. Grillmeier, *op. cit.* pp. 72–3.

of Christ's soul, they replied that the words of Isa. xlii. 1, spoken at Christ's baptism, referred similarly to the 'soul' of the Father. If the words were to be understood τροπικώτερον when spoken of the Father, as would be agreed by all, then there was no reason why they should not be understood in the same way when spoken of the Son.[1] Such exegetical arguments however were not central to the determination of the issues of Apollinarianism, which were fought out rather on wider psychological and soteriological grounds. Yet the repercussions of the controversy on Johannine exegesis can be seen in the work of Theodore and of Cyril, as when both insist with care in the course of their comparatively brief remarks on John i. 14 that Biblical usage shows clearly that 'flesh' may be used to signify human nature as a whole.[2]

---

[1] Epiphanius, *Ancoratus*, 35. Epiphanius attributes these arguments to the Arians, but in this he is almost certainly mistaken (cf. H. de Riedmatten, *op. cit.* p. 113). Cf. the use of the same argument with reference to John i. 14 in Fragment no. 2 of Apollinarius in H. Lietzmann, *op. cit.* p. 204.

[2] T. 23, 14–15; Cyr. *in* John i. 14 (I, 138, 4–17). Theodore appeals to Ps. lxiv. 2 and Cyril to Joel ii. 28.

CHAPTER VIII

THE CHRISTOLOGICAL EXEGESIS OF THEODORE AND CYRIL

The commentator at the beginning of the fifth century had therefore a long tradition behind him, especially in the interpretation of the great Christological texts of the Gospel. The primary feature of that tradition was the clear differentiation between those things which referred to Christ's manhood and those which referred to his God-head. In the third century, it was the demonstration of the existence of these two sets of sayings which had provided an answer to the psilanthropist on the one hand and the docetist on the other, both of whose cases had been founded on an incomplete selection of the relevant evidence. In the fourth century, it was the drawing of a clear distinction between the two sets of sayings which had provided an answer to the Arian, who had combined them in such a way as to produce the picture of one who was neither fully God nor fully man. By the beginning of the fifth century, however, Arianism was no longer the primary issue. It was sufficiently recent, and no doubt also still sufficiently common in popular belief, to ensure that there would be no wholesale abandonment of those techniques which had proved of most importance in countering it.[1] But a new issue had arisen to fill the immediate horizon—namely the manner of the combination of the divine and human in the one Christ.

This also was an issue for which the interpretation of the Fourth Gospel was of especial significance. Long before, Irenaeus had

---

[1] Thus the essence of the Antiochene objection to Cyril's fourth anathema is that it would remove the one effective barrier to Arian and Eunomian exegesis of the great Johannine texts (Cyril, *Ap. pro XII Cap. contra Orientales*, P.G. 76, 333 B; *Ap. contra Theod. pro XII Cap.*, P.G. 76, 409 B, C and 414 A). Cf. also F. A. Sullivan, *The Christology of Theodore of Mopsuestia*, p. 200, with reference to Theodore's Commentary on St John: 'It seems clear that the basic reason for this preoccupation (*sc.* his care to distinguish between what is said of the Word, and what of "Christus in carne") is the need to safeguard the divinity of the Word against the Arian dialectic of such exegetes as Asterius.'

9   129   WSG

claimed that the Gospel was deliberately designed to refute the blasphemous teachings of those who divided the Lord. But the kind of division with which Irenaeus was concerned was of so blatant a character that it had long since been dismissed to the realm of palpably unchristian interpretation. Lip-service to the fact of the unity of Christ's person was paid by all without question or demur, but the difficult question of the manner of that unity was not raised as a matter of great moment until towards the close of the fourth century. In the ensuing controversy the central figure was none other than Cyril himself. Two actions of Cyril in the course of that controversy are of particular significance for our purpose. In the first place, the fourth anathema in his ultimatum to Nestorius reads as follows: 'If anyone distributes between two persons or hypostases the terms used in the evangelical and apostolic writings, whether spoken of Christ by the saints or by him about himself, and attaches some to a man thought of separately from the Word of God, and others as befitting God to the Word of God the Father alone, let him be anathema.' Secondly, at a later stage in the controversy, he extended the range of his attacks from the living Nestorius to his dead predecessors, Diodore and Theodore, as being the sources from which Nestorius had derived his heretical views. This combination of an attack upon the exegetical methods of his opponents and upon the writings of Theodore himself might well lead us to expect a striking difference of method in the Christological exegesis of their two commentaries.

Three further considerations, however, may well serve to modify such expectations. In the first place, both commentaries were written before the outbreak of the Nestorian controversy. And while the differences of approach, to which the controversy gave such violent expression, no doubt go back well before the time of the outbreak itself, we will not expect to find such a clear-cut conflict of exegetical method before the opposition between the two schools in this particular had become fully conscious. In the second place, Cyril seems to have adopted his fourth anathema in large measure as a purely controversial weapon. At any rate, only a year later, once the elimination of Nestorius had been effectively achieved, he was prepared to sign his name to a confession of faith which comes near to a contradiction of it, to the effect that 'of the expressions of evangelists and apostles concerning the Lord, we know that theologians apply some generally as referring to one person, and discriminate others as referring to two natures; and those which are of a divine character they refer to the Godhead of Christ, and those that are lowly to his manhood'.[1] In the third place, it seems probable that the extension of the dispute to include an attack upon Theodore was not desired by Cyril himself. He appears to have engaged in the attack himself partly to satisfy his own more extreme supporters, partly in reaction to the extreme veneration accorded to Theodore by the Antiochenes and partly through fear that the name and writings of Theodore were being used as a means of reintroducing by the back door the teachings of the officially condemned Nestorius.[2] The course of the Nestorian controversy, therefore, would remain fully explicable even if a comparison of the commentaries of Cyril and Theodore should fail to reveal any radical divergence in the pattern of their Christological exegesis.

Certainly the first impression that emerges from such a comparison is one of similarity rather than of difference. Both writers approach the problem with certain important presuppositions in common. There are certain things which cannot on any account be ascribed to divinity. Basically it is any kind of change which is inapplicable to the divine.[3] So general a principle has, of course, many and varied implications. Two examples of particular importance will

[1] See H. Chadwick, 'Eucharist and Christology in the Nestorian Controversy', p. 147 (text in *A.C.O.* II, 1, 1, p. 109, 6–9). In writing to Acacius to justify his reconciliation with the Antiochenes, Cyril divides the words of Scripture concerning Christ into three categories. αἱ μὲν γάρ εἰσι τῶν φωνῶν ὅτι μάλιστα θεοπρεπεῖς· αἱ δὲ οὕτω πάλιν ἀνθρωποπρεπεῖς· αἱ δὲ ὅτι μάλιστα μέσην τινὰ τάξιν ἐπέχουσιν, ἐμφανίζουσαι τὸν υἱὸν θεὸν ὄντα καὶ ἄνθρωπον, ὁμοῦ τε καὶ ἐν ταὐτῷ. It is significant that the examples of the first two categories which spring most readily to his mind are from St John's Gospel (John xiv. 8–9 and x. 30 on the one hand, and viii. 39–40 on the other), but as examples of the third category he turns to Heb. xiii. 8, I Cor. viii. 5–6 and Rom. ix. 3–5 (Cyril, *Ep.* 40; *P.G.* 77, 196 B–D).
[2] H. Chadwick, *op. cit.* p. 148. See Cyril, *Epp.* 69, 70 and 71.
[3] Non enim natura Dei Verbi recipiebat tormentum crucis, neque mox post passionem adveniet ei aliquid novum, quod consolatione repleret corda discipulorum (T. 199, 23–6; John xiv. 28). πέπηγε γὰρ ὄντως ἡ θεία φύσις ἐφ' ἑαυτῇ, τὴν ἐφ' ἕτερόν τι παρατροπὴν οὐκ ἀνεχομένη παθεῖν, ἔχουσα δὲ μᾶλλον ὡσαύτως ἀεί, καὶ ἐν τοῖς ἰδίοις ἑστῶσα πλεονεκτήμασιν (Cyr. *in* John i. 14; 1, 142, 12–15).

suffice at this stage. It renders illegitimate the ascription to divinity of any form of suffering[1] or of any movement or limitation either in space or time.[2] These underlying principles, it will be seen, are expressed in very similar language by both writers, and are regarded by both as absolutely axiomatic. On one occasion Theodore applies this principle where Cyril does not find it necessary to do so. The humble action of the feet-washing, according to Theodore, should be ascribed to 'Domini nostri homo'; whereas, according to Cyril, it is of the essence of the meaning of the sign that it is the act of one who is Lord of all.[3] But this is the exception. It may be allowed to suggest that these presuppositions were held by Theodore in a more rigid form and one which made it more difficult for him to do full justice to the message of the Gospel. But it remains true that any such difference is far smaller than the underlying unity of thought upon the matter.

Two other similar principles are common to both authors. The corollary of our first and basic principle is the inapplicability of such clearly divine characteristics as pre-existence to human nature or to the flesh.[4] This is regarded as equally axiomatic with the first principle, but is not of such importance or extensive application in the interpretation of the Gospel. The third principle is the inadmissibility of applying to the Word of God anything that would

---

[1] Quamvis sit evidens, divinitatem pati non posse;... (T. 51, 27–8; John iii. 16). ὅτι μὲν γὰρ θεὸς ἦν ὁ λόγος ἀθάνατός τε καὶ ἀδιάφθορος, καὶ αὐτὸ κατὰ φύσιν ζωή, καταπτήσσειν οὐκ ἤδει τὸν θάνατον, πᾶσιν οἶμαι προδηλότατον (Cyr. in John vi. 38; 1, 487, 4–7).

[2] Si quis enim de divinitate dicta esse velit haec 'ascendit' et 'descendit', indicium foret magnae stultitiae. Qualis nempe ascensus et descensus erit ei, qui semper est in caelo et in terra? (T. 50, 7–10; John iii. 13). ἐληλυθέναι γεμὴν εἰς τόνδε τὸν κόσμον φησί, μεταχωρεῖν δὲ αὖ πάλιν ἐκ τοῦ κόσμου πρὸς τὸν πατέρα, οὔτε τοῦ πατρὸς ἀπολειφθεὶς ὅτε γέγονεν ἄνθρωπος, οὔτε μὴν τῶν ἐπὶ τῆς γῆς ὅτε μετὰ σαρκὸς ἀπεδήμει πρὸς τὸν πατέρα. θεὸς γάρ ἐστιν ἀληθινὸς ἀρρήτῳ δυνάμει τὰ πάντα πληρῶν, καὶ οὐδενὸς τῶν ὄντων ἀπολιμπανόμενος (Cyr. in John xvi. 28; II, 652, 14–19).   [3] Cf. p. 58 above.

[4] T. 108, 25–7 (John vi. 62); Cyr. in John vi. 38 (1, 489, 2–6). This principle would not of course have been accepted by Origen. Origen sees in John i. 30 with its explicit reference to ἀνήρ clear evidence of the pre-existence of ὁ ἄνθρωπος τοῦ υἱοῦ τοῦ θεοῦ (O. 1, 32). Theodore and Cyril both admit that this verse and John i. 15 refer to Christ's humanity, but are forced to adopt the somewhat strained exegesis that the words refer to men's estimation of him (T. 25, 31–26, 9; 30, 22–36; Cyr. in John i. 15; 1, 145–8; in John i. 30; 1, 171, 17–25) (cf. also Chr. 13, 3).

imply an inferiority to the Father.[1] This principle is not regarded as axiomatic in quite the same sense as the other two, though it is of considerable importance and extensive application. It does not follow obviously from the universally recognised definition of the concept of divinity. It follows rather from an acceptance of the fully developed Nicene faith, with its insistence on Christ's nature as in every possible respect ὁμοούσιος with the Father. For both authors this is the unquestioned standpoint of Christian faith from which the commentaries are written. This principle also, therefore, is common to them both.

It is clear that as long as these principles remain unquestioned, no radical escape from the traditional two-nature exegesis is possible. The interpreter's room for manœuvre is strictly circumscribed. It is possible therefore that an apparent similarity of conclusion may yet conceal a significant difference of approach. Widely differing conclusions are ruled out from the start by these accepted principles. We must be prepared, therefore, to look for evidence of the differences between them not so much in their final conclusions, as in the presence or absence of a desire to manœuvre, even though that desire be necessarily thwarted in expression.

How then do Theodore and Cyril tackle the various problems that inevitably arise in attempting to expound the Christological teaching of the Gospel? In the first place both are agreed that some of the problems that appear to arise are not real problems at all. Language that appears at a superficial reading to be derogatory in some way or another is on a more careful reading seen not to carry any such unfortunate implications. Thus when Jesus speaks of his being unable to do anything apart from his Father, this appears to suggest weakness in the Son, but in reality it does not imply that at all; rather it is expressive of the complete unanimity of their wills.[2]

But not all the difficulties can be solved as easily as this, and the two-nature exegesis has to be called into play. This is regularly employed by Theodore in a neat and systematic way. One set of statements are said to refer to Christ's divine nature,[3] while those of

---

[1] T. 80, 8–11 (John v. 20); Cyr. *in* John v. 19 (1, 319, 11–21).
[2] T. 78, 20–34 (John v. 19); Cyr. *in* John v. 30 (1, 353, 2–354, 5).
[3] E.g. T. 80, 15–18 (John v. 17); T. 108, 25 (John vi. 62).

an opposite character are said to refer to his human nature.[1] This alternation of reference can take place within the context of a single verse or saying. The Gospel itself does not usually make explicit the reference to a particular nature. Everything is attributed to the one person (thus making clear the unity of the two natures in one person), but the variety of phrasing in the Gospel text bears indirect yet equally clear witness to the difference of the natures.[2]

Theodore's treatment of one particular verse may usefully be given in more detail to illustrate the thorough, and even harsh, application of these principles to the text of the Gospel. According to John xvi. 28, Jesus says to his disciples 'I came out from the Father and am come into the world; again I leave the world and go unto the Father'. None of this can be applied literally to Christ's divine nature, because movement is inapplicable to divinity. But the first half cannot be applied at all to Christ's human nature which has no original or natural communion with the Father. It must therefore refer to his divine nature in a non-literal sense. The second half, however, cannot refer to the divine nature, even in a metaphorical sense, because it implies progress towards God. It must refer to the taking up into the Godhead of Christ's human nature. The two halves of the one saying, therefore, must refer to the two different natures. They can be thus combined, because of the unity existing between those two natures. It is in this conception of the union of Christ's human nature with the Father through its union with the Word that the religious significance of the saying is said to consist.[3]

In two cases Theodore has to admit that the wording of the Gospel appears to conflict with his scheme. John iii. 16 appears to associate suffering with the divine nature, by asserting it of the only-begotten Son. This, he claims, is strictly a false attribution, but is allowable,

[1] E.g. T. 30, 29 (John i. 30); T. 33, 6 (John i. 34); T. 80, 3–8 (John v. 20); T. 86, 24–5 (John v. 30); T. 145, 13 (John x. 15); T. 163, 10 (John xi. 42); T. 199, 20–1 (John xiv. 28).
[2] T. 193, 36–194, 7; T. 119, 34–120, 2 (John viii. 16). Cf. Theodore, *Cat. Hom.* 8, 11–12 (John vi. 62; iii. 13). For the exact form in which Theodore describes this attribution of differing characteristics to the one person, see F. A. Sullivan, *op. cit.* pp. 262–3.
[3] T. 217 (cf. also T. 50 on John iii. 13).

because of the unity existing between the two natures, as a means of stressing the great significance of the passion.[1] John vi. 33 speaks of the 'bread of God, which comes down from heaven', thus appearing to assert the heavenly pre-existence of Christ's body. This, he claims, again, cannot be literally true, but is an example of a tendency for Christ to apply to his human nature what strictly belongs to his divinity. This also is allowable because of the fact that his human nature has always been intimately associated with the indwelling divinity. That he is still uneasy about this interpretation, however, is suggested by the fact that he makes the alternative suggestion that Christ may here be referring to his second advent. He appears conscious that this does not really fit the context at all, but remains tempted by the fact that it would provide a much simpler solution of the Christological difficulty.[2]

Such cases, it must be stressed, are for Theodore the exception. In the great majority of cases, he applies the principles of a two-nature exegesis simply and directly. He explains the apparently exceptional cases, and even finds positive religious significance in them. None the less, it seems clear that he still regards them as somewhat unfortunate exceptions, and would have preferred to have been able to apply his system in its simplest form and without any qualification throughout.

Cyril's pattern of exegesis is similar in outline, but significantly different in emphasis. He too makes regular use of a two-nature exegesis, some sayings being applied to Christ in his divine capacity and others to him as man. But he seldom applies it with the neatness or precision of Theodore. He recognises, as Theodore does, that assertions are regularly made by Christ, or about him as a person, which are strictly applicable only to one nature. Jesus declares that he is the light of the world, not that the light of the world dwells in him;[3] he tells his disciples that he will soon leave them, not that his flesh or human presence is to be removed;[4] the Evangelist declares

[1] T. 51–2.
[2] T. 101, 25–102, 7. Chrysostom carefully distinguishes the reference to the bread of life in this verse, which refers to Christ's divinity, and that in *v.* 52, which refers to his body (Chr. 45, 2).
[3] Cyr. *in* John viii. 12 (I, 712, 28–713, 3).
[4] Cyr. *in* John xiii. 33 (II, 381, 19–29).

that Jesus is tired, not that his flesh or his body is tired.[1] Sometimes, as Theodore again also recognises, there appears to be an attribution to the wrong nature, as when the Son of Man is said to have descended from heaven or to ascend where he was before.[2] Theodore had accepted and explained in a similar way these same phenomena, but for him they were exceptional cases to be explained away. For Cyril they are not really exceptions at all; this element of intermingling and apparent confusion is of the essence of the system. While the two natures may (and indeed must) be distinguished in thought, the unity of the person of Christ is the more fundamental reality. In all the instances just quoted he insists most forcefully that here is incontrovertible evidence against those who would divide Christ into two sons.

Both writers are attempting to interpret the Gospel from within a strait-jacket of presuppositions to which the message of the Gospel will not succumb. Theodore applies those presuppositions with the greater rigour, and his interpretation has therefore the greater logical consistency. But this is a doubtful advantage when the logic is an imperfect and not fully applicable human logic. It is significant that Cyril declares himself aware of the inadequacy of human language for describing the wholeness of divine truth, where Theodore makes no such explicit admission.[3] While Cyril does not break free from the limitations which his presuppositions impose on him, the application of them in a looser and more varied manner enables him to do more justice to the Gospel of divine condescension and gives to his interpretation a greater theological potency than that of Theodore.

A similar contrast between the two interpreters may be seen in the language which they use to describe the divine and human elements within the one Christ. Here also we shall find that Theodore is the more systematic, but less satisfying of the two. Theodore has two main pairs of contrasted expressions. The most frequent is the contrast between 'Divina natura' or 'Divinitas' on the one hand and

---

[1] Cyr. *in* John iv. 6 (1, 265–6).

[2] Cyr. *in* John iii. 13 (1, 224); *in* John vi. 62 (1, 550, 21–551, 13).

[3] Cyr. *in* John i. 9 (1, 114, 23–7); *in* John iv. 34 (1, 294, 19–26). Cf. also Apollinarius *in* John xv. 15 (Corderius, p. 384).

'Humana natura' on the other.[1] But he also uses the contrast between 'Deus Verbum' and 'Homo' or 'Homo assumptus'.[2] This second set of terms is clearly the kind of language which is in danger of suggesting the idea of two persons acting together rather than a single person with a twofold nature. Although, as we have seen, he recognises that it is the custom of Scripture to attribute things, whether they be of a divine or human character, simply to the one Christ, he does not always follow a like practice himself. In his own discussions one element of the Christ can be described as the agent of a particular action. Thus it is the 'homo, qui assumptus est', who will come from heaven and will judge all men.[3] It is the 'Domini nostri homo' who performs the feet-washing.[4] While it is true that elsewhere Theodore insists firmly upon the unity of Christ's person, these particular expressions are unfortunate and do appear to imply the action of one element in the Christ in independence of the other. As such they deserve the strictures of Cyril's fourth anathema and the protest contained in his commentary against the use of the phrase, ὁ ἄνθρωπος τοῦ χριστοῦ.[5]

Cyril uses a far more varied set of terms. A selection of the most frequent and characteristic may be given. On the divine side, we

[1] T. 30, 29; 33, 5–6; 50, 7–22; 80, 1–8; 82, 24–9; 86, 23–5; 98, 15–20; 101, 34–102, 3; 108, 22–5; 119, 13–19; 120, 10–12.

[2] T. 83, 25–9; 148, 10–14; 163, 9–12; 182, 19–24; 199, 18–26; 217, 27; 251, 6–10. F. A. Sullivan examines carefully these two sets of contrasted terms and concludes that they are interchangeable and do not correspond to any distinction in the thought of Theodore (op. cit. pp. 206–23).

[3] T. 83, 8–9 (John v. 22). Cf. also T. 176, 2–4.

[4] T. 182, 19–24 (John xiii. 1–15).

[5] Cyr. in John ix. 37 (II, 201, 11–13). The phrase is to be found regularly in the fragments of Eustathius (M. Spanneut, op. cit. Frags. 33, 53, 60, 61, 62 and 63). One of these fragments (no. 63) is directly concerned with the exegesis of St John's Gospel. In John xiv. 6, Eustathius distinguishes between 'the way' as signifying τὴν κατὰ ἄνθρωπον περιβολήν and 'the life and the truth' τὴν τοῦ πατρὸς φύσιν (op. cit. pp. 112–13). A similar exegesis occurs in the Expositio Fidei (Section 4) attributed to Athanasius. But it is possible that this too is really the work of Eustathius as suggested by E. Schwartz (see H. Opitz, Untersuchungen zur Überlieferung der Schriften des Athanasius, p. 178). In Frag. 24 (M. Spanneut, op. cit. pp. 102–3) Eustathius says of John xx. 17 that the words 'I am not yet ascended to my Father' οὐχ ὁ Λόγος ἔφασκε... ἀλλ᾽ αὐτὸς ὁ... ἄνθρωπος. F. A. Sullivan, op. cit. pp. 165–9, argues that this way of speaking appears only in Eustathius' specifically anti-Arian writings and is a direct outcome of his part in the Arian controversy.

find ὡς θεός,[1] θεῖα φύσις or θεότης,[2] and such expressions as ᾗ μέν
ἐστι λόγος καὶ θεός[3] or καθόπερ ἐστὶ λόγος καὶ θεός.[4] On the human
side, we find ὡς ἄνθρωπος,[5] ὡς ἄνθρωπος σχηματίζεται,[6] οἰκονομικῶς,[7] ὡς ἄνθρωπος οἰκονομικῶς[8] and such expressions as ᾗ δὲ γέγονεν
ἄνθρωπος,[9] καθὸ γέγονεν ἄνθρωπος,[10] ὅτε γέγονεν ἄνθρωπος[11] or
καθόπερ ἦν ἄνθρωπος.[12] These lists are far from exhaustive, but are
sufficiently representative to show the main features of Cyril's
manner of expression. At first sight it seems open to a charge of
docetism. The regular use of the phrase ὡς ἄνθρωπος, and more
particularly the fuller phrase ὡς ἄνθρωπος σχηματίζεται, could easily
suggest that the whole human life of Jesus was a pretence, that he was
continually acting as if he were man. But this is a false impression.
Jesus acts ὡς θεός as well as ὡς ἄνθρωπος. He acts in his capacity
as man, not as if he were man. The use of the word σχηματίζεται is
drawn from the use of the word σχῆμα in Phil. ii. 7, a passage which
Cyril is continually quoting and in which it occurs linked with the
phrase ὡς ἄνθρωπος. We cannot easily accuse Cyril of docetism on
the score of such language alone without involving St Paul also in
the charge. σχηματίζεται need not imply any pretence, but simply the
acceptance of the limitations of human form. The actions of Christ are
never the actions of the divine or human element alone. They are
always the actions of the one Christ, sometimes in the light of

[1] Cyr. *in* John i. 38 (I, 193, 13); *in* John viii. 29 (II, 50, 26); *in* John xi. 38 (II, 283,
10); *in* John xvii. 2 (II, 665, 24); *in* John xvii. 6 (II, 679, 18; 684, 9); *in* John xvii.
9 (II, 689, 12); *in* John xx. 17 (III, 124, 17).
[2] Cyr. *in* John vi. 37 (I, 478, 29); *in* John xi. 41–2 (II, 286, 9); *in* John xiv. 16–17
(II, 467, 2–3).
[3] Cyr. *in* John v. 22 (I, 331, 16–17).
[4] Cyr. *in* John xvi. 24 (II, 505, 11).
[5] Cyr. *in* John i. 32 (I, 185, 12; 187, 21); *in* John iii. 35 (I, 257, 11); *in* John iv. 22
(I, 276, 6; 283, 21); *in* John vi. 37 (I, 479, 1); *in* John vii. 39 (I, 697, 25); *in* John
viii. 40 (II, 80, 10–11); *in* John xi. 41 (II, 286, 8); *in* John xii. 27 (II, 318, 18); *in*
John xiv. 16 (II, 467, 2); *in* John xx. 17 (III, 124, 18).
[6] Cyr. *in* John vi. 11 (I, 416, 13–14); *in* John viii. 29 (II, 50, 27).
[7] Cyr. *in* John i. 33 (I, 190, 3); *in* John iii. 16 (I, 226, 20); *in* John v. 36 (I, 373, 25);
in John x. 25 (II, 251, 19).
[8] Cyr. *in* John v. 22 (I, 331, 14–15).
[9] *Ibid.* (I, 331, 18).
[10] Cyr. *in* John vii. 39 (I, 692, 18); *in* John xii. 24 (II, 313, 6).
[11] Cyr. *in* John xv. 9 (II, 570, 13).
[12] Cyr. *in* John vii. 39 (I, 692, 27).

his eternal divinity, sometimes in the light of his newly adopted incarnate status.

The application of this two-nature exegesis is never regarded merely as a necessary activity of later theological reflection. It is regarded as a means of making clear the actual intentions of Jesus as he spoke. The alternation from one mode of speaking to the other is frequently shown to have been motivated by the historical situation of the Gospel setting. This kind of argument is employed both by Theodore and by Cyril, though more frequently by the latter. It is also much used in the homilies of Chrysostom.[1]

Jesus is both God and man with a perfect right to speak as either. The precise form of his speech is therefore determined by the needs of particular occasions.[2] This need is essentially a pedagogic need. Believers need to be given a clear conception alike of the Lord's divinity and of his incarnation.[3] Unbelievers who have failed to accept one approach must be offered some different aspect of the truth.[4] In both cases this involves Jesus as a good teacher in combining the human and divine elements in his teaching and moving frequently from one to the other.

This principle may be illustrated from the treatment of two passages. All three commentators are agreed in applying this principle to the controversy between Jesus and the Jews which followed on the sabbath healing of the man by the pool of Bethesda. Jesus justifies himself by an assertion of his oneness with the Father (John v. 17). When this rouses the fury of the Jews, Jesus rewords his assertion in language which at least appears to give him a humbler relation to the Father and which refers to his human nature (John v. 19, 20).[5] He then goes on to lay claim to the two divine functions

---

[1] Examples of the application of this principle in Catena fragments of fourth- and fifth-century writers show it to have been a widely established principle at the time of Theodore and of Cyril—e.g. Didymus explains the reference of the Son of Man's authority to the sealing of the Father in John vi. 27 as designed to win credibility from the Jews (*P.G.* 39, 1649 A, B). Isidore explains the apparently subordinationist language of John v. 19 as designed at least in part to allay the suspicions of the Jews who thought that he was acting against the Father (Corderius, pp. 151–2).

[2] Cyr. *in* John xvii. 8 (II, 687, 4–8).

[3] Cyr. *in* John xvii. 4 (II, 671); T. 192, 29–32; T. 198, 18–24.

[4] Cyr. *in* John v. 19 (I, 317).

[5] Cyr. *ibid.*; T. 80.

of raising the dead and judging the world, but finally redresses the balance once more and clips the wings of their anger by asserting that the ability to do these things is given to him as Son of Man by the Father (John v. 26, 27).[1]

The second passage is John x. 28–38. Here Jesus begins by claiming that he can give eternal life and that no one can pluck his sheep out of his hand. Then seeing that the Jews ridicule such a claim on the part of one whom they regard as a mere man, he goes on to attribute this safety in a more acceptable manner to the keeping power of the Father, who is greater than all. Finally, in the interests of ensuring true belief, he comes back to the exalted claim of unity with his Father.[2] Chrysostom continues this idea of alternation still further. The rather strange comparison of himself with the 'gods' of old time to whom the word of the Lord came is designed to mitigate the fury of the Jews caused by the claim to equality and evidenced by the desire to stone him. Once this aim has been achieved, Jesus returns to the great claims of *vv*. 37 and 38.[3]

The particular difficulty experienced by the Jews was that of conceiving Jesus, whom they could clearly see to be a man, as being also more than man. Jesus' task in teaching was therefore to lead them on from an existing belief in his humanity to a belief also in his divinity. This could only be done gradually. Chrysostom therefore asserts that it was Jesus' practice to speak frequently of the humbler aspects of his mission, which were comparatively acceptable to his hearers, but only rarely of the more exalted aspects, and even then in an indirect and hidden manner.[4] For the same reason Jesus sometimes begins a discourse with a reference to his humanity so as to forestall an immediate onrush of opposition. He does this even when the reference to his humanity is not strictly apposite, as when, at the beginning of the discourse following the feeding of

---

[1] Cyr. *in* John v. 26–7 (I, 347). For Chrysostom's treatment of the passage, see Chr. 38, 3–4; 39, 1–2.

[2] Cyr. *in* John x. 29–30 (II, 253–4); T. 152, 1–10 (cf. also Theodore, *Cat. Hom.* 4, 14).

[3] Chr. 61, 2. For another striking example of the assertion and application of this principle, see Chrysostom on John xii. 34–7 (Chr. 68, 1–2).

[4] Chr. 27, 1; 64, 1. See p. 116 above for Novatian's assertion of this principle and the exactly contradictory conclusion that he draws from it.

the five thousand, he attributes the gift of the bread that abides to eternal life to the Son of Man.[1] Most frequently of all, it is his regular custom to attribute to the power of his Father things which might have been asserted directly of his own divine nature, in order to avoid giving offence to the Jews.[2] This he does not only in controversial discussion with the still utterly unbelieving Jews, but also, because of their weakness and blindness, in the course of teaching the disciples.[3]

Chrysostom declares that while there can only be one reason for the exalted claims of Jesus, namely their truth, his humbler sayings may have a variety of causes. Of these he lists five—to show that he is not unbegotten, to show that he is not in opposition to God, the fact of the incarnation, the weakness of his hearers, and to teach the lesson of humility.[4] Moreover the Gospel shows that as a teaching method it was at least partially successful. When we read that 'as He spake these things, many believed on Him', the things which he had just been speaking were typically lowly sayings ascribing the source and goal of his actions to the Father. The success, however, was only partial. Such humble sayings can only lead to a partial and incomplete faith, and the subsequent context shows that the faith here spoken of was of such a partial and incomplete kind.[5]

Here then is a radical and by no means altogether unsuccessful attempt to present the two-nature exegesis as something rooted in the historical situation of Jesus' own day. There are, however, three particular types of context to which this kind of exegesis was applied and in which it was not so easy to maintain the note of historical realism. These passages of particular difficulty are ones concerning the ignorance, the prayers and the emotions of Jesus. Each of these problems must be considered in turn.

[1] Cyr. *in* John vi. 27 (I, 441, 16–18).
[2] Cyr. *in* John vi. 37 (I, 478, 27–479, 3); *in* John vi. 57 (I, 538, 22–5); *in* John vii. 16 (I, 604, 15–21); *in* John viii. 28 (II, 37 and 45); *in* John x. 18 (II, 244–6); *in* John x. 25 (II, 251). The principle finds its clearest enunciation in Chrysostom in relation to the words of the Baptist about Jesus (Chr. 30, 1–2; John iii. 31–2).
[3] T. 216, 29–31 (John xiv. 16; xvi. 26–7); Cyr. *in* John xiv. 16 (II, 466, 9–467, 5); *in* John xvii. 12 (II, 700–1).
[4] Chr. 49, 2 (John vii. 18).   [5] Chr. 53, 2 (John viii. 30).

1. THE IGNORANCE OF JESUS

This is not a problem which is raised by the Fourth Gospel in a particularly acute form. There are no passages comparable to the saying of Jesus in Mark xiii. 32, where he expressly denies knowledge of the time of the Parousia. The issue arises primarily out of two questions of Christ. The first question is that to Andrew and his companion 'What seek ye?'. Both Theodore and Cyril insist that this was not asked in ignorance, but to provide the occasion for the beginning of useful conversation.[1] We do in fact use questions in that kind of way, and no great problem arises. The second question is that asking the whereabouts of the tomb of Lazarus. This is not quite so easily or satisfactorily dealt with. Both again explicitly rule out the motive of ignorance. Theodore declares that it was to show that the ensuing miracle was not done with a motive of ostentation. Cyril suggests the positive purpose of getting a good number of people to go in front and show him what he was looking for, thereby attracting a large number to the site of the miracle.[2] So far the arguments used give the questions of Jesus an explanation that can be understood fully in terms of historical realism. In social intercourse questions are used not only for their primary purpose of gaining previously unknown information, but also for other subsidiary purposes. The questions of Jesus are of this latter kind, and have one of these subsidiary purposes in view.[3] But Cyril (who takes the whole matter much further than Theodore) does not press the argument home in this way. For him a question necessarily implies ignorance, and therefore Jesus in asking a question σχη-ματίζεται to be ignorant as man of what he knows as God.[4] The

[1] T. 34, 8–9; Cyr *in*. John i. 38 (1, 193, 12–14). A similar explanation is given by both Theodore and Cyril of Jesus' question to the sick man 'Wouldst thou be made whole?'; but in that case it is the apparent futility of the question rather than the apparent ignorance of Jesus that they are anxious to disprove (T. 70, 25–31; Cyr. *in* John v. 7; 1, 307, 4–12).

[2] T. 162, 6–10; Cyr. *in* John xi. 34 (II, 280, 21–281, 5). This second question concerning the tomb of Lazarus unfortunately occurs in the part of the commentary occurring only in fragmentary form and some of the fragments given by Pusey are of doubtful attribution. Cyril's basic approach to the problem of Christ's ignorance, however, is clear from passages elsewhere in the commentary.

[3] Cf. the phrase οἰκονομῶν τι χρήσιμον with reference to the question in John xi. 34 (Cyr. *in* John viii. 29; II, 51, 8).   [4] Cyr. *in* John viii. 29 (II, 50, 26–7).

word σχηματίζεται, as we have already argued, does not necessarily imply a pretence, though it is not easy to see how else it is to be translated here.[1] In the course of the discussion, he employs two other synonyms for it—ἄγνοιαν σοφίζεται, ὑπεπλάττετο τὴν ἐρώτησιν.[2] This has given rise to considerable debate as to whether or not Christ's ignorance according to Cyril is to be regarded as real.[3] This is not a question which should be treated in isolation from the other aspects of Christ's humanity. Ignorance is a part of the human σχῆμα which Christ had adopted in his incarnation; in that sense it must be regarded as real. But this ignorance co-exists in the same person with a divine omniscience. The relationship between them can only be expressed in the same kind of paradox with which Cyril speaks of the Logos suffering impassibly.[4]

It is interesting to notice that Cyril uses another argument of a very different kind. He points out that the Old Testament attributes to the Father the question 'Adam, where art thou?', which is of a nature very similar to that asked by Jesus in John xi. 34.[5] In the case of Genesis iii. 9, there is no question of an incarnation. If therefore a question can legitimately be attributed to the Father on the grounds of the necessarily anthropomorphic use of language about God, it can be accounted for on the lips of Jesus in a similar way. If he had pressed home this argument, Cyril could have avoided the whole question of Christ's ignorance as an incarnational problem in the course of actual exegesis of the Fourth Gospel. But his concern in the commentary is not merely exegetical but doctrinal, and within that wider sphere the problem is inescapable.

Finally both Cyril and Theodore make one further point of

[1] See p. 138 above.
[2] Cyr. in John xi. 34 (II, 281, 9); in John viii. 29 (II, 51, 8).
[3] See J. Liébaert, La Doctrine Christologique de Saint Cyrille d'Alexandrie avant la Querelle Nestorienne, pp. 87–100.
[4] See H. Du Manoir de Juaye, Dogme et Spiritualité chez Saint Cyrille d'Alexandrie, p. 162; R. V. Sellers, Two Ancient Christologies, p. 88 n. 8.
[5] Cyr. in John xi. 34 (II, 281, 6–12). The authenticity of the Cyrilline passage is uncertain, but the same point is made by Severian of Gabala, Homily 2, ed. Aucher, p. 29 (=ps-Hippolytus, On the Raising of Lazarus, p. 221). In Tertullian we find the converse of Cyril and Severian's argument. The asking of a question in Gen. iii. 9 is evidence of a pre-incarnational assumption of human affections on the part of the Son (Adv. Prax. 16, 4).

importance. It would be absurd, they say, to ascribe ignorance of the whereabouts of Lazarus' tomb to one who knew about the fact of his death from a distance.[1] Thus a denial of ignorance on the part of the Jesus of the Fourth Gospel need not be based on alien Greek categories of omniscience, but on the overall picture of the Johannine Christ presented by the Gospel itself.

2. THE PRAYERS OF JESUS

If there is no evidence of ignorance on the part of the Johannine Christ, there are clear examples of him as one who prayed to his Father. Three passages may be considered.

In John iv. 22 Jesus identifies himself with the Jews and declares 'We worship what we know'. Here, says Cyril, he must be speaking as man because as God he does not worship but is worshipped. This is a part of his σχῆμα ταπεινώσεως, and is intended for our imitation.[2] Chrysostom, always much concerned with the original historical setting, claims that his words are deliberately framed to conform with the Samaritan woman's partial belief in him as a Jewish prophet.[3]

In John vi. 11 Jesus gives thanks to his Father before performing the miracle of the loaves and fishes. All three commentators agree that he intended to provide us with an example of the importance of grace at meals. Cyril and Chrysostom also add the customary explanation that in consideration for the weakness of his hearers he wishes to play down his own divine honour and show clearly that he is not setting himself up in opposition to the Father.[4]

But the issue arises most acutely with chapter xvii. Theodore insists repeatedly that this is not ordinary prayer, but prophecy under the form of prayer; it is the substance and not the form that is to be regarded. The form is a kind of parable, not to be taken

[1] T. 162, 7–8; Cyr. *in* John viii. 29 (II, 51, 2–7); *in* John xi. 34 (II, 280, 19–21). The second of the Cyrilline passages is a fragment of doubtful attribution; it is very similar in wording to the passage in Theodore and should probably be attributed to him. In any event the point is certainly made by both authors and in fact goes back to Athanasius, *Or. Con. Ar.* 3, 37.
[2] Cyr. *in* John iv. 22 (I, 276–7).
[3] Chr. 33, 1.
[4] T. 94, 28–32; Cyr. *in* John vi. 11 (I, 416); Chr. 42, 2, 3.

literally. The reason for this form of prayer is to help the disciples. While their faith in him was so weak that they might not have much faith in the words of encouragement that he had spoken to them in the upper room, yet they would hardly be able to doubt that God would hear his prayers.[1] Chrysostom also insists that it is not really a prayer, but a conversation held for the encouragement of the disciples. When the Evangelist begins the next chapter with the words 'When Jesus had spoken these words...', he is deliberately referring to the so-called prayer as a conversation with the disciples.[2] In addition to this immediate historical purpose, Jesus was deliberately giving instruction by example on how to pray.[3] Cyril also starts with a reference to the concept of the prayer as an example,[4] but he is conscious even in this context that the concept of example is only a small part of the significance of Christ's actions.[5] Because he does not separate Christ's humanity so rigidly from his divinity, he is in less danger of isolating the concept of example from the deeper ideas of redemption and of the divine transformation of human nature. Once again we find language used to describe his praying similar to that used with reference to his ignorance. τὸ τῆς αἰτήσεως πλάττεται σχῆμα καὶ ὡς οὐκ ἔχων αἰτεῖ.[6]

It seems undeniable that in all such discussions a sense of the reality of Christ's prayers has been lost. But one important point needs to be made in defence of the commentators. In two of the passages quoted explicit reference is made to John xi. 42.[7] There Jesus declares that his prayer of thanks to his father is strictly superfluous, but has been uttered 'because of the multitude which standeth around...

---

[1] T. 219, 1–11; 222, 20–3; 228, 23–8; 229, 34–230, 13. The phrase used is σχῆμα προσευχῆς (T. Frag. 406, 15–16), involving the use of the same word which plays so large a part in the writings of Cyril. But the fact that Theodore has here to introduce a special word of qualification, which does not figure in his normal assertions about the actions of Christ's humanity, seems to imply that there was for him a special degree of unreality attaching to the prayers of Jesus.

[2] Chr. 83, 1 (John xviii. 1).

[3] Chr. 80, 1 (John xvii. 1).

[4] Cyr. *in* John xvii. 1 (II, 685, 15–16).

[5] Cyr. *in* John xvii. 4 (II, 671–2); *in* John xvii. 14 (II, 709, 13–710, 18).

[6] Cyr. *in* John xvii. 5 (II, 677, 1–2). Cf. also *in* John vi. 11 (I, 416, 13–14) and *in* John xi. 42 (II, 286–7).

[7] Cyr. *in* John vi. 11 (I, 416); Chr. 80, 1.

that they may believe that thou didst send me'. If the commentators' interpretation of the prayers of Jesus is to be charged with introducing an element of unreality or even of docetism, can the Evangelist himself escape the same charge?

3. THE EMOTIONS OF JESUS

As Chrysostom points out, it is the fourth Evangelist with his description of the tears of Jesus and his perturbation of spirit who provides the most striking examples of Christ's full humanity outside the passion story.[1] There are four references to the perturbation of Jesus, two during the raising of Lazarus (John xi. 33 and 38), one at the prospect of the passion (John xii. 27), and one at the disclosure of the traitor (John xiii. 21). Theodore finds no special difficulty in these texts. John xii. 27 contains an explicit reference to the soul, that is, the human soul, of Jesus. The others are an expression of his anger at the faithlessness of the Jews or the treachery of Judas. The reference to the spirit in xi. 33 and xiii. 21 is a reference to the supernatural source of foreknowledge about the attitude of the Jews and the action of Judas, which is the cause of his anger.[2] The tears of Jesus are not allowed so natural an explanation. Tears of ordinary human grief would clearly be superfluous when he was just about to raise Lazarus to life again. They must, therefore, be intended as an example for us of the appropriate extent of human grief.[3]

Cyril agrees that the tears of Jesus have an exemplary purpose. To show that mourning should not be overdone, Christ allows his ἰδία σάρξ to weep a little, although being ἄδακρυς ὅσον εἰς ἰδίαν φύσιν.[4] This is just the kind of explanation that we would expect. Of the four passages that speak of Christ's perturbation he gives a much more distinctive interpretation which appears to involve the idea of conflict between the divine and human elements in Christ. The perturbation of John xiii. 21 arises from the Spirit's hatred of evil, but its particular form probably arises from the difficulties of the

[1] Chr. 63, 2 (John xi. 35 and 38).   [2] T. 162, 3–6; 172, 27–9; 185, 17–26.
[3] T. 162, 11–14 (John xi. 35). Cf. Isidore: ἐδάκρυσεν ὡς φιλοσοφίας ἄγαλμα ὁ Χριστὸς ἐπὶ Λαζάρου (Cramer, p. 318).
[4] Cyr. in John xi. 36 (II, 282, 3–10). Similar language about Christ allowing his body to weep and to hunger is to be found in Athanasius, Or. Con. Ar. 3, 55.

flesh in having to carry so violent an emotion.[1] In John xi. 33 it is rather a question of the Spirit putting a stern check upon the natural grief of the flesh—a treatment which the flesh does not find it easy to bear.[2] Christ is said to be acting ὡς θεὸς παιδαγωγικῶς.[3] If the educative significance were intended to be simply by way of example, we would expect it to be a matter of action as man rather than as God.[4] In any event the idea of example, if present at all, is soon left behind. It is rather a divine conquest of fear and cowardice by the second Adam, which once achieved in him can become available to all. Just as Christ's death was necessary for the conquest of death, so his grief and fear were necessary if man was to be freed from them.[5]

If some of these interpretations, which speak of Christ's actions as unnecessary to him but enacted as examples to us, seem at times to destroy the reality of his human nature, they have also their positive value. Even the exemplarist explanations, and still more the deeper level of explanation given at times by Cyril, are a recognition of the truth that the most important fact about Christ's life is its redemptive significance. The concern about Christology was not a barren intellectual concern; it was intimately connected with a concern about soteriology.[6] If there seems at times to be a disproportionate emphasis upon the exact nature of the belief that Jesus is the Christ, the Son of God, which the Gospel desires to inculcate, it is because the exact form of that belief was felt to be all-important for the ensuing reception of life in his name. The Gospel was seen to be not merely a handbook of intellectual orthodoxy, but a gospel of salvation. To that aspect of its interpretation we must now turn.

[1] Cyr. in John xiii. 21 (II, 363, 17–29).
[2] Cyr. in John xi. 33 (II, 279–80).   [3] Cyr. in John xi. 38 (II, 283, 10).
[4] Cf. the comment of Chrysostom on John xii. 27, when he insists that it must refer to the οἰκονομία rather than the θεότης; otherwise it would be of no value to us as an example (Chr. 67, 1).
[5] Cyr. in John xii. 27 (II, 315–16; 320, 13–23). Unfortunately these last three texts occur in the section of the Gospel where Cyril's commentary survives only in fragmentary form. J. Liébaert (op. cit. pp. 131–7) has shown good ground for not attributing II, 317, 7–318, 10 to Cyril. But there seems no reason for doubting the authenticity of the passages on which our interpretation is based. This line of interpretation is not original with Cyril, though it is very considerably developed by him. The germ of the idea is to be found in Athanasius (Or. Con. Ar. 3, 57). Cf. also Chr. 63, 1 (John xi. 33).
[6] Cf. H. Chadwick, op. cit. pp. 152–3.

CHAPTER IX

THE GOSPEL OF SALVATION

The dominant conception of salvation in the whole tradition of early Greek theology is the bridging of the gap between the human and the divine, the mortal and the immortal, in the person of the God-man Christ Jesus. The nature of the union of human and divine in his person is thus directly related to the nature of the salvation that he brought. In this basic presupposition Theodore and Cyril are at one. Moreover, if there is any one major strand of New Testament thought from which this whole tradition springs it is the thought of the Fourth Gospel. Therefore a comparison of their exegesis of this aspect of the Gospel's thought provides a useful medium for the comparison of their fundamental religious ideas and of the extent of their rooting in the Biblical tradition.

Theodore's exposition of this redemptive function of the incarnation is, as we would expect, the simpler but not necessarily the more profound. God-the-word is by nature united to the Father. The 'homo assumptus' is similarly united by nature to us. God-the-word has through the mediation of the Spirit taken this 'man' into the closest 'conjunctio' or 'familiaritas' with himself. What Christ's 'man' or human nature has first received, we receive in our turn, in so far as it is possible for us to do so. We are linked through our oneness with Christ's human nature in the first place to the Word, and thereby are brought to the ultimate goal of 'familiaritas' with the Father.[1]

The main emphasis here is on the idea that the taking of Christ's humanity into 'familiaritas' with the Father makes that same course possible for us. The similarity between our progress and his[2] is very close indeed. As Theodore conceives of the union between God-

[1] T. 225, 36–226, 15 (John xvii. 11). Comparison with the surviving Greek fragments (esp. T. Frag. 406, 7–14) shows that 'conjunctio' and 'familiaritas' normally correspond to συνάφεια and οἰκείωσις in the original.

[2] In exposition of Theodore's thought, it becomes necessary to use the personal pronoun with reference to Christ's humanity.

the-word and the 'homo assumptus' as effected by the mediation of the Spirit, the parallelism can be fully developed.¹ When Jesus declares that he must go away before the Paraclete can come, he is implying that the Spirit must first complete the work of leading him to glory and can then be given to the disciples in prospect of the same goal.² The climactic moment in this process of raising mortal human nature to the realm of immortality was the resurrection. It was the Spirit who effected the resurrection of the 'Christus in carne', and it is the Spirit who will effect the same for us.³

It is clear that in such a scheme it is Christ's oneness as man with us that is of primary importance, and it is upon this that Theodore lays most stress. The taking up of that humanity into full 'familiaritas' with the Father is conceived, in some sense at least, as a process culminating in the resurrection and ascension.⁴ Such a view inevitably wears something of an adoptionist air. It is, however, clearly not adoptionist in the fullest sense of the word. Although he speaks of the mediating role of the Spirit in the Word's assumption of the 'man', the crucial moment of this union is still the moment of conception and not of baptism.⁵ The relationship of the Word to the Father has its role to play in this scheme, but it is a less important one. Theodore is entirely orthodox and holds firmly to the Nicene view that the Word is ὁμοούσιος with the Father, but the idea is not greatly stressed in expositions of the message of salvation.

In Cyril, Christ's oneness with us as man and his oneness with the Father as God receive a more equal emphasis. The completeness of his identification with man on the one hand and with God on the other are of equal importance in order that he may provide the link

¹ T. 26, 18–22 (John i. 16); T. 33, 5–21 (John i. 33–4); T. 59, 20–6 (John iii. 34); T. 201, 10–23 (John xv. 1–5); T. 212, 15–213, 3; T. 225, 17–19.
² T. 209, 14–22 (John xvi. 7).
³ T. 224, 37–225, 10.
⁴ T. 195, 9–10: 'Ego post resurrectionem adhaesionem perfectam cum Patre recipiam.' Cf. Sullivan, op. cit. p. 253: 'It is only in heaven that this union (sc. between the Word and the man) reaches its ultimate perfection.'
⁵ Theodore, De Incarnatione, VII (H. B. Swete: Appendix A, Fragments of the Dogmatic Works of Theodore, p. 296, 19–20). It is true, however, that Cyril shows himself very much more concerned about the question—cf. his extensive refutation of any such idea in John i. 32–3 (I, 174–90).

between the two.¹ That he is ὁμοούσιος with the Father and by nature God in the fullest sense of the word receives emphatic and repeated affirmation. In the voluntary self-humiliation of his incarnation he has become as truly one with us. This act of self-emptying is regularly described as being on our account (δι᾽ ἡμᾶς) and so is every aspect of it.² It is on our account that he receives the Spirit at his baptism;³ it is in order that the good effect may be passed on to us that at the tomb of Lazarus he controls and conquers that weakness of human flesh through which we are so easily overwhelmed by grief;⁴ it was δι᾽ ἡμᾶς καὶ ὑπὲρ ἡμῶν that he bore the indignities of wrongful scourging and of mockery;⁵ it was on our account and not on his own that he sanctified himself, that is to say his own flesh;⁶ it was δι᾽ ἡμᾶς καὶ ὑπὲρ ἡμῶν that he died and rose again, and finally entered into his glory, thus achieving the first appearance of man in the courts of heaven.⁷ It is clear that the idea of the progressive advancement of the human nature of Christ, which is so marked a feature of Theodore's scheme, is to be found here also. In fact, in the striking treatment of the overcoming of the human emotions it receives perhaps its most surprising and extreme manifestation.⁸ It is clear also that the phrase δι᾽ ἡμᾶς has a very wide range of meaning —he receives the Spirit for us in a very different sense from that in

¹ Cyr. *in* John i. 13 (I, 136, 4–9); *in* John v. 46 (I, 393, 11–15); *in* John vi. 42 (I, 503, 8–14); *in* John x. 14–15 (II, 232, 21–233, 3); *in* John xiv. 3 (II, 404, 17–25); *in* John xiv. 6 (II, 410, 23–31); *in* John xiv. 20 (II, 486, 11–15); *in* John xvi. 7 (II, 619, 13–27); *in* John xvii. 22–3 (III, 1–4).

² Cyr. *in* John xvii. 11 (II, 695, 5–6); *in* John xx. 17 (III, 124, 13–14).

³ Cyr. *in* John i. 32–3 (I, 185, 9–10).

⁴ Cyr. *in* John xi. 33 (II, 280, 12–14).

⁵ Cyr. *in* John xix. 1–3 (III, 61, 6–13).

⁶ Cyr. *in* John xvii. 19 (II, 724, 20–5); frag. *in* John x. 36 (J. Reuss, *Biblica*, vol. xxv, 1944, p. 208). The same point is made by Origen in *Num. Hom.* 11, 8, where he ingeniously upholds the unity of Christ's person by the quotation of Heb. ii. 11. Apollinarius, who emphasises that the whole incarnation is the process of sanctification, also insists that the unity of Christ's person is the reason for his speaking of 'sanctifying himself' rather than more specifically of sanctifying his flesh (*De Unione* 10–11; Lietzmann, *op. cit.* pp. 189–90).

⁷ Cyr. *in* John i. 29 (I, 170–1); *in* John xiv. 3 (II, 403–4). Cf. the interesting comment of Apollinarius on John xvi. 10. The Spirit will convict the world of δικαιοσύνη after Christ's ascension, because our justification is rooted in the ascension whereby σὰρξ ἐξ ἡμῶν καὶ εἶδος ἀνθρώπινον are on the throne (Corderius, p. 392).

⁸ See pp. 146–7 above.

which he receives scourging and mockery for us; his death is on our behalf in a different sense from that in which his resurrection is. Yet all these affect us for the same fundamental reason—namely our oneness with him as man. πάντες γὰρ ἦμεν ἐν αὐτῷ καθὸ γέγονεν ἄνθρωπος.[1] The culmination of this unity with him as man is that he raises us to his status. We receive a change of nature so that we are no longer ordinary men but heavenly men,[2] sons of God,[3] and even to be described as θεοί,[4] though all these titles require due and careful qualification. Our sonship is different from his in being an adoptive one; our divinity is κατὰ χάριν and not κατὰ φύσιν.[5]

It is clear that these schemes of thought bear a real relation to the Gospel's conception of salvation mediated through the person of Christ. It is not so clear to what extent they can be regarded as strict exegesis of the ideas of the Gospel. According to the Gospel, certain relationships with Christ are open to us because as man he is one with us. But because he is also God, these relationships (of faith, knowledge or vision) are in reality relationships with the Father.[6] In the seventeenth chapter, these ideas are brought to a climax in the notion of union. Our union with Christ is determinative both of a union with one another and a union with Father and Son, which are analogous to (καθώς) the union of mutual indwelling that exists between the Father and the Son.[7] It is this great notion of man's goal as a full participation in the life of God, mediated to

[1] Cyr. in John i. 32–3 (I, 185, 7–8). Cf. also in John i. 14 (I, 141, 6); in John i. 29 (I, 171, 2–3); in John xiv. 20 (II, 486, 19); in John xvi. 33 (II, 657, 20–1); in John xvii. 22–3 (III, 4, 15–16).

[2] Cyr. in John xvii. 20–1 (II, 737, 19–23).

[3] Cyr. in John i. 12 (I, 133, 15–134, 11); in John xiv. 3 (II, 404, 28–9). See also the references in the next note; the title θεοί always occurs coupled with that of υἱοί or τέκνα.

[4] Cyr. in John i. 13 (I, 136, 27–31); in John i. 14 (I, 141, 27); in John i. 18 (I, 156, 27); in John vi. 15 (I, 423, 29); in John xv. 9–10 (II, 571, 13); in John xvii. 11 (II, 695, 10); in John xx. 17 (III, 122, 23).

[5] Cyr. in John i. 12 (I, 133, 25–6: ὁ μὲν γάρ ἐστιν υἱὸς ἐκ πατρὸς ὑπάρχων ἀληθινός, θετοὶ δὲ ἡμεῖς); in John i. 18 (I, 156, 25–7: εἰ γὰρ ὄντως θεός ἐστι μονογενής, πῶς οὐκ ἔστι κατὰ φύσιν ἕτερος ὡς πρὸς ἐκείνους, οἵπερ εἰσὶ κατὰ θέσιν θεοὶ καὶ υἱοί;); in John vi. 15 (I, 423, 26–424, 1); in John viii. 42 (II, 84, 17–20).

[6] John xii. 44; John viii. 19; John xiv. 9.

[7] John xvii. 21.

him by Christ, which lies at the heart of the soteriology both of
Theodore and of Cyril.[1] Yet it was not easy for exegetes who were
so self-consciously aware of the difference between the human and
the divine to do full justice to the idea of man entering into that very
union of Father and Son, which lies at the centre of the life of the
Godhead. Can our ultimate union with the Father really be 'even
as' that which exists eternally between him and the Son? Chrysostom
is quite explicit that it cannot. Four times in the course of his comparatively brief comments on the closing verses of the seventeenth
chapter he repeats his insistence that, in view of the radical difference
between divine and human nature, the word καθώς cannot be understood to imply an exact parallelism or equality.[2] The same point is
made with great clarity and emphasis by Apollinarius in the surviving
Catena fragments on the relevant portions of the Gospel.[3]

The starting-point of Theodore's thought is that in Christ there
are two separable natures co-existing in perfect harmony. So the
essence of the problem of salvation is the raising of our human nature

[1] This notion had also played an important part in the thought of Origen. See
especially *De Principiis*, 3, 6, 1 where Origen claims that the idea of union is an
advance on the idea of likeness, and that it rules out as an absurdity the idea that our
future existence could be a bodily one. Cf. also *De Princ.* 1, 6, 2; *Comm. Rom.* 4, 9.

[2] Chr. 82, 1 and 2 (John xvii. 14–26). Essentially the same point is made with
equal insistence by Chrysostom in Chr. 75, 2. He there insists that, in the text 'I am
in the Father and you in me and I in you' (John xiv. 20), the word 'in' is being used
in two different senses. ἐπὶ μὲν οὖν τοῦ πατρός, οὐσίας ἐστίν. ἐπὶ δὲ αὐτῶν,
ὁμονοίας καὶ βοηθείας τῆς παρὰ τοῦ θεοῦ τὸ εἰρημένον. Similarly in John xx. 21,
'As the Father hath sent me, even so send I you', the καθώς and the repetition of
the same word ἀποστέλλω must not be understood to imply an absolute identity
between the two sendings. Cf. the comment of Augustine that the 'as' of John
xvii. 18 and 23 both signify cause and not equality (*Tract. Joh.* 110, 5).

[3] The general point is most clearly put in his comment on John xiv. 12. ἄρτι
μὲν τὴν φυσικὴν ἑνότητα ἑαυτοῦ πρὸς τὸν πατέρα διεξῄει, φέρει δὲ ἐφεξῆς καὶ τὴν
κατὰ χάριν ἑαυτοῦ πρὸς τοὺς ἀποστόλους ἕνωσιν. τοῦτο γὰρ ὁμοίωμα ἐκείνου,
καὶ μίμησις τοῦ κατὰ φύσιν τὸ κατὰ χάριν (Corderius, pp. 360–1). On John xv.
10 ('If ye keep my commandments, ye shall abide in my love; even as I have kept
my Father's commandments and abide in his love') he points out three differences
between Christ and us. (1) Christ's obedience was κατὰ φύσιν and without effort,
stress or training. (2) Our obedience is in hope of reward. (3) Christ's love is
directed to the Father, ours to Christ (*ibid.* pp. 381–2). On John xvii. 16 ('They
are not of the world, even as I am not of the world') he says that while Christ is
not of the world κατὰ φύσιν and κατ' ἀλήθειαν, the disciples are only so καθ'
ὁμοίωσιν (*ibid.* p. 414).

to enjoy the same kind of perfect harmony with God. In effect there are four rather than three terms in his mediatorial sequence. We are related to Christ's human nature; that is perfectly joined to the divine Word, which in turn is consubstantial with the Father. Through its conjunction with the divine Word, Christ's human nature is brought into perfect harmony ('familiaritas') with the Father, and our human nature can be brought to the same goal. And since what is true of Christ's human nature may in the Gospel be applied simply to Christ without qualification, Theodore can say that we are brought into the same union with the Father as Christ (that is, Christ's 'homo' or human nature) enjoys. He is enabled to give full force to the καθώς by applying the relevant saying to Christ's human nature alone.[1]

Cyril's starting-point is the concept of the one Christ, who is both God and man, and for him the goal is rather the transformation of the human into the divine. We are linked to Christ as man, and the same Christ as God is consubstantial with the Father. If, therefore, Cyril were to give the καθώς of chapter xvii its fullest force, he would have to say that we are brought by Christ into a relation of consubstantiality with the Father. He goes a long way in that direction, but is reluctant to press the point home. Our goal is a participation in the divine nature, which justifies, as we have seen, an ascription of the title θεοί. This can be described as involving our being changed into another nature,[2] but the divinity that we receive is imparted and therefore clearly to be distinguished from the intrinsic divinity of the Son. Our relationship to the Father is thus not exactly the same as that of Christ.[3] This qualification of the complete identity of the mediated relationship with its archetype is justified in two ways. One line of argument is to say that Christ's σάρξ itself, in ascending to an unconfused union with the Logos and through the Logos to the Father, is brought only into a moral and not a 'natural'

[1] T. 226, 12–15 (John xvii. 11); cf. Theodore, *Cat. Hom.* 10, 18 (John xvii. 20–1).
[2] Cyr. *in* John xvii. 20–1 (II, 737, 15–23). Cf. also *in* John i. 29 (I, 170, 19–20) when Christ is described as being ἀναμορφώσεως τῆς εἰς θεὸν ὑπόθεσις.
[3] The same difficulty, which is here being dealt with in its most radical form in terms of union with God, also occurs in Cyril's treatment of Christ's role as mediator of the knowledge and vision of God (cf. pp. 86 and 93 above).

relationship with the Father.[1] But this is not the main line of argument used, and, despite Cyril's protestations that it does not destroy the unity of the Christ, it is an argument which fits rather with Theodore's than with Cyril's interpretation of the person of Christ. The main line of argument is to point out that the union of Christ with the Father is used as an analogy not only of our ultimate relationship with God, but also of the unity of the Church. This unity is clearly a moral one and no more, and it follows, therefore, that the antitype cannot be intended to resemble its archetype in every detail.[2] But in using this argument Cyril is primarily concerned to provide a safeguard, not against an overstatement of the ultimate unity of man and God, but against an understatement of the unity of the Godhead. He does not show any serious anxiety that men will so overpress the analogy of the consubstantial unity of the Godhead as to assert a strictly parallel unity between redeemed mankind and the Father; he is extremely anxious to denounce the reverse argument, which had been used by the anti-modalist writers of the third century and taken up by the Arians, which claimed that the relationship of unity within the Godhead must correspond exactly to the unity of the Church, and can therefore be no more than a unity of social concord.[3] His emphasis, therefore, always rests upon the unqualified nature of the unity within the Godhead, and the unity, which is man's goal, is described in language which approaches, though it never quite reaches, the same level of unity. The believer's union with *Christ* is described as being exactly parallel to that existing between Christ and the Father—namely a 'natural' union as contrasted with a purely 'moral' union of mutual love.[4] Concerning the nature of our ultimate union with God he is more guarded, but with careful qualification he does go so far as to declare

[1] Cyr. *in* John xvii. 22–3 (III, 2, 2–21). The crucial words are σχετικῶς δηλονότι καὶ οὐ φυσικῶς.

[2] Cyr. *in* John xvii. 20–1 (II, 731, 23–732, 11). It is interesting to contrast the comment of Barrett on the same passage: 'The unity of the Church is strictly analogous to the unity of the Father and the Son' (Barrett, p. 427).

[3] Cyr. *in* John xvii. 20–1 (II, 732, 12–733, 27); *in* John xiv. 20 (II, 476–9). For the use of John xvii in this way in the third century, see especially Hippolytus, *Con. Noet.* 7. Cf. p. 125 above.

[4] Cyr. *in* John xiv. 20 (II, 481, 7–11).

that men are brought by the mediation of the Son into 'some sort of natural liaison' with God himself.[1]

These accounts of the soteriological ideas of Theodore and of Cyril have been designed to bring out as clearly as possible the main character of their thought as centring on the mediatorial significance of the conjunction of divine and human in the person of Christ. In order to achieve this, some abstraction from the wholeness of their thought has been necessary. If we were to regard the accounts given as a comprehensive statement of their soteriologies, we would be guilty of serious falsification in two respects. In the first place, both give (as any scheme of thought with Biblical roots must do) far more importance to the fact of Christ's death than we have yet done justice to. Secondly, nothing has been said of the means by which our unity with Christ as man is made the effective medium of our receiving the benefits that stem from him. Something must now be said on these two questions.

The death of Christ is not normally treated as a separate or isolated phenomenon, but in the closest conjunction with the whole movement of the incarnation. As we have seen, it was for Cyril one of those things which Christ did effectively for us.[2] Similarly Theodore insists that it was particularly by his death that he dealt with the interrelated problems of death and sin.[3] But where these ideas are taken further and developed in greater detail, it is usually done in traditional terms, which bear no close exegetical relation to the particular text of the Gospel which may have given rise to the discussion. This is perhaps the inevitable outcome of the fact that the Gospel itself does not seem to have any full or clearly developed interpretation of its own of the significance of the cross. The one particular line of interpretation in the Gospel which receives the most interesting development in the commentaries is that of the cross as a judgment upon Satan. Theodore and Chrysostom develop this idea in very much the same way. Because of sin, Satan has the right to inflict men with death. Christ, as sinless, could follow Elijah

---

[1] Cyril, *Dialogue* I, *P.G.* 75, 693 D–696 A. (φυσικὸν ὥσπερ τινὰ τὸν τῆς συναφείας λαχοῦσα τρόπον) (John xvii. 21–3); Cyr. *in* John xvii. 20–1 (II, 734, 8–10).

[2] See. p. 150 above.

[3] T. 29, 20–8 (John i. 29).

and Enoch and simply leave the world without dying. But this would benefit no-one but himself. He allows himself, therefore, to be killed. But Satan in killing him acts unjustly, and will be condemned for it by the judgment of God. Christ will then be released from the death unjustly imposed on him, and will be able to free also those who are joined to him.[1]

This leads naturally to the second question. Who are those who are joined to him and how are they so joined? Cyril, as we have seen, insists that the principle of union is that we are joined to him, or more accurately we are incorporated in him on the basis of our shared humanity. This, as he clearly recognises, is bound to suggest the somewhat surprising conclusion that all men share automatically in his benefits. This conclusion he does not hesitate to draw. What Christ did, he did for the whole human race, and the whole human race will share in the basic fruit of his work—namely enabling our mortality to rise again out of death. But for some this participation in Christ's resurrection will be of doubtful benefit. They will rise again only to hear their sentence of dismissal to the eternal punishments of hell. Thus the sharing in Christ's resurrection is something common to every member of the human race, but for the entry into life in its fullest sense some differentiating principle is required. This is variously given as faith in Christ, living the good life or partaking of the life-giving flesh.[2] It is this last idea which receives the most detailed and significant development. Cyril accepts the general principle that 'the flesh profiteth nothing'. But Christ's flesh is different. Because it is the body not of any ordinary person but of the Word of God, which is Life itself by its very nature, it also receives by virtue of the closeness of the union the property of being able to give life, which is inherent in the Word.[3] This endowment of the flesh is the fruit of Christ's sanctifying of himself, that is his

---

[1] T. 174, 10–175, 2; Chr. 67, 2 (John xii. 31). Cf. Theodore, *Cat. Hom.* 5, 18 (John xiv. 30; xii. 31–2). Cyril also has the idea that Satan expects the cross to be his victory, not recognising the true nature of his victim. But he appears to be thinking more in antagonistic than judicial terms (Cyr. *in* John xiii. 27–8; II, 373).

[2] Cyr. *in* John x. 10 (II, 220–1), where this distinction is given an exegetical basis in the idea of abundant life; *in* John x. 14–15 (II, 233); *in* John vi. 51 (I, 520–1).

[3] Cyr. *in* John vi. 63 (I, 551–2). Cf. Apollinarius in John vi. 53–5 (Corderius, p. 192).

body,[1] and it is illustrated by the way that he used his body as a kind of assistant in two of the miracles of resurrection, where it might have been expected that he would work simply by the divine word of command.[2] Christ's body is therefore life-giving, and it can be quite literally mixed with our bodies.[3] This enables the more stubborn element of our earthly bodies to be prepared for immortality, just as our souls are endowed with newness of life by the direct action of the Holy Spirit.[4] It provides a union with Christ which is not merely πνευματικός but also σωματικός.[5]

Theodore's answer to the question is markedly different. For him our natural birth as men only succeeds in uniting us to Adam and the way of death. It does link us with Christ's human nature, but if that link is to achieve its end of bringing us into true relationship with his divine nature, there must be the affinity not only of natural birth but also of spiritual birth. This is effected in the rebirth of baptism, which corresponds both to Christ's baptism, at which the Spirit descended and which was a type of his resurrection, and also to his resurrection itself. So our baptism is the point of the effective operation of the Spirit upon us and a type of our ultimate resurrection. It is thus the essential link which grafts us into the way first marked out by Christ, whereby human nature can be raised to fellowship with God.[6] Theodore does admit a general Eucharistic reference in chapter vi, but he does not develop it in detail, and clearly does not regard it as fundamental to the soteriological thought of the Gospel. Thus both authors regard a sacramental means of union with Christ as an essential element in the Gospel's scheme of salvation, but it is upon different sacraments that they place the primary emphasis.

[1] Cyr. *in* John xvii. 12–13 (II, 706–7).
[2] Cyr. *in* John vi. 53 (I, 530, 8–13).
[3] Cyr. *in* John vi. 35 (I, 475, 23–5).
[4] Cyr. *in* John vi. 53 (I, 531, 12–16).
[5] Cyr. *in* John xv. 1 (II, 543, 1–544, 14); *in* John xvii. 20–1 (II, 734, 19–736, 21); *in* John xvii. 22–3 (III, 2, 27–31).
[6] T. 55–8. Cf. also T. 33, 5–21 (John i. 33–4); T. 46–7 (John iii. 3–5); T. 196, 25–6 (John xiv. 20); T. 201, 13–15 (John xv. 1–5); T. 212–13; T. 229.

EPILOGUE

AN ASSESSMENT

There is no title that the Fathers would have coveted more for themselves than that of Biblical theologians. Later scholars may point with justice to the influence of Greek metaphysical thought upon their writings and their understanding of the Gospel, but in conscious aim and intention their overriding purpose was to interpret the message of the Bible. We have studied some of their greatest representatives consciously engaged in executing that work of interpretation upon what they and the consensus of opinion in the Church after them have normally regarded as the greatest of the books of Scripture. How are we to assess and to evaluate their work as commentators?

First of all, the acuteness of observation and attention to detail, which is a general characteristic of all their work, must be quoted as a valuable mark of all the commentaries. In almost every discussion of the commentaries with which we have been concerned, this point is noted as a meritorious feature of the work in question.[1] With so carefully constructed a writing as St John's Gospel, this is an indispensable characteristic of the good commentator.[2]

Nevertheless there are other even more important elements in the equipment of the good commentator, and these are not so universally present in the work of the Fathers. Of prime importance is a certain breadth of spiritual discernment, which can appreciate the deep theological character of the author's thought and which recognises that he is seeking to express ultimate truths about the divine dealing

---

[1] With reference to Heracleon's commentary, see G. Salmon in *D.C.B.* vol. II, pp. 898–9; Loewenich, *op. cit.* p. 93; H. E. W. Turner, *The Pattern of Christian Truth*, p. 184 n. 1; for Origen's commentary, see H. Smith, *Ante-Nicene Exegesis of the Gospels*, p. 60; for Theodore, see H. B. Swete in *D.C.B.* vol. IV, p. 947. In each case examples are given of the use of small details in the actual work of exegesis, on which the author's favourable judgment is based.

[2] Cf. Lightfoot, p. 349: 'Anyone who studies St John's Gospel for long is likely to be impressed...by the extreme care with which it is written, a care extending to the smallest details.'

with the world, which are not and cannot be perfectly amenable to any one system of human logic. It is here that the greatness of Origen's work lies. His exposition of the fundamental theological concepts of the Gospel is an achievement of great and lasting value. It is precisely here also that the weakness of Theodore's work is to be found. For all the honesty of his approach, the directness and practical good sense of many of his comments, his commentary as a whole is a disappointing book. He has attempted to expound the meaning of the Gospel too narrowly within the confines of his own way of thought. To borrow a phrase from Origen, it is as if he has never lain upon the Evangelist's breast; his mind has never found spiritual communion with the mind of St John, and therefore he cannot reveal the Gospel's most precious secrets to us. His work never does full justice to the whole range and depth of the theological meaning of the Gospel. Chrysostom, writing for the pulpit rather than the study, lacks something of the precision of Theodore, and also thereby something of the rigidity of his thought. But as a work of interpretation, his homilies suffer from the same fundamental weakness as the work of his fellow-Antiochene—in the words of Westcott there is 'a lack of spontaneous sympathy for the more mysterious parts of the Gospel'.[1]

But alongside this all-important characteristic of spiritual affinity and theological discernment, there is need for the more pedestrian virtue of good sense, of the ability to distinguish between the higher ranges of a bold but profound theological thought and the wild flights of fancy. Much of the thought of the second and third centuries lacked the control of this practical virtue. In particular, it is the absence of this virtue which vitiates the work of Origen as a commentator. Side by side with examples of profound theological exposition stand passages of allegorical interpretation, which are entirely arbitrary in method and utterly unrelated in content to the meaning of the Gospel.

The fragments of Heracleon are hardly sufficient to allow the passing of a firm judgment upon his work, but it is evident that it is open to the same kind of criticism. It was no doubt his allegorical interpretations that particularly attracted Origen's interest, and the

[1] Westcott, vol. I, Introduction, p. cxc.

proportion of allegory in the fragments may therefore well be greater than the proportion in his work as a whole. Origen indeed criticises him not only for unjustifiable allegorising, but also on occasions for failure to allegorise, and it is certainly evident that his whole approach is less arbitrarily allegorical than that of the majority of Gnostic exegetes. In fact, he does not appear to be any more arbitrary in method than Origen. The real difference between them is not one of method but of theological concern. The heart of Heracleon's theological interest was a celestial drama of salvation, of which the events on this earth were a kind of shadow. In this he stands further from St John than Origen does. The content of his allegorical interpretations therefore tends to be further removed from the true meaning of the Gospel.[1]

Cyril, writing two centuries after Origen, represents the maturity, as opposed to the infancy or adolescence, of the Alexandrian school. This difference is clearly marked in the difference of their commentaries. Something of the freshness, the vigour, the theological penetration of Origen has gone; but a sense of balance and good sense has come to check the excesses of the earlier scholar. Cyril's commentary is a profound work of theological interpretation, sustained throughout with a high level of consistency. It goes beyond the range of simple exegesis. His openly avowed concern for a δογματικωτέρα ἐξήγησις and his passionate advocacy of the ways of orthodoxy have led him to blur the distinction between exegesis of the author's meaning on the one hand and the full development of a theological system, which, though not the direct teaching of the Gospel, seems to be the only adequate outcome of reflection on its message, on the other. From the narrower standpoint of the strict work of commentary, this is a weakness; but it is not unmitigated loss. There is perhaps something about the theological nature of the Gospel which makes the maintenance of such a distinction incompatible with a fully satisfying treatment of its message. Certainly the Gospel lives under Cyril's hand. For him the central theme of Christian faith was the work of Christ as mediator between the

---

[1] Cf. Loewenich, *op. cit.* pp. 92–5. See also J. Daniélou, *Origène*, pp. 190–5 (E.T. pp. 191–6) for the influence of this aspect of Heracleon's exegesis on Origen himself.

sinful finite life of earth and the perfect eternal life of heaven. The foundation stone of that faith was the Fourth Gospel. For him, therefore, there is no difference between the meaning of the Fourth Gospel and the full body of Christian faith. In expounding the meaning of the Gospel, he is expounding the heart of his own religious faith.

BIBLIOGRAPHY

A. COMMENTARIES ON THE GOSPEL

(1) *Ancient*

Origen, ed. A. E. Brooke, Cambridge, 1896. (Paragraph numbers are identical with those of the edition of E. Preuschen in *G.C.S.*)

John Chrysostom, *P.G.* 59.

Theodore of Mopsuestia, *Corpus Scriptorum Christianorum Orientalium: Scriptores Syri*, Series 4, Tomus III, interpretatus est J. M. Vosté, Louvain, 1940. Greek fragments in R. Devreesse, *Essai sur Théodore de Mopsueste*, pp. 305–419, Vatican, 1948.

Cyril of Alexandria, ed. P. E. Pusey, Oxford, 1872. (Volume, page and line reference to Pusey's edition are given in brackets.)

Augustine, *Corpus Christianorum, Series Latina* 36, Turnhout, 1954.

Corderius, *Catena Patrum Graecorum in S. Johannem*, Antwerp, 1630.

Cramer, *Catena in Evangelia SS. Lucae et Johannis*, Oxford, 1841.

In the case of Cyril's commentary, the verse of the Gospel on which comment is being made is included in the basic reference; in all other cases it is given in brackets after the reference if it is not already obvious from the context and if the comment is of interest as exegesis of the particular text.

(2) *Modern*

C. K. Barrett, *Gospel according to St John*, London, 1955.

J. H. Bernard, *I.C.C.* (2 vols.), Edinburgh, 1928.

C. H. Dodd, *Interpretation of the Fourth Gospel*, Cambridge, 1953.

E. C. Hoskyns, *The Fourth Gospel*, 2nd ed., London, 1947.

R. H. Lightfoot, *St John's Gospel*, Oxford, 1956.

G. H. C. Macgregor, *The Gospel of John* (Moffatt Commentary), London, 1928.

W. Temple, *Readings in St John's Gospel*, London, 1947.

B. F. Westcott, *The Gospel according to St John* (2 vols.), London, 1908.

B. PRINCIPAL OTHER WORKS CONSULTED

(1) *Ancient*

Adamantius, *Dialogos, G.C.S.*, ed. W. Bakhuyzen, Leipzig, 1901.

Anastasius Sinaita, *Contra Monophysitas, P.G.* 89.

Apollinarius, *Works* and *Fragments* in: H. Lietzmann, *Apollinaris von Laodicea und seine Schule*, Tübingen, 1904.

Asterius, *Fragments* in: G. Bardy, *Recherches sur Saint Lucien d'Antioche et son École*, Paris, 1936.

Athanasius of Alexandria, *De Incarnatione*, *P.G.* 25.

—— *Orationes Contra Arianos*, 1–3, *P.G.* 26.

ps-Athanasius, *Expositio Fidei*, *P.G.* 25.

Augustine, *De Consensu Evangelistarum*, *C.S.E.L.* 43.

Chrysostom, *Opera*, *P.G.* 47–64.

Clement of Alexandria, *Paidagogos* and *Stromateis*, *G.C.S.*, ed. O. Stählin, Leipzig, 1905–9.

—— *Excerpta ex Theodoto*, ed. F. M. M. Sagnard, Paris, 1948.

Cyprian, *Opera*, *C.S.E.L.* 3.

Cyril of Alexandria, *Opera*, *P.G.* 68–77.

Cyril of Jerusalem, *Catecheses*, *P.G.* 33.

Didymus, *Opera*, *P.G.* 39.

Dionysius of Alexandria, *Letters and Other Remains*, ed. C. L. Feltoe, Cambridge, 1904.

Epiphanius, *Ancoratus* and *Panarion*, *G.C.S.*, ed. K. Holl, Leipzig, 1915–33.

Eusebius of Caesarea, *Contra Marcellum* and *De Ecclesiastica Theologia*, *G.C.S.*, ed. E. Klostermann, Leipzig, 1906.

—— *Demonstratio Evangelica*, *G.C.S.*, ed. I. Heikel, Leipzig, 1913, referred to as *Dem. Ev.*

—— *Historia Ecclesiastica*, *G.C.S.*, ed. E. Schwartz, Leipzig, 1903–9, referred to as *H.E.*

—— *Quaestiones Evangelicae*, *P.G.* 22.

Eustathius of Antioch, *Fragments* in: M. Spanneut, *Recherches sur les écrits d'Eustathe d'Antioche*, Lille, 1948.

Gregory Nazianzen, *The Five Theological Orations*, ed. A. J. Mason, Cambridge, 1899, cited as *Theol. Or.*

Hegemonius, *Acta Archelai*, *G.C.S.*, ed. H. Beesan, Leipzig, 1906.

Heracleon, *Fragments*, ed. A. E. Brooke, Cambridge, 1891.

Hippolytus, *Elenchos*, *G.C.S.*, ed. P. Wendland, Leipzig, 1916.

—— *Contra Noetum*, ed. E. Schwartz, in: *Zwei Predigten Hippolyti*, Munich, 1936.

ps-Hippolytus, *On the Raising of Lazarus*, *G.C.S.*, ed. H. Achelis, Leipzig, 1897.

Irenaeus, *Adversus Haereses*, *P.G.* 7 (volume and page of the edition of W. W. Harvey, Cambridge, 1857, are also given in brackets).

Isidore, *Epistles*, *P.G.* 78.

Jerome, *Epistles*, ed. J. Labourt, vols. 1–5, Paris, 1949–55.

Novatian, *De Trinitate*, ed. W. Yorke Fausset, Cambridge, 1909.

Origen, *Contra Celsum* and *De Oratione*, *G.C.S.*, ed. P. Koetschau, Leipzig, 1899.

—— *De principiis*, *G.C.S.*, ed. P. Koetschau, Leipzig, 1913.

—— *Exegetical Works*, editions in *G.C.S.* when available: otherwise *P.G.* 12–14.

—— *Fragments on the Psalms*, in: J. B. Pitra, *Analecta Sacra*, vols. 2 and 3, Paris, 1884 and 1883.

—— *Fragments on the Epistle to the Ephesians*, J. A. F. Gregg, in: *J.T.S.* vol. III, 1901–2.

Pamphilus, *Apologia pro Origene*, *P.G.* 17.

Tertullian, *Opera, Corpus Christianorum, Series Latina*, vols. 1, 2. Turnhout, 1954.

Theodore of Mopsuestia, *Catechetical Homilies*, ed. R. Tonneau, Studi e Testi 145, Vatican, 1949.

—— *Dogmatic Fragments*, ed. H. B. Swete, Appendix to vol. II of *Theodore of Mopsuestia's Commentaries on the Minor Epistles of St Paul*, Cambridge, 1882.

(?Valentinus), *Evangelium Veritatis*, ed. M. Malinine, H. C. Puech and G. Quispel, Zürich, 1956.

(2) *Modern*

B. Altaner, *Patrologie*, Freibourg, 1951.

G. Bardy, *Commentaires Patristiques de la Bible*, Supplément au Dictionnaire de la Bible, vol. II, pp. 73–103, Paris, 1934.

—— *Exégèse Patristique*, Supplément au Dictionnaire de la Bible, vol. IV, pp. 569–91, Paris, 1949.

—— *Recherches sur Saint Lucien d'Antioche et son École*, Paris, 1936.

H. N. Bate, 'Some Technical Terms of Greek Exegesis', *J.T.S.* vol. XXIV (1922), pp. 59–66.

J. F. Bethune-Baker, *An Introduction to the Early History of Christian Doctrine*, 8th ed., London, 1949.

C. Bigg, *Christian Platonists of Alexandria*, Oxford, 1913.

M. E. Boismard, 'Critique Textuelle et Citations Patristiques', *R.B.* vol. LVII (1950), pp. 388–408.

F. M. Braun, 'Qui ex Deo natus est', *Aux sources de la tradition Chrétienne: mélanges offerts à M. Maurice Goguel*, pp. 11–31, Neuchatel, 1950.

A. E. Brooke, 'The Extant Fragments of Heracleon', *Texts and Studies*, vol. I, no. 4, 1891.

R. P. Casey, 'Clement and the Two Divine Logoi', *J.T.S.* vol. XXV (1923), pp. 43–56.

H. Chadwick, 'Eucharist and Christology in the Nestorian Controversy', *J.T.S.* new ser. vol. II (1951), pp. 145–64.

J. Daniélou, *Bible et Liturgie*, Paris, 1951.

—— *Origène*, Paris, 1948. (E.T. by W. Mitchell, London and New York, 1955.)

R. Devreesse, *Essai sur Théodore de Mopsueste*, Studi e Testi 141, Vatican, 1948.

—— 'La Méthode Exégétique de Théodore de Mopsueste', *R.B.* vol. LIII (1946), pp. 207–41.

—— 'Notes sur les Chaînes Grecques de Saint Jean', *R.B.* vol. XXXVI (1927), pp. 192–215.

BIBLIOGRAPHY

H. Du Manoir de Juaye, *Dogme et Spiritualité chez St Cyrille d'Alexandrie*, Paris, 1944.

A. Grillmeier, 'Die theologische und sprachliche Vorbereitung der christologischen Formel von Chalkedon', in: *Das Konzil von Chalkedon*, vol. I, pp. 5–202, Würzburg, 1951.

J. Guillet, 'Les Exégèses d'Alexandrie et d'Antioche: Conflit ou Malentendu?', *R.S.R.* vol. XXXIV (1947), pp. 257–302.

R. Hanson, *Origen's Doctrine of Tradition*, London, 1954.

A. Harnack, *Der kirchengeschichtliche Ertrag der exegetischen Arbeiten des Origenes*, Leipzig, 1919.

A. Kerrigan, *St Cyril of Alexandria: Interpreter of the Old Testament*, Rome, 1952.

J. Liébaert, *La Doctrine Christologique de Saint Cyrille d'Alexandrie avant la Querelle Nestorienne*, Lille, 1951.

H. Lietzmann, *Apollinaris von Laodicea und seine Schule*, Tübingen, 1904.

W. von Loewenich, *Das Johannes–Verständnis im zweiten Jahrhundert*, Giessen, 1932.

H. de Lubac, *Histoire et Esprit: l'Intelligence de l'Écriture d'après Origène*, Paris, 1950.

—— Introduction to *Origène: Homélies sur la Genèse*, Paris, 1944.

—— 'Typologie et Allégorisme', *R.S.R.* vol. XXXIV (1947), pp. 180–226.

M. Malinine, H. C. Puech and G. Quispel, *Evangelium Veritatis*, Zürich, 1956.

C. Martin, 'Note sur l'homélie εἰς τὸν τετραήμερον Λάζαρον attribuée à saint Hippolyte de Rome', *R.H.E.* vol. XXII (1926), pp. 68–70.

J. Mehlmann, 'A note on John i. 3', *Exp. T.*, Aug. 1956, pp. 340–1.

L. Pirot, *L'œuvre exégétique de Théodore de Mopsueste*, Rome, 1913.

G. L. Prestige, *God in Patristic Thought*, 2nd ed., London, 1952.

J. Quasten, *Patrology*, vols. I and II (Utrecht, 1950–3).

C. E. Raven, *Apollinarianism*, Cambridge, 1923.

J. Reuss, 'Cyril von Alexandrien und sein Kommentar zum Johannes-Evangelium', *Biblica*, vol. XXV (1944), pp. 207–9.

H. de Riedmatten, *Les Actes du Procès de Paul de Samosate*, Friebourg en Suisse, 1952.

—— 'Some Neglected Aspects of Apollinarist Christology', *Dominican Studies*, vol. I (1948), pp. 239–60.

G. Salmon, Art. 'Heracleon' in Smith and Wace, *D.C.B.* vol. II, pp. 897–901.

J. N. Sanders, *The Fourth Gospel in the Early Church*, Cambridge, 1943.

R. V. Sellers, *The Council of Chalcedon*, London, 1953.

—— *Eustathius of Antioch and his Place in the Early History of Christian Doctrine*, Cambridge, 1928.

—— *Two Ancient Christologies*, London, 1940.

H. Smith, *Ante-Nicene Exegesis of the Gospels*, 6 vols., London, 1925.

M. Spanneut, *Recherches sur les écrits d'Eustathe d'Antioche*, Lille, 1948.

F. A. Sullivan, *The Christology of Theodore of Mopsuestia*, Rome, 1956.

BIBLIOGRAPHY

H. B. Swete, Art. 'Theodorus of Mopsuestia' in Smith and Wace, *D.C.B.* vol. IV, pp. 934–48.

C. H. Turner, 'The Early Greek Commentators on the Gospel according to St Matthew', *J.T.S.* vol. XII (1911), pp. 99–112.

—— 'Greek Patristic Commentaries on the Pauline Epistles', Hastings, *Dictionary of the Bible*, extra volume, pp. 484–531.

—— 'The Punctuation of John vii. 37–8', *J.T.S.* vol. XXIV (1922), pp. 66–70.

H. E. W. Turner, *The Pattern of Christian Truth*, London, 1954.

J. M. Vosté, 'Le Commentaire de Théodore de Mopsueste sur Saint Jean, d'après la Version Syriaque', *R.B.* vol. XXXII (1923), pp. 522–51.

—— 'La Chronologie de l'activité littéraire de Théodore de Mopsueste', *R.B.* vol. XXXIV (1925), pp. 54–81.

INDEX OF PROPER NAMES

167

INDEX OF TEXTS

(a) BIBLICAL

(b) PATRISTIC

In this index only those authors whose works have been most frequently quoted are included; authors whose works have been less extensively used are included in the index of proper names.

INDEX OF TEXTS